Genders, Transgenders and Sexualities in Japan

Despite over a century of academic research into Japan and its customs, many inaccurate preconceptions about Japanese society remain, particularly regarding Japan's complex sex and gender system. *Genders, Transgenders and Sexualities in Japan* is the first collection to take a genuinely comparative look at the changing notions of gender and sexuality in Japan, highlighting the diversity that has long existed among Japanese people.

Based on extensive Japanese language materials and fieldwork, the authors examine how various nonconformist individuals have questioned received notions about sex and gender. From young women opposed to marriage, to heterosexual men who wish to be more involved in family life, the essays investigate the variety and complexity of Japanese people's experiences relating to traditional gender roles. In addition, the personal histories of feminist women, gay men, lesbians and transgender individuals are considered as these groups increasingly work together to challenge what it means to be a responsible citizen of modern Japan.

Featuring chapters written by key Japanese and Western scholars, *Genders, Transgenders and Sexualities in Japan* gives an overview of the important changes taking place in gender and sexuality studies. Including essays on previously overlooked histories, identities and communities, this illuminating collection will be of interest to students and researchers in the fields of Asian studies, anthropology and sexuality and gender studies.

Mark McLelland is a research fellow in the Centre for Critical and Cultural Studies at the University of Queensland. He is the author of *Queer Japan from the Pacific War to the Internet Age* and *Male Homosexuality in Modern Japan* and co-editor of *Japanese Cybercultures*.

Romit Dasgupta lectures in Japanese language, Japanese Studies, and Asian Studies in the School of Social and Cultural Studies at the University of Western Australia.

Asia's Transformations
Edited by Mark Selden, *Binghamton and Cornell Universities, USA*

The books in this series explore the political, social, economic and cultural consequences of Asia's transformations in the twentieth and twenty-first centuries. The series emphasizes the tumultuous interplay of local, national, regional and global forces as Asia bids to become the hub of the world economy. While focusing on the contemporary, it also looks back to analyse the antecedents of Asia's contested rise.

This series comprises several strands:

Asia's Transformations aims to address the needs of students and teachers, and the titles will be published in hardback and paperback. Titles include:

China in War and Revolution, 1895–1949
Peter Zarrow

Confronting the Bush Doctrine
Critical views from the Asia-Pacific
Edited by Mel Gurtov and Peter Van Ness

Japan's Quiet Transformation
Social change and civil society in the 21st century
Jeff Kingston

State and Society in 21st Century China
Edited by Peter Hays Gries and Stanley Rosen

The Battle for Asia
From decolonization to globalization
Mark T. Berger

Ethnicity in Asia
Edited by Colin Mackerras

Chinese Society, 2nd edition
Change, conflict and resistance
Edited by Elizabeth J. Perry and Mark Selden

The Resurgence of East Asia
500, 150 and 50 Year Perspectives
Edited by Giovanni Arrighi, Takeshi Hamashita and Mark Selden

The Making of Modern Korea
Adrian Buzo

Korean Society
Civil society, democracy and the state
Edited by Charles K. Armstrong

Remaking the Chinese State
Strategies, society and security
Edited by Chien-min Chao and Bruce J. Dickson

Mao's Children in the New China
Voices from the Red Guard
generation
Yarong Jiang and David Ashley

Opium, Empire and the Global Political Economy
Carl A. Trocki

Japan's Comfort Women
Sexual slavery and prostitution during
World War II and the US Occupation
Yuki Tanaka

Hong Kong's History
State and society under colonial rule
Edited by Tak-Wing Ngo

Debating Human Rights
Critical essays from the United States
and Asia
Edited by Peter Van Ness

Asia's Great Cities
Each volume aims to capture the heartbeat of the contemporary city from multiple perspectives emblematic of the authors' own deep familiarity with the distinctive faces of the city, its history, society, culture, politics and economics, and its evolving position in national, regional and global frameworks. While most volumes emphasize urban developments since the Second World War, some pay close attention to the legacy of the *longue durée* in shaping the contemporary. Thematic and comparative volumes address such themes as urbanization, economic and financial linkages, architecture and space, wealth and power, gendered relationships, planning and anarchy, and ethnographies in national and regional perspective. Titles include:

Singapore
Wealth, power and the culture of control
Carl A. Trocki

Representing Calcutta
Modernity, nationalism and the colonial
uncanny
Swati Chattopadhyay

Hong Kong
Global city
Stephen Chiu and Tai-Lok Lui

Shanghai
Global city
Jeff Wasserstrom

Beijing in the Modern World
David Strand and Madeline Yue Dong

Bangkok
Place, practice and representation
Marc Askew

Asia.com is a series which focuses on the ways in which new information and communication technologies are influencing politics, society and culture in Asia. Titles include:

The Internet in Indonesia's New Democracy
David T. Hill and Krishna Sen

Asia.com
Asia encounters the Internet
*Edited by K. C. Ho, Randolph Kluver
and Kenneth C. C. Yang*

Japanese Cybercultures
*Edited by Mark McLelland and
Nanette Gottlieb*

Literature and Society is a series that seeks to demonstrate the ways in which Asian literature is influenced by the politics, society and culture in which it is produced. Titles include:

Chinese Women Writers and the Feminist Imagination (1905–1945)
Haiping Yan

The Body in Postwar Japanese Fiction
Edited by Douglas N. Slaymaker

Routledge Studies in Asia's Transformations is a forum for innovative new research intended for a high-level specialist readership, and the titles will be available in hardback only. Titles include:

1. **Genders, Transgenders and Sexualities in Japan**
   Edited by Mark McLelland and Romit Dasgupta

2. **Developmental Dilemmas**
   Land reform and institutional change in China
   Edited by Peter Ho

3. **Japanese Industrial Governance**
   Protectionism and the licensing state
   Yul Sohn

4. **Remaking Citizenship in Hong Kong**
   Community, nation and the global city
   Edited by Agnes S. Ku and Ngai Pun

5. **Chinese Media, Global Contexts**
   Edited by Chin-Chuan Lee

6. **Imperialism in South East Asia**
   'A fleeting, passing phase'
   Nicholas Tarling

7. **Internationalizing the Pacific**
   The United States, Japan and the Institute of Pacific Relations in war and peace, 1919–1945
   Tomoko Akami

8. **Koreans in Japan**
   Critical voices from the margin
   Edited by Sonia Ryang

9. **The American Occupation of Japan and Okinawa***
   Literature and memory
   Michael Molasky

* Now available in paperback

Critical Asian Scholarship is a series intended to showcase the most important individual contributions to scholarship in Asian Studies. Each of the volumes presents a leading Asian scholar addressing themes that are central to his or her most significant and lasting contribution to Asian studies. The series is committed to the rich variety of research and writing on Asia, and is not restricted to any particular discipline, theoretical approach or geographical expertise.

China's Past, China's Future
Engergy, food, environment
Vaclav Smil

China Unbound
Evolving perspectives on the Chinese past
Paul A. Cohen

Women and the Family in Chinese History
Patricia Buckley Ebrey

Southeast Asia
A testament
George McT. Kahin

Genders, Transgenders and Sexualities in Japan

Edited by Mark McLelland and
Romit Dasgupta

LONDON AND NEW YORK

First published 2005
by Routledge
2 Park Square, Milton Park, Abingdon, Oxon OX14 4RN

Simultaneously published in the USA and Canada
by Routledge
270 Madison Ave, New York, NY 10016

Routledge is an imprint of the Taylor & Francis Group

Transferred to Digital Printing 2006

© 2005 Editorial matter and selection, Mark McLelland and Romit Dasgupta;
Individual chapters, the contributors

Typeset in Times by Keystroke, Jacaranda Lodge, Wolverhampton

All rights reserved. No part of this book may be reprinted or reproduced or utilized in any form or by any electronic, mechanical, or other means, now known or hereafter invented, including photocopying and recording, or in any information storage or retrieval system, without permission in writing from the publishers.

British Library Cataloguing in Publication Data
A catalogue record for this book is available from the British Library

Library of Congress Cataloging in Publication Data
Genders, transgenders, and sexualities in Japan / edited by Mark Mclelland and Romit Dasgupta.
p. cm. – (Asia's transformations)
Includes bibliographical references and index.
1. Gender identity–Japan. 2. Homosexuality–Japan. 3. Transsexualism–Japan.
I. McLelland, Mark, 1966– II. Dasgupta, Romit. III. Series.
HQ1075.5.J3G46 2005
305.3'0952--dc22
2004030609

ISBN10: 0–415–35370–X (hbk)
ISBN10: 0–415–40585–8 (pbk)

ISBN13: 978–0–415–35370–0 (hbk)
ISBN13: 978–0–415–40585–0 (pbk)

Printed and bound by CPI Antony Rowe, Eastbourne

Contents

List of contributors	ix
Acknowledgements	xiii
Note on the text	xv

1 **Introduction** 1
MARK MCLELLAND AND ROMIT DASGUPTA

2 **Hegemonic gender in Japanese as a foreign language education: Australian perspectives** 15
YURIKO NAGATA AND KRISTEN SULLIVAN

3 **The origins of "queer studies" in postwar Japan** 33
HITOSHI ISHIDA, MARK MCLELLAND AND TAKANORI MURAKAMI

4 **Transgendering *shōjo shōsetsu*: girls' inter-text/sex-uality** 49
TOMOKO AOYAMA

5 **From *The Well of Loneliness* to the *akarui rezubian*: Western translations and Japanese lesbian identities** 65
BEVERLY CURRAN AND JAMES WELKER

6 **The politics of *okama* and *onabe*: uses and abuses of terminology regarding homosexuality and transgender** 81
WIM LUNSING

7 **Salarymen doing queer: gay men and the heterosexual public sphere** 96
MARK MCLELLAND

8 Being male in a female world: masculinity and gender in
   Okinawan shamanism   111
   MATTHEW ALLEN

9 "Understanding through the body:" the masquerades of
   Mishima Yukio and Morimura Yasumasa   126
   VERA MACKIE

10 An introduction to men's studies   145
   KIMIO ITŌ

11 Rethinking Japanese masculinities: recent research trends   153
   FUTOSHI TAGA

12 Salarymen doing straight: heterosexual men and the dynamics
   of gender conformity   168
   ROMIT DASGUPTA

13 Feminist futures in Japan: exploring the work of Haruka
   Yōko and Kitahara Minori   183
   LAURA DALES

14 Commodified romance in a Tokyo host club   200
   AKIKO TAKEYAMA

   Index   216

Contributors

Matthew Allen is Associate Professor of Japanese History at the University of Auckland. Major publications include *Undermining the Japanese Miracle* (Cambridge, 1994) and *Identity and Resistance in Okinawa* (Rowman and Littlefield, 2002). He has published extensively in anthropology, psychiatry and history journals, and in edited volumes on Japan and Asia.

Tomoko Aoyama is a Senior Lecturer in the School of Languages and Comparative Cultural Studies at the University of Queensland. She is currently writing a book on food and eating in modern Japanese literature. Her recent publications have appeared in *Monumenta Nipponica* (58: 4) and *Asian Masculinities* (RoutledgeCurzon, 2003).

Beverley Curran is an Associate Professor in the Department of Creativity and Culture (Multicultural Studies) at Aichi Shukutoku University in Nagoya, Japan. *Rezubian nikki*, her collaborative Japanese translation of Nicole Brossard's *Journal intime* was published in 2000 (Kokubunsha).

Laura Dales is a PhD candidate and tutor in the Discipline of Asian Studies at the University of Western Australia. Her research interests include studies of Japanese and other Asian feminisms, agency and resistance and gender issues in contemporary Japan. She recently contributed a chapter to the book *Women and Agency in Asia* (Marshall Cavendish, 2005).

Romit Dasgupta lectures in Japanese, Japanese Studies and Asian Studies in the School of Social and Cultural Studies at the University of Western Australia. He has published in *Japanese Studies*, *Japanese Cybercultures* (Routledge, 2003), *East Asian Masculinities: The Meaning and Practice of Manhood in China and Japan* (RoutledgeCurzon, 2003) and *The Encyclopedia of Contemporary Japanese Culture* (Routledge, 2002).

Hitoshi Ishida is an Adjunct Lecturer at Meijigakuin University, Kanagawa. His numerous publications include contributions to journals and edited volumes on Japanese popular culture, gender studies and the history of homosexuality and transgenderism in Japan. He is a member of Chuo University's Research Group on the Social History of Transgenderism in Postwar Japan.

x Contributors

Kimio Itō is a Professor in the Faculty of Human Sciences at Osaka University. In 1991, along with a group of concerned researchers and community members, he established the first men's group in Japan, the *Menzu Ribu Kenkyūkai* (Men's Liberation Research Association). In 1992 he offered the first-ever university course in Men's Studies at Kyoto University. His best-known publications include *Otokorashisa no yukue* (The path of manliness), *Danseigaku nyūmon* (An introduction to men's studies) and *Jendā de manabu shakaigaku* (Studying sociology through gender).

Wim Lunsing is an anthropologist who has taught at Oxford Brookes and Copenhagen Universities and was recently a Research Fellow at Tokyo University. He is the author of *Beyond Common Sense: Sexuality and Gender in Contemporary Japan* (Kegan Paul, 2001) and numerous papers on sexuality, gender and research methods and ethics. His latest project concerns individual ways of dealing with the changing employment situation in Japan.

Vera Mackie is Australian Research Council Professorial Research Fellow in History at the University of Melbourne. Major publications include *Gurōbaruka to jendā hyōshō* (Ochanomizu Shobō, 2003), *Feminism in Modern Japan: Citizenship, Embodiment and Sexuality* (Cambridge, 2003) and *Creating Socialist Women in Japan: Gender, Labour and Activism* (Cambridge, [1997] 2002).

Mark McLelland is an Australian Research Council Postdoctoral Fellow in the Centre for Critical and Cultural Studies at the University of Queensland. Major publications include *Queer Japan from the Pacific War to the Internet Age* (Rowman and Littlefield, 2005), *Male Homosexuality in Modern Japan* (RoutledgeCurzon, 2000) and the edited volume *Japanese Cybercultures* (Routledge, 2003).

Takanori Murakami is an assistant researcher in the Seijo University Institute of Folklore Studies.

Yuriko Nagata lectures in the School of Languages and Comparative Cultural Studies at the University of Queensland. She is the author of *Unwanted Aliens* (University of Queensland Press, 1996), *Oosutoraria Nihonjin kyōseishūyō no kiroku* (Kobunken, 2002) and co-editor of *Navigating Boundaries: The Asian Diaspora in Torres Strait* (Pandanus Books, 2004).

Kristen Sullivan teaches English at the Shimonoseki City University. Her honours thesis investigated the linguistic construction of Japanese masculinities.

Futoshi Taga is an Associate Professor in the Faculty of Literature, Kurume University, Japan. His major publications include *Dansei no jendā keisei* (Tōyōkan Shuppansha, 2001) and chapters in *Asian Masculinities* (RoutledgeCurzon, 2003) and *Handbook of Studies on Men and Masculinities* (Sage, 2004).

Akiko Takeyama is a PhD candidate in cultural anthropology at the University of Illinois at Urbana-Champaign. Her research interests lie in gender, sexuality and popular culture. She is currently a Japan Foundation doctoral fellow conducting fieldwork in Japan for her thesis.

James Welker is a PhD student in the Department of East-Asian Languages and Culture at the University of Illinois at Urbana-Champaign. His publications include "Telling her story: narrating a lesbian community," in *Japanstudien: Jahrbuch des Deutschen Instituts für Japanstudien* vol. 16 (2004) and "Drawing out lesbians: representations of lesbian desire in *shōjo* manga," in *Lesbian Voices: Canada and Beyond* (New Delhi: Allied Publishing, in press).

Acknowledgements

The editors would like to thank Terri-Ann White, the Director of the Institute of Advanced Studies at the University of Western Australia, for financial assistance toward translation and travel costs which enabled several participants in this collection to present their work at a workshop at the University of Western Australia. We would also like to thank the University of Queensland's Arts Faculty Research Concentration in Asian Identities for funding a similar workshop at the University of Queensland. We would also like to join Vera Mackie in thanking Hosoe Eikoh, Morimura Yasumasa and Shinoyama Kishin for permission to reproduce their artwork.

We are particularly grateful to all our contributors who, despite their heavy teaching loads and numerous other academic duties, managed to meet the deadlines and respond with cheer to our last-minute demands for revisions and alterations. Series editor Mark Selden, too, was tremendously helpful with his always timely and constructive criticism. A team effort such as this can never be accomplished without everyone involved giving freely of their time and efforts. We thank you all.

Note on the text

Contributors excepted, all Japanese names are listed in Japanese order – surname followed by given name. When romanizing Japanese terms, long vowels have been represented by macrons except in terms that are commonly written in English – including place names such as Tokyo, and period reigns like Showa and Taisho. Capitalization has generally been avoided when transliterating Japanese except in instances when these terms would normally be capitalized in English, including personal and place names.

1 Introduction

Mark McLelland and Romit Dasgupta

More than a century and a half after *Japonisme* first swept the salons of Europe, Japan, far more so than other more populous countries of "the Orient," still provides Western media with an endless supply of exotic and enticing images. Recent movies such as *Kill Bill*, *The Last Samurai*, *Lost in Translation* and *Japanese Story* have presented viewers with a repertoire of familiar characters – from samurai, yakuza, geisha and ninja, to the more quotidian salaryman. These movies, populated by all our favorite Japanese characters, seem so very satisfying (and credible) because they offer, as Edward Said points out, "a world elsewhere, apart from the ordinary attachments, sentiments, and values of *our* world in the West" (1995: 190).

This longstanding fascination with *Things Japanese* (the title of an 1891 collection by Basil Hall Chamberlain) is perhaps best illustrated by Arthur Golden's (1998) best-seller *Memoirs of a Geisha*, the success of which saw the release of numerous other works about Japan's traditional "floating world." Indeed, travelers passing through airport bookshops in the early years of the present century will no doubt have noticed entire *shelves* dedicated to books on this topic. It would be unlikely that a book about a Chinese or an Indian courtesan, no matter how skillfully written, would have gained the same popularity. *Memoirs of a Geisha* was able to become so popular because it confirmed (admittedly in the context of a skillfully written and engaging narrative) everything that we think we already *know* about Japan.[1] It is the very "authentic" feel of the novel Anne Allison (2001) identifies as a major factor behind its success. As Allison observes, the novel resonates because it fits so well with widespread orientalist notions that are routinely entertained about Japan in societies of the West. She comments that the book is "Orientalist in the Saidean sense of treating the 'Orient' as innately different from the 'West' whose culture homogenizes as well as differentiates 'them' from 'us'" (2001: 382).

While this repertoire of characters borrowed from Japanese history makes for engaging cinema, it does little to advance our understanding of Japan's complex modern society which is subject to the same global trends and influences that are resulting in demographic and social shifts in other post-industrial nations such as the US, the UK and Australia. Notions of "homogeneity" and, more recently, "hegemony," have come under attack from a variety of theorists who have analyzed how the shift from "traditional" to "modern" ways of living, thinking and working have been characterized by increasing differentiation and segmentation – within populations as much as markets. Giddens (1992), for instance, notes the development and proliferation of diverse "lifestyle sectors" within previously undifferentiated communities which are challenging received notions about how certain types of individuals should live their lives. Traditionally, gender has been a major divide structuring the kinds of lifestyle choices that individuals have been able to make but, in contemporary society, gender exerts less and less influence on an individual's chosen life path. Issues of gender are increasingly complicated by the rise of a new category – sexuality, or better sexual orientation – which has emerged in Japan, as it has in the US and elsewhere, as a major node around which individuals are constructing their lifestyles.

This collection of essays focuses on changing notions of gender and sexuality in Japan in order to highlight the diversity which exists (and which, to an extent, has long existed) among Japanese people. Following the recent trend toward pluralizing concepts such as "gender" in order to highlight the diversity that these terms tend to mask when used in the singular, we present a series of essays focusing on a wide range of Japanese genders, transgenders and sexualities. We include the term transgenders here to stress that despite the proliferation of "masculinities" and "femininities" in contemporary societies, increasing numbers of people are choosing to live outside this binary structure; that is they prefer to live beyond or between conventional gender categories. Drawing extensively upon Japanese-language materials, as well as fieldwork with a range of Japanese individuals and communities, the authors in this collection present much new information about recent changes in Japanese constructions of gender and sexuality. We begin by considering the nature and the scope of research into Japanese gender and sexuality up until now.

Beyond homogeneity?

Vera Mackie has observed that Japanese "models of citizenship implicitly privilege the male, white-collar 'citizen in a suit'" (2000: 246) and it is due to the marginalized position that women have occupied in a range of social situations that we have such a wealth of studies of Japanese women. These include studies ranging from the prewar "peasant" femininities enacted by village women described in Smith and Wiswell's (1982) *Women of Suye Mura* to the urban women's political activism outlined by Mackie (1997) in *Creating Socialist Women in Japan* and Sievers's (1983) history of early feminist thought, *Flowers in Salt: The Beginning of Feminist Consciousness in Modern Japan*. Other important studies of contemporary women include Kelsky's (2001) *Women on the Verge: Japanese Women, Western Dreams*, an investigation of Japanese women's internationalism, and LeBlanc's (1999) study of women's participation in local politics, *Bicycle Citizens: The Political World of the Japanese Housewife*.

In contrast to these numerous investigations into a range of Japanese women's lifestyles and philosophies, little attention has been paid to the variety that exists among Japanese men. Indeed, it is not much of an exaggeration to state that "we know virtually nothing about the practices Japanese men use to construct their masculinity" (Sturtz Streetharan 2004: 82). The lack of even a single monograph which takes the construction of masculinity in Japan as its focus testifies to this extreme imbalance. To an extent, as Taga points out in his chapter in this volume, male experience has historically been taken as paradigmatic of human experience and only women's lives have been seen as different, problematic, deficient or in some other way "marked" and thereby in need of specific study.

While human experience is typically portrayed through the lives and achievements of men, to the extent that men as a category have been studied, there has also been a pronounced focus upon relatively elite men. The "salaryman" has for a long time been seen as the be-all and end-all of Japanese masculinity and it is his life and values that have attracted the most research (Vogel 1963; Plath 1964; Ballon 1969; Rohlen 1974; Clark 1979; van Helvoort 1979; Beck and Beck 1994). While this trend began with works such as Vogel (1963) and to a certain extent even Dore (1958), perhaps the most influential work on the salaryman has been that by Japanese anthropologist Nakane Chie. In 1967 Nakane devoted an entire chapter to the description of the "Characteristics and Value Orientation of Japanese Man" in her influential work *Tate shakai no ningen kankei: tan'itsu shakai no riron* (Inter-personal relationships in a vertically structured society: a theory of a homogenous society), translated into English in 1970 as *Japanese Society*. This book was warmly received in Japan and it was translated into English with government support so as to provide a textbook explaining Japan to the West. Still in print after over 30 years and frequently set as an introductory reader on Japanese anthropology courses, countless students have used this book as a resource in developing their understanding of Japan and Nakane's theories, particularly her description of Japan as an "homogenous society," have exerted a strong influence, not only on the discipline of Japanese studies, but via popular journalism, upon media representations of Japan in general. Three decades later, Nakane's description of *the* Japanese man (as if all men in Japan shared the same characteristics and all possessed a single value orientation) is clearly seen as a *nihonjinron* (Japanese uniqueness)[2] argument, but it is only in the last few years that studies problematizing Nakane's depiction of the elite, heterosexually married, white-collar salaryman as the paradigmatic embodiment of Japanese masculinity have become available in English. These include Fowler's (1996) investigation of Tokyo's day laborers, *San'ya Blues: Laboring Life in Contemporary Tokyo*, Roberson's (1998) study of male factory workers, *Japanese Working Class Lives: An Ethnographic Study of Factory Workers*, and Roberson and Suzuki's (2003) pioneering collection *Men and Masculinities in Contemporary Japan*, which is significantly subtitled *Dislocating the Salaryman Doxa*.

Likewise, it is only in the past few years that English scholarship has shown an interest in previously overlooked "marginal" or "liminal" sexual and gender identities (although in terms of the historical record, these patterns of behavior were hardly marginal at the time). Leupp's (1995) *Male Colors: The Construction of Homosexuality in Tokugawa Japan*, Pflugfelder's (1999) *Cartographies of*

Desire: Male-Male Sexuality in Japanese Discourse 1600–1950 and McLelland's (2000) *Male Homosexuality in Modern Japan* have traced developments in male homosexual identity and practice from the Tokugawa period through to the end of the last century, while Robertson's (1998) *Takarazuka: Sexual Politics and Popular Culture in Modern Japan* and Chalmers's (2002) *Emerging Lesbian Voices from Japan* have looked at lesbian identities from the Taisho period until the 1990s.

Lunsing's (2001) *Beyond Common Sense: Sexuality and Gender in Contemporary Japan* and McLelland's (2005) *Queer Japan from the Pacific War to the Internet Age* are so far the most comparative, looking at a wide variety of "non-standard" lifestyles and relationships. Lunsing finds that, contrary to received opinion, many people in contemporary Japan live outside hegemonic sex and gender roles and relationships and McLelland's work shows that spaces have *always* existed for the expression of non-heterosexual desires and gender variant identities throughout the postwar period. In addition, important new work on gendered language use, such as Smith and Okamoto's (2005) *Japanese Language, Gender, and Ideology: Cultural Models and Real People*, has problematized much previous scholarship that assumed a binary relationship between "men" and "women." There are, in fact, multiple masculinities and femininities in Japan as well as a range of transgender identities; Japanese sexualities, too, are similarly diverse.

Yet, while this growing interest in the English literature on the diversity of Japanese sex and gender expression is to be welcomed, it remains slight in comparison with the now extensive amount of research into multiple genders and sexualities published in Japanese. The ongoing boom in publications relating to masculinities/men's studies, for instance, exemplifies the proliferation of voices and debates related to genders and sexualities taking place in Japan today. A whole body of work published over the past decade or so, by scholars and/or activists including Amano and Kimura (2003), Asai *et al.* (2001), Taga (2001), Shibuya (2001), Nishikawa and Ogino (1999), Sunaga (1999), Inoue *et al.* (1998), Nakamura and Nakamura (1997), Toyoda (1997), and Itō (1996, 1993), among others, attests to the richness and diversity of debates revolving around interrogations of "masculinity" as a gender construct. Yet, despite the significant influence of these works on discourse about genders and sexualities in contemporary Japan, very little of this material has been translated into English or is even referenced in English-language scholarship on gender in Japan.

This is unfortunate since this developing body of theory is not simply an academic preserve but, via popular media such as the internet,[3] NHK's education channel (Itō 2003), high-brow (but widely read) journals such as *AERA*, *Gendai shisō* and *imago*, and the mainstream press, is influencing the manner in which masculinity and gender are thought about in the Japanese context. Indeed, this discussion now takes place at all levels of society – for instance, in its July 1997 issue, the popular men's magazine *Bart* ran a feature entitled "Kanzennaru 'danseigaku' de otoko ni nare!" (Become a man through mastering "men's studies"!), the first of many such features to present men's studies as a trendy activity.

Publications in Japanese about previously overlooked gender and sexual identities and practices, in particular, have undergone something of a boom in the last decade. Ueno Chizuko (1992, 1994) pioneered innovative critiques of Japanese sexuality from a feminist perspective and a new wave of trendy, young women writers including Haruka Yōko (2000a, 2000b) has further mainstreamed feminist critique in Japanese pop culture. Also, important landmarks in gay studies include Fushimi (1991, 2002), Yajima (1997) and Itō, S. (1992); in lesbian studies Yajima (1999), Kakefuda (1992) and *Bessatsu Takarajima* (1987), and in queer studies Kuia Sutadiizu Henshū Iinkai (1996, 1997). A number of attempts have also been made to explore connections between gay theory and feminism, including Itō and Ochiai (1998) and Saitō and Fushimi (1997). There are also a growing number of books about the lives and experiences of transgender individuals – including Harima and Souma (2004), Miyazaki (2000), Komatsu (2000) and Toyama (1999) and at least one university association dedicated to uncovering Japanese transgender history – Sengo Nihon Toransujendā Shakaishi Kenkyūkai (Postwar Japan Transgender Social History Study Group) – which has been responsible for a series of publications detailing otherwise unrecorded aspects of transgender history (Yajima 2000; Sugiura 2001; Mitsuhashi 2004). Sex workers, too, long written about by non-practitioners of the trade as a social problem, have recently found a voice in a series of publications (Hasurā 2000; Matsuzawa 2000a, 2000b, 2003) which stress that sex work, as often as not, results from personal choice not social privation. The plurality of debate, now aided and abetted by the internet, around issues concerning sexuality and gender is such that it is no longer possible to talk about Japanese "men" or "women" as homogenous categories and it is important that some of this discussion should be translated into English and become more widely known.

This volume, featuring chapters written by key Japanese authors as well as Western scholars who draw heavily on Japanese-language materials and debates, gives, for the first time in English, an overview of the important changes taking place in gender and sexuality studies within Japanese scholarship as well as the wide variety of gender and sexual identities negotiated by Japanese people themselves. The chapters in this collection depict the plurality of gender positions that are negotiated and expressed by people in Japan whose lives have fallen outside the purview of previous gender scholarship and whose experience has not been accorded a place in the curriculum. While also engaging with Western and Japanese gender theories, the main aim of the chapters in the book is to investigate the wide variety and complexity of Japanese people's lived experience relating to gender and sexual expression through paying close attention to ethnographic detail as well as Japanese discourse and cultural products.

What is new about this collection is that it brings together essays on a range of topics that would normally be segregated into specific collections dealing with "women," "men," or "sexual minorities." This kind of segregation is, however, highly misleading since, as the chapters that follow illustrate, much discussion is taking place in Japan *between* these categories – popular feminism in Japan, for instance, is now critiquing the previously central role that heterosexuality has played in feminist theory and Japan's newly emerging men's groups have had to deal with issues relating to homosexuality and homophobia. The relatively new discipline of men's studies has necessarily been influenced by prior feminist theory and there is much discussion between male, female, and increasingly, transgender gender theorists. Sexual minorities, of course, have *always* needed to consider the constraints of hegemonic norms in the realms of gender performance and sexual behavior and a range of queer communities are not just in communication with each other but are increasingly in contact with representatives of men's studies and feminism. In the realm of popular culture, too, openly gay and transgendered authors have recently gained a wider audience and several have won major literary prizes. In 2000, for instance, the prestigious Akutagawa award went to Fujino Chiya, a male-to-female transsexual, for her novel featuring a range of queer characters and in 2003 Fushimi Noriaki, Japan's most visible gay critic and author, received the 40th annual Bungei prize for his debut novel featuring a gay protagonist. The success of these novels testifies to the broad appeal of their themes.

Yet, despite this plurality, as other chapters in this collection show, hegemonic notions about gendered behavior remain strong in certain constituencies. Heterosexual men, in particular, in comparison with other groups in Japanese society, seem to be less able to change their ideas to fit new social structures and exigencies. This is despite the very real challenges to traditional notions surrounding masculinity, particularly in the wake of the social and economic changes of the 1990s. As some of the chapters in the second half of the book highlight, there are contradictory and complex dynamics at work in the ways notions of masculinity are being re-configured. On the one hand, there is an increasing recognition of the personal and societal cost to individual men of subscribing to a gender ideology which defines masculinity through work and being the family provider, the *daikokubashira* (literally, central supporting pillar) of the household. On the other hand, the corporate re-structurings and employment insecurity of the 1990s as well as today's harsher economic climate, may in fact have made it more difficult for men to disengage themselves from those expectations, and make more radical lifestyle choices.

Overview of the book

Nagata and Sullivan's chapter (Chapter 2) on gender stereotyping in Japanese language textbooks is a useful place to start when considering the aims of this collection. As these authors point out, current Japanese language teaching resources tend to teach "gender-appropriate" language within a somewhat narrow and anachronistic framework and are hardly adequate to the lived realities of language use in Japan today. This is because language (precisely because there has, traditionally, been a cultural emphasis on men's and women's speech) is the site of considerable contestation.

Nagata and Sullivan, writing from their respective positions as teacher and student, express frustration at textbooks which "perpetuate and reproduce normative gender stereotyping and gendered language norms." However, they conclude that it is not only the textbooks that are at fault but also "an inability to teach *outside* cultural and gender norms by teachers." They suggest that many Japanese language teachers are themselves over-invested in conservative, outmoded notions about the singularity of Japanese culture and that change, if it is to come, will more likely be in response to student demands for a more socially inclusive curriculum.

Nagata points to a classroom exercise in which students were to act in a play featuring the characters of a popular TV drama they had been studying as a language resource. In their dramatization the students imagined a scenario in which several characters came out as lesbian and gay. However, no commercial JFL materials currently exist which acknowledge or help students describe the language (let alone the realities) of lesbian and gay life in contemporary Japan. This is despite the fact that the students were not imposing their own local concerns on the classroom but simply rehearsing what is now a common plot device in many Japanese movies and home dramas where *kamingu auto* (coming out), in conjunction with the verb *suru* (to do) has become an indigenized Japanese term and is widely understood (see McLelland 2003; also Chapter 7 this volume).

That Japanese studies, as it has been narrowly conceived, has overlooked the enormous variety of sexual and gender identities expressed by Japanese people in the postwar period is underlined by Chapter 3 by Ishida, McLelland and Murakami which draws on Japan's postwar "perverse press." These authors, who have been involved with Chuo University's seminar on postwar transgender history, draw on Foucault to show how a large body of archival material concerning the lives and experience of a wide range of sexual and gender nonconformists has been overlooked by both Japanese and English-language scholars since it has been considered to contain only "naïve" and "hierarchically inferior" knowledge. They point out how the many hundreds of editions of "perverse" magazines published in the immediate postwar decade offer an alternative resource for understanding the development of sex and gender identities during this period. Since these reports contain many first-person narratives from a range of sexual and gender minorities, the authors argue that these "subjugated knowledges" should be recovered and used to rethink received opinions about Japanese sexual and gender history. The sheer variety of this literature is testimony to the possibilities that have *always* existed in Japanese society for expressing sexual and gender difference, even at a time when mainstream notions about gender were considered to be at their most hegemonic.

The representation of sexual and gender diversity is, of course, not a postwar development; there are multiple examples in the literary record, from the gender-switching siblings of the Heian period *Torikaebaya monogatari* (Willig 1983), through the homoerotic "acolyte tales" of the medieval era (Childs 1980), the samurai love stories of the Tokugawa period (Ihara 1990), the *ero guro nansensu* (erotic, grotesque nonsense) stories of the 1920s, to reports concerning practitioners of "Lesbos love" in the postwar "perverse press" (McLelland 2004). However, as Aoyama points out in Chapter 4, interest in gender and sexually ambivalent characters has also long been conspicuous in the genre of *shōjo shōsetsu*, or girls' fiction. Indeed, Aoyama notes how "bishōnen (beautiful boys), androgyny, transgender, transsexuality and male homosexuality" are "favorite themes" in a variety of media created and consumed by women and girls, from the all-female theater troupe, the Takarazuka, to online YAOI fandom. It is this widespread appeal of "queer" themes and characters – well beyond communities who might be defined as sexually or gender variant – that is so fascinating in the case of Japanese culture and which can seem startling to English readers not acquainted with Japan.

Carrying on the literary theme, Curran and Welker in Chapter 5 discuss the long association that lesbians in Japan have had with literature – not so much as authors or characters, but as translators. They point out that "lesbian" as an identity category in Japan was brought about through a process of translation, as a range of Western terminology relating to women's same-sex love was rendered into Japanese from the middle of the Meiji period onwards. Far from being passive subjects of this process, however, Curran and Welker demonstrate that women with same-sex orientations such as Hiratsuka Raichō and Yoshiya Nobuko were themselves pivotal agents in this process of acculturation through their work as translators, editors and critics of Western sexological and literary texts. Importantly, they show how lesbians working together as translators is an important and ongoing cultural practice in Japan with the Rezubian shōsetsu hon'yaku wākushoppu (Lesbian novel translation workshop) at the Tokyo lesbian space LOUD (Lesbians Of Undeniable Drive) being the most current example.

Lunsing's and McLelland's chapters, too, focus on sexual minorities in today's Japan but from a more political angle. Lunsing, in Chapter 6, considers the problematic nature of the categories and labels used to discuss gay, lesbian and transgender people in Japan, stressing that while there is much confusion about this issue in mainstream society, members of sexual minorities themselves also violently disagree about the use of "appropriate" language. Just as Nagata and Sullivan point out that it is problematic to be too prescriptive about the use of "gender-appropriate" language for men and women, Lunsing argues that recent discussions in Japan point to the impossibility of giving the variety of terms for sex and gender difference fixed meanings. A rise in "*tōjisha*" consciousness (that is, the "people [directly] concerned") has meant that individuals are resisting the old paternalism (of experts, professionals, the press or even self-proclaimed leaders of minority rights' groups) and are stressing their right to self-determination and expression. The irony of this position is that it makes group or collective activism all the more problematic since it is difficult for individuals with such a strong sense of personal difference to forge a common sense of identity or agree upon specific strategies for change.

McLelland, in Chapter 7, also notes the upsurge in discourse about the rights of individuals to self-define which is being promulgated via new media such as the internet. McLelland argues that until recently many gay Japanese men who have worked as salarymen were prepared to suppress their sexual identities and live as *kakure homo* (or hidden homosexuals) in the workplace. However, numerous factors have recently led to dissatisfaction with the suppression of more personal, individual traits in favor of workplace harmony. These include the collapse of

Japan's economic boom and the growing reality of job insecurity that faces most workers – fewer Japanese men now anticipate working their entire careers in the context of one office or firm. A parallel and related development is the rise in the number of men's groups and the proliferation of discussions about masculinity taking place both in academia and more widely in the media. This new realm of enquiry, rather than taking masculinity as a given, is increasingly seeing it as a problem and the previously hegemonic associations between masculine identity, productive employment and reproductive married life are beginning to unravel. As McLelland argues, the public sphere is not a neutral space but still heavily invested in rigid, hegemonic notions about gender and sexual practice. However, young men are increasingly challenging the myth that their lives lived in the workplace should be devoid of "personal" input or that their private selves should be sacrificed in favor of saving public face.

While Lunsing's and McLelland's chapters draw attention to new ways in which members of sexual and gender minorities are becoming more politically conscious through recovering and celebrating their differences, Allen's chapter (Chapter 8) reminds us that Japan has always contained specific spaces in which sexual or gender ambivalence has not only been accepted but, at times, has contributed toward an individual's sense of well-being and success. Most work in this area has looked at the role that transgender people have been allotted in Japan's vast entertainment sphere (Robertson 1998; McLelland 2005) but Allen provides an analysis of how adopting certain transgender attributes has helped a young man find his place in the context of Okinawa's woman-dominated religious world. He comments that "Akihiro has transformed *himself* into a performative *herself*. In doing so he has made himself receptive to a cosmological perspective rarely available to males. And in gaining access to this cultural knowledge he has reconstructed his gender." It is important to recognize that while this transgenderism may seem queer to Western eyes, it actually makes sense in the context of Okinawa's indigenous religious world-view.

Mackie's Chapter 9, too, deals with the performative nature of gender in the context of two seemingly dissimilar Japanese artists and cultural critics – Mishima Yukio and Morimura Yasumasa. Taking as her starting point the observation by Morimura that in terms of gender performance he and Mishima had made similar, though contrasting, gender choices – Morimura emphasizing the feminine and Mishima the masculine – Mackie explores how both artists have engaged in a very public series of gender "masquerades." Mackie shows how both Morimura and Mishima have projected a variety of gendered selves through a process of citation, deploying international as well as local gender images in their self-fashioning. In so doing, her chapter underlines the provisional, constructed, "citational" nature of all gender categories.

The chapters outlined so far might be considered to focus on previously sidelined or marginal sex and gender identities. By contrast, those by Itō (Chapter 10) and Taga (Chapter 11) reveal how even "mainstream" notions of masculinity are increasingly fractured and open to difference and contestation. The socio-economic and cultural shifts accompanying the Bubble Economy years of the 1980s and the economic downturn and corporate re-structuring of the 1990s allowed previously muted concerns about the assumptions and ideals surrounding hegemonic masculinity to emerge as an audible form of public discourse. As many of the guarantees underpinning hegemonic masculinity began to unravel over these years, there was increasing realization that individual men could be victims of the patriarchal gender ideology which had been axiomatic to Japan's industrial-capitalist project. This applied even to those men ostensibly close to the hegemonic ideal, such as middle-aged salarymen forced to re-assess their lives as a consequence of becoming victims of corporate re-structuring. Taga's chapter connects this problematization of masculinity to the emergence of men's studies and research into men and masculinities, as a distinct strand within gender and sexuality research in Japan from the 1990s. His chapter situates the emergence of this body of research and literature within the various socio-cultural shifts that have occurred during this period and provides an overview of the major works that have emerged.

Of the various writers and activists in the area of men's studies discussed in Taga's chapter, arguably the most high-profile figure is Kimio Itō who was one of the driving forces behind the emergence of men's studies as a discipline in the 1990s. Through his writings – aimed at both academic and general readerships – as well as through community activities such as seminars, public lectures, and media appearances, he drew attention to some of the problematic aspects of hegemonic masculinity in Japan. In Chapter 10, the translated excerpts from one of his best-known works, *Danseigaku nyūmon* (An introduction to men's studies, 1996), included in this volume will give English-language readers a taste of some of the issues and challenges which underlay the interrogation of masculinity in the 1990s.

However, despite the increased interrogation of masculinity as a construct and a new stress on the plurality of men's lives, Dasgupta's chapter (Chapter 12) provides an important reality check. Although attitudes may be changing in Japan, certain notions about masculinity, in particular, remain hegemonic. Dasgupta reminds us that the ideological expectations of the discourse linking masculinity with being a husband, father, and provider, continues to exert power over many men's lives. Yet, rather than being slaves to these ideologies, Dasgupta is careful to point out how the salarymen in his sample variously contest, negotiate and comply with these hegemonic demands.

If Japanese men are slow to change, it seems that women have fewer problems when imagining new ways of living and loving. Both Dales (Chapter 13) and Takeyama (Chapter 14) analyze new discourses of romantic love that are being produced and consumed by Japanese women in the context of a sex-goods business and a host club. Both chapters point out how the conditions of late-capitalism in Japan intersect with dominant ideologies of gender and sexuality in contradictory ways. On the one hand, Japan's trajectory of modernity was premised on a gender ideology marginalizing women (and men who did not subscribe to the expectations of hegemonic masculinity). However, the conditions of late-capitalist society with its stress on service and consumption have opened up increased space for women to participate in the labor market and also exercise their power as consumers. While

Japan's "floating world" of sexual entertainment has traditionally been structured in terms of men as consumers and women as service providers, women are increasingly using their purchasing power to obtain services from men, encouraging a more self-conscious and "instrumental" attitude toward sexual satisfaction among some women.

Conclusion: where to from here?

As outlined above, there is a rapidly expanding body of research on gender and sexual diversity in Japan in Japanese and to a lesser extent in English. However, there have been few projects *bringing together* researchers and activists – whether Japanese or Western – working on these different strands. Thus, there has been limited opportunity for investigations of such (seemingly) disparate topics as female patrons of male host clubs, lesbian translators or salarymen's views of marriage to be discussed alongside each other as examples of sexual and gender diversity in Japan. Sexuality and gender are not autochthonous forces which exist independent of wider social structures and ideologies. Constructs of masculinity exist in dependence upon femininity and a wide range of masculinities and femininities are necessarily structured in relation to certain forms which are privileged, if no longer hegemonic, in contemporary societies. Studies of particular sex and gender identities are, of course, still valuable and necessary, but what we hope to encourage through presenting a wide range of sexual and gender communities, identities and ideologies in this collection, is the development of a comparative approach which does not pigeon-hole and ultimately sideline sex and gender expressions which do not fit preconceived notions about Japanese society.

Notes

1. This was brought home to Mark McLelland while at the doctor's. When McLelland mentioned to the doctor that he worked in the field of Japanese Studies, the doctor was keen to praise *Memoirs of a Geisha* which both he and his wife had enjoyed. When McLelland mentioned that although a good read, the book was a *fictional* tale by an *American* man, the doctor disagreed, arguing that it was based on the author's translation of the memoirs of an actual geisha. (This is, in fact, just a literary device deployed by the author – as he explains in a postscript, "the character of Sayuri and her story are completely invented," Golden 1998: 433.)
2. Commencing in the 1930s, *nihonjinron* or "debate about Japaneseness" refers to a genre of popular literature offering essentialist descriptions of and arguments for Japanese uniqueness. See Befu (2001) for a history and analysis.
3. There are numerous internet sites devoted to various aspects of masculinity – one example is the Men's Lib Tokyo site which provides a variety of resources and links: http://www.eqg.org/~yeswhome/MensLib/index.html (accessed 3 November 2004).

References

Allison, A. (2001) "Memoirs of the Orient," *Journal of Japanese Studies*, 27(2): 381–398.
Amano, M. and R. Kimura (eds). (2003) *Jendā de manabu kyōiku* (The study of education through gender), Kyoto: Sekai Shisōsha.

Asai, H., S. Itō and Y. Murase (eds). (2001) *Nihon no otoko wa doko kara kite, doko e iku no ka* (Where have Japanese men come from, where will they go?), Tokyo: Jūgatsusha.

Ballon, R. (1969) *The Japanese Employee*, Tokyo: Sophia University Press.

Bart. (1997) "Kanzennaru 'danseigaku' de otoko ni nare!" (Become a man by mastering "men's studies"), 7(4): 10–20.

Beck, J. and M. Beck. (1994) *The Change of a Lifetime: Employment Practices among Japan's Managerial Elite*, Honolulu: University of Hawaii Press.

Befu, H. (2001) *Hegemony of Homogeneity: An Anthropological Analysis of Nihonjinron*, Melbourne: TransPacific Press.

Bessatsu Takarajima. (1987) *Onna o ai suru onna no monogatari* (Stories of women-loving women), Tokyo: JICC shuppan.

Chalmers, S. (2002) *Emerging Lesbian Voices from Japan*, London: RoutledgeCurzon.

Chamberlain, B. (1891) *Things Japanese*, London: Kegan Paul, Trench, Trubner & Co.

Childs, M. (1980) "Chigo monogatari: love stories or Buddhist sermons?" *Monumenta Nipponica*, 35(2): 127–151.

Clark, R. (1979) *The Japanese Company*, New Haven, CT: Yale University Press.

Dore, R. (1958) *City Life in Japan: A Study of a Tokyo Ward*, London: Routledge and Kegan Paul.

Fowler, E. (1996) *San'ya Blues: Laboring Life in Contemporary Tokyo*, Ithaca, NY: Cornell University Press.

Fushimi, N. (2002) *"Gei" to iu keiken* (The experience called "gay"), Tokyo: Potto Shuppan.

—— (1991) *Puraibēto gei raifu* (Private gay life), Tokyo: Gakuyō Shobō.

Harima, K. and S. Souma (eds). (2004) *Seidōitsusei shōgai 30 nin no kamingauto* (Thirty sufferers from gender identity disorder come out), Tokyo: Sōyōsha.

Haruka, Y. (2000a) *Tōdai de Ueno Chizuko ni kenka wo manabu* (Learning to fight with Ueno Chizuko at Tokyo University), Tokyo: Chikuma Bookstore.

—— (2000b) *Kekkon shimasen* (I won't marry), Tokyo: Kodansha.

Hasurā, A. (2000) *Baita nikki* (A whore's diary), Tokyo: Isshi Puresu.

Ihara, S. (1990) *The Great Mirror of Male Love*, trans. P. Schalow, Stanford, CA: Stanford University Press.

Inoue, T., C. Ueno and Y. Ehara (eds). (1998) *Danseigaku: Nihon no feminizumu bessatsu* (Men's studies: special edition of Japanese feminism series), Tokyo: Iwanami Shoten.

Giddens, A. (1992) *The Transformation of Intimacy: Sexuality, Love and Eroticism in Modern Societies*, Cambridge: Polity Press.

Golden, A. (1998) *Memoirs of a Geisha*, London: Vintage.

Itō, K. (2003) *Otokorashisa no shinwa* (Myths of masculinity), NHK ningen kōza (NHK human lecture series), aired between August and September.

—— (1996) *Danseigaku nyūmon* (An introduction to men's studies), Tokyo: Sakuhinsha.

—— (1993) *"Otokorashisa" no yukue: danseibunka no bunkashakaigaku* (Tracing "masculinity:" the cultural sociology of male culture), Tokyo: Shinyōsha.

Itō, S. (1992) *Otoko futarigurashi: boku no gei puraido sengen* (Two men living together: my gay pride declaration), Tokyo: Tarōjirōsha

Itō, S. and K. Ochiai. (1998) *Jibun rashiku ikiru: dōseiai to feminizumu* (Live like oneself: homosexuality and feminism), Kyoto: Kamogawa booklet.

Kakefuda, H. (1992) *Rezubian de aru to iu koto* (On being "lesbian"), Tokyo: Kawade Shobō Shinsha.

Kelsky, K. (2001) *Women on the Verge: Japanese Women, Western Dreams*, Durham, NC: Duke University Press.

Komatsu, A. (2000) *Nyūhāfu ga kimeta: "watashi" rashii ikikata* (On deciding to be a new-half and living like myself), Tokyo: KK Ronguserāzu.
Kuia Sutadiizu Henshū Iinkai (eds). (1997) *Kuia sutadiizu '97* (Queer studies '97), Tokyo: Nanatsumori Shokan.
—— (1996). *Kuia sutadiizu '96* (Queer studies '96), Tokyo: Nanatsumori Shokan.
LeBlanc, R. (1999) *Bicycle Citizens: The Political World of the Japanese Housewife*, Berkeley, CA: University of California Press.
Leupp, G. (1995) *Male Colors: The Construction of Homosexuality in Tokugawa Japan*, Berkeley, CA: University of California Press.
Lunsing, W. (2001) *Beyond Common Sense: Sexuality and Gender in Contemporary Japan*, London: Kegan Paul International.
Mackie, V. (2000) "The dimensions of citizenship in modern Japan: gender, class, ethnicity and sexuality," in A. Vandenberg (ed.) *Citizenship and Democracy in a Global Era*, London: Macmillan.
—— (1997) *Creating Socialist Women in Japan: Gender, Labour and Activism 1900–1937*, Cambridge: Cambridge University Press.
McLelland, M. (2005) *Queer Japan from the Pacific War to the Internet Age*, Lanham, MD: Rowman and Littlefield.
—— (2004) "From sailor-suits to sadists: 'Lesbos love' as reflected in Japan's postwar 'perverse press'," *U.S.-Japan Women's Journal*, 27: 1–25.
—— (2003) "Gay men, masculinity and the media in Japan," in K. Louie and M. Low (eds) *Asian Masculinities: The Meaning and Practice of Manhood in China and Japan*, London: RoutledgeCurzon.
—— (2000) *Male Homosexuality in Modern Japan: Cultural Myths and Social Realities*, London: RoutledgeCurzon.
Matsuzawa, K. (ed.). (2003) *Watashi ga kimeta 2* (I decided, volume 2), Tokyo: Potto Shuppan.
—— (2000a) *Watashi ga kimeta* (I decided), Tokyo: Potto Shuppan.
—— (2000b) *Uru uranai wa watashi ga kimeru* (I decide whether or not to sell), Tokyo: Potto Shuppan.
Mitsuhashi, J. (2004) *Josō aikō dansei A-shi no raifuhisutorii* (Life history of Mr A: a male lover of MtF cross-dressers), Tokyo: Chūō Daigaku Sengo Nihon Toransujendā Shakaishi Kenkyūkai.
Miyazaki, R. (2000) *Watashi wa toransujendā* (I am transgendered), Tokyo: Neoraifu.
Nakamura, A. and T. Nakamura (eds). (1997) *Otoko ga miete kuru jibun sagashi no 100 satsu* (100 books for men's search for self), Kyoto: Kamogawa Shuppan.
Nakane, C. (1970) *Japanese Society*, Berkeley, CA: University of California Press.
Nishikawa, Y. and M. Ogino (eds). (1999) *Kyōdō kenkyū: dansei-ron* (Joint research on debates on masculinity), Kyoto: Jinbun Shoin.
Pflugfelder, G. (1999) *Cartographies of Desire: Male-Male Sexuality in Japanese Discourse 1600–1950*, Berkeley, CA: University of California Press.
Plath, D. (1964) *The After Hours: Modern Japan and the Search for Enjoyment*, Westport, CT: Greenwood Press.
Roberson, J. (1998) *Japanese Working Class Lives: An Ethnographic Study of Factory Workers*, London: Routledge.
Roberson, J. and N. Suzuki (eds). (2003) *Men and Masculinities in Contemporary Japan: Dislocating the Salaryman Doxa*, London: RoutledgeCurzon.
Robertson, J. (1998) *Takarazuka: Sexual Politics and Popular Culture in Modern Japan*, Berkeley, CA: University of California Press.

Rohlen, T. (1974) *For Harmony and Strength: Japanese White-Collar Organization in Anthropological Perspective*, Berkeley, CA: University of California Press.

Said, E. (1995) *Orientalism*, Harmondsworth: Penguin.

Saitō, A. and N. Fushimi. (1997) *Kairaku no gijutsu* (The art of pleasure), Tokyo: Kawade Bunko.

Sengo Nihon Toransujendā Shakaishi Kenkyūkai (eds). (2001) *Sengo Nihon toransujendā shakaishi (vol. 3) kisō kenkyū shiryō* (Postwar Japan transgender social history, vol. 3, Basic research resources), Tokyo: Chuo University.

Shibuya, T. (2001) "'Feminusuto dansei-kenkyū' no shiten to kōzō: Nihon no danseigaku oyobi dansei hihan wo chūshin ni" (A view and vision of "feminist studies on men and masculinities": focusing on a critique of men's studies and research on men in Japan), *Shakaigaku Hyōron*, 51(4): 447–463.

Sievers, S. (1983) *Flowers in Salt: The Beginnings of Feminist Consciousness in Modern Japan*, Stanford, CA: Stanford University Press.

Smith, J. and S. Okamoto (eds). (2005) *Japanese Language, Gender, and Ideology: Cultural Models and Real People*, Oxford: Oxford University Press.

Smith, R. and E. Wiswell. (1982) *The Women of Suye Mura*, Chicago: University of Chicago Press.

Sturtz Streetharn, C. (2004) "Students, *sarariiman* (pl.), and seniors: Japanese men's use of 'manly' speech register," *Language in Society*, 33: 81–107.

Sugiura, I. (2001) *Matsuba Yukari no raifuhisutorii* (Matsuba Yukari life history), Tokyo: Chūō Daigaku Sengo Nihon Toransujendā Shakaishi Kenkyūkai.

Sunaga, F. (1999) *Hage wo ikiru* (Living with baldness), Tokyo: Keisō Shobō.

Taga, F. (2001) *Dansei no jendā keisei* (The gender formation of men), Tokyo: Tōyōkan Shuppansha.

Toyama, H. (1999) *Otoko toshite ikiru joseitachi: Miss Dandy* (Women living as men: Miss Dandy), Tokyo: Shinchōsha.

Toyoda, M. (1997) *Otoko ga "otokorashisa" wo suteru toki* (When men discard "manliness"), Tokyo: Asuka Shinsha.

Ueno, C. (1994) *Seiairon* (Debates on sexuality), Tokyo: Kawade Bunko.

—— (1992) *Sukāto no shita no gekijō* (Theatre under the skirt), Tokyo: Kawade Bunko.

van Helvoort, E. (1979) *The Japanese Working Man: What Choice? What Reward?* Tenterton, Kent: Paul Norbury Publications.

Vogel, E. (1963) *Japan's New Middle Class: The Salaryman and His Family in a Tokyo Suburb*, Berkeley, CA: University of California Press.

Willig, R. (trans.). (1983) *The Changelings: A Classical Japanese Court Tale*, Stanford, CA: Stanford University Press.

Yajima, M. (2000) *Okama dō wo iku: Yatsuse Yumi no kenkyū* (On the *okama* road: Yatsuse Yumi's research), Tokyo: Chūō Daigaku Sengo Nihon Toransujendā Shakaishi Kenkyūkai.

—— (1999) *Josei dōseiaisha no raifuhisutorii* (Female homosexuals' life histories), Tokyo: Gakubunsha.

—— (1997) *Dansei dōseiaisha no raifuhisutorii* (Male homosexuals' life histories), Tokyo: Gakubunsha.

2 Hegemonic gender in Japanese as a foreign language education
Australian perspectives

Yuriko Nagata and Kristen Sullivan

Introduction

The treatment of culture in foreign language teaching has been the subject of vigorous pedagogical and theoretical investigation over the past two decades. Liddicoat *et al*. write, "The nature of language learning has become more complex, integrating new subject matter reflecting the increased importance of culture" (1997: 28). These investigations have resulted in a greater awareness of cultural stereotyping in foreign language teaching resources. The teaching of Japanese as a foreign language (JFL) has also been affected by developments in this area.[1] The argument is that cultural stereotyping in textbooks published for tertiary learners projects a vision of Japan which does not reflect reality. This chapter specifically looks at gender stereotyping in such materials that perpetuate and reproduce normative gender stereotyping and gendered language norms. Inherent in such cultural and gender stereotyping in JFL teaching materials are ideologies of "Japaneseness," often referred to as *nihonjinron* (theory of Japanese uniqueness) sentiments, which actively influence how Japanese see themselves and how Japan is portrayed to the outside world. Such notions of "Japaneseness" and the crafting of "desirable" ways of "being Japanese" are interwoven into the Japanese language that appears in Japanese learning materials, and are reinforced through JFL education.

This chapter draws on studies of gender stereotyping in JFL textbooks to examine how norms of gender and gendered language circulating in the JFL learning environment influence both learners' and teachers' negotiations with gender and language. *Onna kotoba* (women's language) is frequently presented to the JFL learner as the language of all Japanese women and, importantly, a specific kind of femininity is attached to it. We suggest that a reconsideration of how gendered language is described and dealt with in the classroom and how gender is incorporated into the linguistic and cultural content of courses is a necessary step in the advancement of JFL education. Of particular importance is a reevaluation of how gendered language is presented in textbooks.

While this chapter examines actual language use – specifically at a grammatical level – we can similarly examine the way "gender-marked" lexicons are taught, and also what counts as "appropriate" content in JFL learning materials and classroom interactions. Moreover, since both authors are women, we specifically focus on the experiences of women students and teachers. Considering that both learners (Kinoshita Thomson and Iida 2002: 185) and teachers (Marriott *et al.* 1994) of Japanese in Australia are predominantly women (each approximately 70 percent), this inquiry is of particular importance and highlights the need for further analysis. At the same time, this high proportion of female participants in JFL also suggests that the range of language male students are exposed to may not always reflect "male" experiences, which is another topic in need of consideration.

As the aim of the chapter is to examine the experiences of those who participate in the JFL classroom, it is appropriate that it has been co-written by a teacher and a student of Japanese. The key text on which the theoretical discussions draw is a dialogue between the authors about *our* experiences with gender norms and JFL as teacher/student. This dialogue developed through the recounting of personal experiences, extended discussions on theoretical texts, and e-mail communication. It appears here, for purpose of conciseness, as an edited compilation of several discussions, prefaced with a *Y* (for Yuriko, teacher) or *K* (for Kristen, learner) to indicate the speaker. Moreover, where it seems appropriate, we have presented the original dialogue in a soliloquized form. While the perspectives and experiences presented here are necessarily personal, we believe they nicely illustrate the current state of gender in JFL education as well as key issues that need to be further addressed both in the Australian context and beyond.

Gender stereotyping in JFL textbooks: existing studies

A language lesson is a curricular as well as a social event (Hutchinson and Torres 1994). There is usually a teacher, a learner, or learners as well as teaching materials, which often include a textbook. Learners see a textbook as a framework/guide which helps them organize their learning both inside and outside the classroom. The role of the textbook is often central in classrooms since most teachers carry enormous teaching loads with little time for research, materials development or reflection. While good teachers constantly try to devise their own materials, in reality, the development of supplementary materials is increasingly difficult due to copyright restrictions and the time it takes. University language teachers in Australia, and elsewhere, are required to perform a difficult balancing act between materials development and research. In the increasingly "publish or perish" environment in Australian universities, tertiary language teachers are supposed to produce research papers as well as develop teaching materials since the latter are not acknowledged as publications for purposes of promotion or the gaining of tenure.

Yet, despite the central role played by textbooks in the JFL learning experience, there are still relatively few studies which focus on the gender norms which are promulgated through this medium. Evaluative studies of existing JFL textbooks undertaken so far argue that they are in serious need of revision so that they represent a more diverse view of the gender reality. Here we will briefly outline the findings of these studies.

In her examination of gender stereotyping in ten JFL textbooks, Nagata (1992) found that they suffered from gender bias through omission, proportional representation and stereotypical representation, especially in terms of their illustrations and the social roles allocated to female characters. Siegal and Okamoto's study (1996) looked at language, gender and social roles in five widely used Japanese textbooks. They argue that representations in the textbooks "reflect a 'normative' ideology – especially beliefs and values focused on middle-class 'white-collar' homogeneity and rigid 'traditional' sex roles" (ibid.: 667). Maree (1997a) analyzed Japanese–English dictionaries used by JFL learners and found gender bias in definitions, examples, illustrations and translations that favored men.

In a more recent study of business Japanese textbooks, Kinoshita Thomson and Otsuji (2003: 185) also found that "the textbooks present a stereotypical and exaggerated version of social practices of the Japanese business community, based on idealized native-Japanese norms." Female characters in the textbooks they analyzed were found to have less access to managerial positions, and fewer opportunities to participate in business, than they do in reality. They claim that "gendered textbooks will have a gendered impact on the learners who use them" (ibid.: 202) and thus call for "textbooks which provide more diverse perspectives of the Japanese business community" (ibid.: 185). Finally, Kawasaki and McDougall's (2003) empirical study looks at gendered language norms, and specifically examines the female and male characters' use of sentence final particles in the model dialogues of three JFL textbooks (ibid.: 45). From this analysis they conclude that "the textbooks are presenting an over-generalized, indeed incorrect, picture of Japanese society" (ibid.: 53).

These studies demonstrate the extent to which gender stereotyping and dominant gender norms permeate JFL textbooks. What remains to be investigated, however, is how JFL learners and teachers feel about and respond to such representations. This is the question which we will address in the dialogues that follow.

Encountering gender norms: JFL classroom experiences

As they reach more advanced levels of study in Japanese, learners are gradually exposed to gender norms through various gender-marked features, both linguistic and meta-linguistic. Kristen began studying Japanese at the age of 11 (Grade 6) at a time when the Australian government was keen to promote Asian languages in schools. She reflects on how she became aware of gendered aspects of the Japanese language:

> *K*: It was in my senior years of high school. Our Japanese teacher pointed out how certain *kanji* [Chinese characters] featuring the radical for "woman" can be understood as derogatory. She then mentioned how sentence-final particles tend to be different for men and women. The class being made up entirely of female students, she taught us that Japanese women tend to use the *-wa* final particle instead of the neutral *-yo*. Of course, we were told about the "appropriate" use of gendered pronouns way back in primary school.

Yuriko is a Japanese native speaker and has taught all levels of Japanese at two Australian universities: she has been in her current position for 14 years. She was an EFL (English as a Foreign Language) teacher before becoming a JFL teacher and was already conscious of gender bias in EFL learning materials:

> Y: Students should be informed about such aspects of the language along with other linguistic features as a form of socio-linguistic knowledge. They want to know if it's there. But I think it's also important for students to receive additional explanation from the teacher regarding the neutralization of gender differences in Japanese today. This should be done right from the beginner's level. However, many students in Australia and other countries are already aware of the need for social equity, let alone the various forms of discrimination in the societies they live in. Because they already bring such social literacy into the foreign language classroom, such pre-existing knowledge has to be taken into account and the level of treatment of these matters adjusted accordingly.

> K: I totally agree. But I feel that kind of balance between teaching about linguistic norms and actual language use is still lacking in even intermediate and advanced course materials. When I first started studying Japanese at university, gendered linguistic differences became more obvious through the texts and audio materials we were using. But this wasn't offset with any alternative texts or explanations about the diversity in actual language usage.

Kanada (cited by Nagata 1995: 9) argues that, "not to address the social issues manifest in all language use is at best inadequate and at worst irresponsible." As indicated in the recent analyses of JFL textbooks discussed above, the characterization of speakers in JFL textbooks is also extremely normative:

> Y: I think JFL textbooks are often so predictable with the characterization of speakers in those so-called "model" dialogues. It is so often the case in textbooks targeting general adult learners that the main characters are salarymen[2] and their colleagues and wives. In university set textbooks, it is often the case that the professors are men, and the telephone operators and secretaries are women.

As a result of the repetitiveness of the context, settings and topics, lexical items also become predictable. Lexical items such as "husband" and "wife" are among these, and are often among the first terms that students study where they become aware of their discriminatory meaning. The sexist connotations of these terms make their use awkward for some, which renders the lack of critical attention to them in textbooks problematic:

> Y: Students ask if there are any non-derogatory alternatives. I introduce neutral words such as *tsuma* [my wife] for *kanai* [my woman in the house]

and *otto* [my husband] for *shujin* [my master]. They are relatively straightforward. But there aren't really good alternatives for referring to someone else's husband and wife if you don't want to use *goshujin* [your master] or *okusan* [your woman in the back]. *Otsureai* [your spouse] sounds very archaic. *Pātonā* [partner] can be used, but it's a little awkward to say ~*san no pātonā* or *pātonā no kata*. One member of a group called *Kairyu* in Kyoto said that *ottosan* is beginning to be heard.[3] Nothing really works well.

K: When I was in Japan I felt awkward referring to somebody's husband as *goshujin*, but didn't know of any appropriate substitutes. Actually, there was one time when a volunteer at the university where I was studying told me that she didn't refer to her husband as *shujin* but *pātonā*, or the English "husband." I remember then not knowing how I should refer to her husband, wary of classroom teachings about the correct and incorrect ways to refer to your interlocutor and their significant others, and a couple of times even referred to him as her *otto-san*. Looking back now, *pātonā-san* would probably have been a good alternative.

All these terms *shujin*, *goshujin*, *kanai* and *okusan* are still widely used in Japan, despite the fact that they have been subject to recurrent discussions among Japanese feminists since the late nineteenth century. According to the *Asahi Shinbun*, many women are reluctant to use *shujin*, or do not like to be addressed as *okusan*.[4] Gender-based discriminatory terms are, however, attracting increasing attention in the media. In its eighth edition in 1997, the *Kisha Handobukku*, a stylebook for journalists, provided a list of some gender-based discriminatory terms for the first time.[5] However, *shujin*, *goshujin*, *kanai* and *okusan* were not listed among them.

The projection of gender norms by other means is also problematic. Gender stereotyping in JFL is at times extreme in its conformity to gendered language norms and certain meta-linguistic features:

K: It's not just the issue of discriminatory language but gendered language in textbooks that used to frustrate me. The dialogues between male and female characters in the textbooks were always marked by the "gender-appropriate" pronouns, sentence-final particles and usage of polite language, etc. I couldn't stand it. Audio materials are just as bad, and my friends and I cringed at those super high-pitched voices that were always used for the female characters.

Y: There is nothing wrong with high-pitched voices. What bothers me is this use of pitch to depict certain gendered images of women in Japan as polite, indirect and empathetic.

K: Actually, I used to wonder why such high-pitched voices were almost always used for female characters when most of the Japanese women I knew, like my teachers and friends, all talked in relatively low voices.

> *Y:* My dilemma is that such audiotapes are "better than nothing" – the students need to be exposed to a variety of native speaker voices, not just mine. The only way to gain some balance in the classroom is to bring in as many authentic voices as possible – either by live or by other audio-visual resources.

Various well-meaning classroom activities such as role-plays can also make some students feel extremely uncomfortable:

> *Y:* Listening to such recordings is one thing, but asking students, regardless of their gender, to reproduce them is another. In the past I always felt awkward and sort of embarrassed hearing a female student read the female part in *onna kotoba*, particularly the sentence final particle *dawa*. I feel it creates embarrassment on all sides – both for the teacher and the student. Some students make fun of representations of *onna kotoba* by exaggerating the female speech style through the use of meta-linguistic features such as facial or hand gestures. I always wonder what is going through their minds when they do this.
>
> *K:* I often wondered what my classmates were thinking too – if they felt the same way as I did. When I was still at an intermediate level, I didn't question the accuracy of these gendered representations, or whether they were consistent for all Japanese speakers. Instead, I started to think negatively about this aspect of Japanese.

Ohara, in her research on the relationship between voice pitch and gendered identities in Japanese, demonstrated that "a high pitched voice is a resource for projecting femininity in Japanese culture" (2001: 247) and "the female English-Japanese bilinguals' decisions about their voice pitch were deeply entrenched in their perceptions of gender and femininity in Japanese culture" (ibid.: 248). One such learner commented:

> Sometimes it would really disgust me, seeing those Japanese girls, they were not even girls, some of them were in their late twenties, but they would use those real high voices to try to impress and make themselves look real cute for men. I decided that there was no way I wanted to do that.
>
> (ibid.: 244)

Of the several examples of gender stereotyping we have discussed in this section, norms of gendered language usage – particularly *onna kotoba* – have also been highlighted elsewhere as creating conflicts for female learners, especially in their own everyday use of Japanese (Siegal 1995; Siegal and Okamoto 1996; Maree 2000). The remainder of the chapter will, therefore, focus on this issue.

Gendered language in Japanese: theoretical developments

While conceptualizations of gendered language in Japanese have developed dramatically over the past two decades, JFL teaching materials continue to promote dominant norms of language and gender, and under-represent other possibilities. These norms have been perpetuated by certain streams of *joseigo kenkyū* (women's language research). Through an unproblematized reliance on static notions of gender in terms of biological essentialism and binary dualisms, these studies theorize gendered language as *reflecting* gender "realities." In other words, they create essentialist distinctions between women's and men's speech, confounding gender marked language into the rigid categories of "women's language" – the language of all women – and "men's language" – the language of all men. There was a preoccupation in earlier research (e.g. Abe, Ide, Shibamoto and others) with debating whether the existence of gendered language was to be understood in positive or negative terms. This left unquestioned the direct correlation between gender and language, and the actual theoretical understandings of gender that were employed.

However, the assumptions of these earlier theories have become the subject of investigation since the early 1990s, and new research has questioned the notion of a "one-to-one relationship of gender to speech" (Okamoto, cited in Maree 2003). This research has been influenced by new understandings of sentence-final-particles as indexical functions,[6] as well as the recognition of the importance of analyzing "actual speech"[7] and the incorporation of context into analysis. Two main strands of research have developed – one that is concerned with locating linguistic diversity through analyzing "actual speech," and the other with locating the ideological construction of *onna kotoba* – as methods to challenge the discourse of "Japanese women's language" (Yukawa and Saito 2002).

One of the most commonly cited findings of empirical studies of women's actual speech relates to the use of *otoko kotoba* (men's language), particularly by young, but also by some middle-aged women (Matsumoto 2002). Okamoto's investigation of young women's use of "masculine" speech is one example of recent research that reveals how actual speech differs from gendered language norms. Her work also highlights the level of linguistic diversity, both between and within groups of women (Okamoto and Sato 1992; Okamoto 1995, 1996, 1997), which problematizes claims of a homogenous community of Japanese women speakers. Okamoto locates the linguistic agency of Japanese speakers, arguing that speech styles are strategically chosen "based on consideration of multiple social aspects of the context as well as on [the speaker's] linguistic ideology, or beliefs and attitudes concerning language use" (1997: 795). As a result of this research, there is now increasing evidence that the language actually used by Japanese women often deviates from "gender appropriate" norms.[8]

Inoue's genealogy of Japanese women's language also contributes significantly to the deconstruction of the discourse of *onna kotoba*. By examining "linguistic modernization movements," she demonstrates how current understandings of women's language did not develop along a stable historical lineage – as primordialist discourses would have us believe. Instead, they were "carved out, selected, and (re)constructed as Japanese women's language" during Japan's modernization in the late nineteenth century (2002: 385).

While the individual research projects discussed here have been diverse, one of the most important understandings they have provided is that *onna kotoba* and *otoko kotoba* are not empirical categories, but thoroughly ideological and cultural.

Hegemonic gender in Japanese as a foreign language

Recent inquiries into "Japanese women's language" have challenged essentialist views of gendered language norms and called for new approaches to the treatment of gender and language.[9] It is this reading of *onna kotoba* as ideology that allows us to investigate the perpetuation of gendered norms in JFL as another means of maintaining control over the image of "Japan."

As noted by Inoue (2002), the issue of Japanese women's (linguistic and gender) identity seems to stand out as a major area of contention in Japanese society. In her article about young Japanese women's use of "masculine" language, Okamoto (1995: 297) quotes from a "letter to the editor" by a 59-year-old man concerned with the increasing use of men's language and "dirty words" by women. The writer calls for the preservation of "attractive and adorable women's language." This type of argument reduces women and their (linguistic) identities to token symbols of essentialist cultural claims – pawns in the transmission of culture. Teaching language to foreigners can be seen as one such vehicle of cultural transmission. It is also another arena in which images of Japan are monitored – rendering invisible the lives, experiences, and *voices* of those on the margins. The writer in this example seems to be particularly aware of this, warning that "[i]f we teach men's language to female foreigners, we will inevitably end up teaching the wrong Japanese culture" (Okamoto 1995: 297).

Assimilation into "*the* Japanese Culture" is continually presented to the JFL learner in Japan as an obvious goal and a step toward achieving linguistic proficiency and cultural competence. This expectation of foreign students is reflected in Kristen's testimonial:

> K: As an exchange student in Japan, one of our main objectives is to "become as Japanese as possible" – success is measured by the degree we can emulate the "perfect native speaker." At many times during my exchange I did consider this to be a primary goal. Actually, I was often introduced to people as "more Japanese than Japanese" [*nihonjin yori nihonjinmitai*], and this was meant to be the ultimate compliment – like a statement saying that I had "made it" as an exchange student. This aim comes into question, though, when the homogenized image of what it means becomes unstable. So I wasn't entirely comfortable with using or subverting gendered linguistic norms as an outsider to whom cultural assimilation was proposed as a goal, even if those proposing it did not necessarily expect complete success.

In an interview with Satomi Mishina (1994: 430), Sachiko Ide states that:

If she [the non-native student of Japanese] wants to interact with Japanese people using Japanese, she should follow what we actually do. That's how people communicate in the society. It's like the air; this is what makes us feel comfortable. This is our social norm.

However, it is the question of which "Japanese people" and which "social norms" unproblematically referred to by Ide in the quote above that is the main issue here. As argued elsewhere by Maree (2003; 1997b), it is the totalizing effect of Ide's (1993) talk of "us Japanese women" in her theorizations of "Japanese women's language" that is pernicious because it discounts the diverse experiences of female speakers of Japanese.

The backlash faced by the "gender-free" – let alone "gender-multiple" – education movement gives us some insight into the continuing strength of conservatives in Japan. Their argument against the call to remove gender stereotyping in textbooks is that "the ideology behind 'gender free' education is dangerous as it denies the traditional Japanese culture which has formed the minds of Japanese people" (Tsuruta 2003: 4). This argument for maintaining "traditional" notions of gender and nation among conservatives demonstrates the broader context in which JFL is situated. In other words, this image of "Japan" is ideologically constructed, so any call to dismantle it – for example, by challenging normative notions of gender – will be seen as an assault on tradition by those who stand to benefit from maintaining the current hetero-gender order. This means that when we consider challenging the current state of gender in JFL, we need to keep in mind that the crafting of textbooks is inherently interconnected with the question of who and what is to count under the rubric of "Japan."

Negotiating with gender norms

The learner

Kristen spent one year as an exchange student at a university in the south-west of Japan. This was when she first experienced diversity in the actual usage of gendered language:

> K: When I was on exchange I started to realize that the extent of gendered language norms stretched far beyond what we were taught in the classroom. But as I started talking with and listening to more and more native Japanese speakers, and engaging with Japanese texts, especially spoken media, I also saw just how diverse and colorful the language actually is, and the level of diversity among speakers. The Japanese I encountered was very different from that presented to us in JFL textbooks. This encouraged me to experiment more with my own language use.

However, this can also come about when learners become confronted and feel in conflict with gender language norms:

K: It was when I was communicating in Japanese every day and gradually reaching a more advanced speaking level that this actually became a practical issue for me. I felt that I had to make certain linguistic decisions. Namely, whether or not to conform to gendered language norms in my own speech. Based on my own gender ideologies and beliefs, I personally felt uncomfortable doing this. I found that I lacked the necessary background to inform the linguistic decisions I needed to make, though.

This was compounded by the constant appearance of this image of the "right way for girls to talk" in Japanese and the occasional good-natured "advice" from teachers or acquaintances about using the appropriate language. Personally, it was awkward to be told that I had to talk a certain way because I was "a girl" especially because I felt the "appropriate language" for "my gender" didn't necessarily reflect my own desired terms of self-expression.

According to Kramsch (cited in Siegal and Okamoto 1996: 674–675):

learners should be encouraged to acquire a "critical cultural literacy," that is, a contextual competence based on a critical understanding of the new world that a second language provides, such as attitudes, beliefs, values, expectations, and behaviors; from that understanding, learners are enabled to find their own voice in a second language.

K: I have my preferred style of speaking in English, which can sometimes draw criticism or surprise. But I'm fully aware that speaking in certain ways in particular circumstances is more beneficial, and is indeed more desirable, and I can use this cultural knowledge to my advantage. While I'm confident and fluent in switching in English, translating this attitude to Japanese proved harder in the beginning. A lack of background knowledge and my positioning as a female foreign student made it hard for me to balance my dual aims of "proficiency" and "creating my own style in Japanese."

I always dreaded criticism of how I talked, or making a "mistake" when I was an exchange student. But, at the same time, I wanted to find a way of speaking in Japanese that was more reflective of myself. After being in Japan for a while, I started to speak in different ways with different people to gauge their impression of the appropriateness of the language I was using. To this "experiment" I received a number of interesting responses, from people shocked, concerned or amused if I used *otoko kotoba*, to those who made no comments at all. In many ways, doing this helped me create my personal speaking style in Japanese.

This concept of the learner "creating their own style" or "finding their own voice" in the new language is a recent development in second language acquisition theory (Siegal and Okamoto 1996; Ohara 2001; Pavlenko and Piller 2001). Kristen's account reveals how the second language acquisition process is far from neutral but is rather a deeply subjective experience. Pavlenko and Piller (2001: 29) argue that many second language acquisition theories view second language learners as "passive vessels for input and output." Such traditional pedagogies create the myth of the "idealized learner" (Rampton, cited in Siegal and Okamoto 1996: 674) whose linguistic goal is to become the perfect "native speaker" (Siegal and Okamoto 1996: 674). Non-compliance with language norms is, therefore, viewed in terms of incorrectness and failure (Ohara 2001: 241–242).

Siegal and Okamoto (1996: 674) introduce the concept of "learner positionality," arguing that "[t]he issues concerning 'norms' in language textbooks need to be considered not only in light of social and linguistic diversity, but also from the perspective of the learner – the learner's social position, goals, and values." In other words, they call for the recognition of the learner's multiple subjectivities and goals in the JFL learning environment, and the possibility of "learner conflict regarding appropriate target language use" (ibid.: 675). Such a teaching pedagogy regards the dual aims of informing learners about gendered linguistic "norms" and providing them with the critical cultural understanding necessary for *their own* language use in multiple contextual settings as equally important. The literature often describes the learner's negotiation with gendered language norms as resulting from "a conflict concerning how they view themselves, their view of Japanese women and 'women's language' and the language they need to use to speak appropriately in various situations" (Siegal 1995: 241; see also Ohara 2001). This means that facilitating a critical understanding and appreciation of the diversity of the target culture and its people must also be considered a goal in the JFL classroom (Siegal and Okamoto 1996; Ohara 2001; Pavlenko and Piller 2001).

The teacher

Siegal and Okamoto remind us of the important role the teacher plays in this process, writing that "[w]e hope that language teachers carefully reflect on how and what they are teaching" (1996: 675). The teacher plays a unique role in cultivating a comfortable and safe learning environment. Yuriko's story reveals that it is not just students but teachers, too, who engage and negotiate with language and gender.

Like many other Japanese nationals who are teaching in Australian universities, Yuriko is a Japanese-English bilingual:

> *Y:* With my family in Japan, I speak in the way I always do with them – in the neutral register with an occasional masculine touch. My sister is the same. When I visit my old friends in Japan, I can almost hear myself constantly adjusting my style or register depending on who I am talking to and where I am. Sometimes I find myself putting on a bit more of a "feminine" touch, not so much in the language itself, but through my body language, like how I sit or what I wear.

Yuriko talks about experiences where her speech was commented upon in Japan:

> Y: Some years ago, I was visiting an old friend at a university in Japan to have a work-related meeting with her and two other colleagues of hers, whom I was meeting for the first time. As the meeting progressed, I decided to switch to a less formal register with them as I detected a quite informal approach from her colleagues. Later that night she confided that she thought I should have kept the formal register throughout. I didn't agree with her sense of language use, but the point is that I was made to feel "inappropriate" because I was visiting from outside Japan.

On another occasion:

> Y: I was visiting an American professor of linguistics who had been living in Japan for quite some time. During our introductory conversation he suddenly commented that I didn't raise the tone of my voice when introducing myself to him and spoke with a rather low voice throughout. I took his comment as a compliment.

As evident in the classroom experiences Yuriko discussed, a teacher's personal gender ideologies can make it extremely uncomfortable for them to teach within the confines of the binary gender norms depicted in many JFL textbooks.

Teachers carry their own gender identity and ideologies into the classroom, even if they are not immediately obvious or openly revealed to the students. This becomes *their* "positionality" in the choice of teaching materials, content and teaching philosophy – which is crucial in creating a classroom in which students are encouraged to raise issues, give opinions and experiment with their language use (Summerhawk 1998).

While the teacher plays an important role in selecting teaching materials and determining how the classroom is to be managed, the role of students in creating dynamic and meaningful classroom experiences should not be overlooked:

> Y: For example, I used a Japanese family TV drama in an advanced Japanese course a few years ago. The characterization in the drama itself was pretty stereotypical, but it's one of the few audio-visual JFL materials available. The final oral assessment of the course was a group presentation of a play based on the drama, but set ten years later. I was thrilled to see how creative my students were with characterization and plots. For example, some of the students developed characters which later came out as gay or lesbian. The language used in their scripts was also original and not restricted to gender norms. These classroom experiences really give me an important insight into what interests students. For me, students are the source of inspiration for material development. I am now compiling some new material, let's just call it "The Japan which Has Not Appeared in JFL Textbooks." This text is a collection of interviews (in the original dialect)

with lots of people of different occupations, ages, regions, ethnic backgrounds and sexualities.

In a conventional classroom with a conventional textbook, "gay" and "lesbian" would never appear as lexicons, let alone as actual characters. In this example, the students' input into the JFL classroom significantly enriched the learning content. By bringing the outside world (e.g. Australia) into the classroom, students can provide learning input – the kind of input that conventional textbooks cannot provide. This notion of input is what Kramsch (1993: 5) defines as "quality input." In such a learning environment, the teacher is no longer the privileged "owner" of knowledge, and learning at an advanced tertiary level becomes what it should ideally be: independent and meaningful. This type of approach is one way that the JFL classroom can move away from the exclusive engagement with materials that project homogenized images of Japan.

However, the reverse is also true, and an inability to teach *outside* cultural and gender norms by teachers is probably a more typical description of the JFL education at present. As is evident from the discussions so far, much work remains to be done to disrupt this element of control over the representation of "Japan." While we now see critiques of *nihonjinron* arguments and a general shift toward a more critical and diversity-embracing research agenda in Japanese Studies, JFL is comparatively lagging behind, and seems to be unable to disengage itself from the traditional perceptions of the Japanese people, Japan and Japanese culture. Within this matrix, the teacher plays the role of cultural and ideological facilitator and retains control over what is to be introduced and discussed in the classroom. Without disrupting this element of control, chances for a significant transformation in how gender and sexuality can be incorporated in JFL seem futile.

How this is to be achieved remains an important challenge. As we have seen, significant impetus for change can be expected to come from the students themselves. Another possibility is the inclusion of more diverse images, contexts and characters in JFL teaching materials, which would allow the introduction of "unconventional" themes. For teachers who do not necessarily take issues of gender into account, or those who do but are unsure how it can be better incorporated, the provision of unconventional materials can be seen as a first step. However, while the introduction of such teaching materials is important, there needs to be a drastic change in basic pedagogical methods and mentalities within the JFL culture itself before there can be a significant transformation in how gender is incorporated in JFL. Perhaps JFL *teachers* themselves needs to be provided with a critical cultural awareness of Japan and greater sociolinguistic understanding of Japanese just as it has been suggested is crucial for learners of foreign languages.

Conclusion

This chapter has focused on the issue of gender and JFL, and in particular on the experiences of women learners and teachers. However, we would like to suggest that these arguments are equally relevant to the needs of male learners and teachers as well as to the area of sexuality and JFL. The "actual speech" of men and the cultural discourses of *otoko kotoba* (men's language) and *onē kotoba* (camp speech) in particular, remain very under-researched. We must not assume that "men" make up a homogenous community of speakers to whom issues of gender and linguistic negotiation are irrelevant. In a similar vein, Anna Livia and Kira Hall (1997: 3) point out that sexuality and sexual orientation remain marginal criteria for analysis in the area of linguistic research. This is further accentuated when the aspect of second language acquisition is included. While there have been some recent studies on Japanese language and sexuality,[10] intersections between sexuality and JFL and the experiences of lesbian, gay, bisexual, transgender and queer identified learners and teachers with language norms have yet to be considered. This reflects their comparative absence in Japanese Studies. We argue that new paradigms for doing JFL need to include issues of both gender and sexuality. This process necessarily involves challenging existing frameworks and ideological assumptions that have influenced understandings of "Japan" and the Japanese language, and through this the current formation of JFL education.

Notes

1 Teaching of Japanese culture is done in a curriculum area called *nihonjijō* in JFL education in Japan. It is in this area where theoretical debates have occurred. Representative researchers in this area include Hasegawa Tsuneo, Hosokawa Hideo, J.V. Neustupny, Sunakawa Yuichi, Kawakami Ikuo, Sasaki Michiko and Kadokura Masami.
2 See Dasgupta (2003) for an anecdote about just how widespread the figure of the salaryman is as the representative of Japanese men among Japanese Studies students. McLelland (Chapter 7, this volume) also points out how the image of the salaryman is uppermost in the minds of most Western people when they think about Japanese men.
3 Personal communication with Ms Y. Murazawa, 2 August 2004.
4 Cited by M. Saito. Available online: http://homepage.mac.com/saitohmasami/public_html/guideline.html (accessed 26 September 2004). See also Takeyama (Chapter 14, this volume) for a discussion of women who do not like to be referred to as Mr so-and-so's wife.
5 Available online: http://homepage.mac.com/saitohmasami/public_html/guideline.html (accessed 26 September 2004).
6 See Ochs (1992) for gender indexicals, Silverstein (1976) for the concept of indexicality and Maree (1997b, 2003) for an overview that incorporates J.L. Austin's speech act theory.
7 This new trend toward analyzing "actual speech" examples, as opposed to native speaker introspection, anecdotal evidence or self-report surveys, derives from a re-evaluation of previous research methodologies which have been found to report only how people think they speak or should speak. Bias in sampling choice typically favored middle-class, middle-aged and (presumably) heterosexual research participants. This last point has recently been problematized by Maree and Ogawa and (Shibamoto) Smith. The over-representation of speakers from the Yamanote region of Tokyo has also been the subject of critique. See, for example, J. S. Shibamoto (1985) and Takano Shoji (2000).
8 This concern with locating diversity in gendered language use has recently been extended to include male speakers and Cindi Sturtz (Streetharan) has argued that region and life stage influence men's (non-)use of gendered language. While she does

not report locating instances of men's linguistic gender transgression, this has been documented, and indeed is obvious in the speech of transgender television talents such as Mikawa Ken'ichi and among some gay men, as *onē kotoba*. The term *onē kotoba* comes from *onēsan kotoba*, literally meaning "big-sister speech" (McLelland 2000: 47), or camp speech. While it features the linguistic forms typically associated with the feminine, its usage conveys different meanings from that of normative heterosexual femininity (Hirano 1994: 92–93). As quoted in Ogawa and (Shibamoto) Smith (1997: 403), Fushimi Noriaki stresses *onē kotoba*'s "performative (*enshutsuteki*) nature." See the earlier work of Janet S. Shibamoto (1985, 1986) for a very brief look at male speakers in "a-typical gender roles" and Mark McLelland (2000) and Wim Lunsing (2003) for descriptions of *onē kotoba* and gendered language use by gay and transgendered men.

9 However, there has also been important criticism of the "heterogender bias" and "conflation of gender and sexuality" even among these new research models. See the work of Claire Maree for an analysis.
10 See the works of Claire Maree (1997b, 2000, 2003), Naoko Ogawa and Janet S. (Shibamoto) Smith (1997), and James Valentine (1997a).

References

Abe, H. N. (1995) "From stereotype to context: the study of Japanese women's speech," *Feminist Studies*, 21(3): 647–671.
Dasgupta, R. (2003) "Creating corporate warriors: the 'salaryman' and masculinity in Japan," in K. Louie and M. Low (eds) *Asian Masculinities: The Meaning and Practice of Manhood in China and Japan*, London and New York: Routledge.
Hirano, H. (1994) *Anchi heterosekushizumu* (Anti-heterosexism), Tokyo: Pandora/Gendai Shokan.
Hutchinson, T. and E. Torres. (1994) "The textbook as agent of change," *ELT Journal*, 48: 315–328.
Ide, S. (1993) "Sekai no joseigo, Nihon no joseigo – joseigo kenkyū no shintenkai wo motomete" (Global women's language, Japan's women's language – searching for new developments in the field of women's language research), *Nihongogaku*, 12(6): 4–12.
Inoue, M. (2002) "Gender, language, and modernity: toward an effective history of Japanese women's language," *American Ethnologist*, 29(2): 392–422.
Kawasaki, K. and K. McDougal. (2003) "Implications of representations of casual conversation: a case study in gender-associated sentence final particles," *Japanese-Language Education around the Globe*, The Japan Foundation Japanese Language Institute, 13: 41–57.
Kinoshita Thomson, C. and S. Iida. (2002) "Gendered language in Japanese: learner perceptions in Australia," *Japanese-Language Education around the Globe*, The Japan Foundation Japanese Language Institute, 12: 1–20.
Kinoshita Thomson, C. and E. Otsuji. (2003) "Evaluating business Japanese textbooks: issues of gender," *Japanese Studies*, 23(2): 185–203.
Kramsch, C. (1993) *Context and Culture in Language Teaching*, Oxford: Oxford University Press.
Liddicoat, A., C. Crozet, L. Jansen and G. Schmidt. (1997) "The role of language learning in academic education: an overview," *Australian Review of Applied Linguistics*, 20(2): 19–32.
Livia, A. and K. Hall (eds). (1997) "'It's a girl!' Bringing performativity back to

linguistics," in A. Livia and K. Hall (eds) *Queerly Phrased*, New York: Oxford University Press.
Lo Bianco, J. (2003) "Culture: visible, invisible and multiple," in J. Lo Bianco and C. Crozet (eds) *Teaching Invisible Culture: Classroom Practice and Theory*, Melbourne: Language Australia.
Lunsing, W. (2003) "What masculinity?: Transgender practices among Japanese 'men'," in K. Louie and M. Low (eds) *Asian Masculinities: The Meaning and Practice of Manhood in China and Japan*, London and New York: Routledge.
McLelland, M. (2000) *Male Homosexuality in Modern Japan: Cultural Myths and Social Realities*, London: RoutledgeCurzon.
Maree, C. (2003) "'Ore wa ore dakara' (Because I'm me): a study of gender and language in the documentary *Shinjuku Boys*," *Intersections: Gender, History & Culture in the Asian Context* (9). Online. Available: <http://wwwsshe.murdoch.edu.au/intersections/issue9/maree.html> (accessed 20 April 2003).
—— (2000) "Kotoba no wana no negoshiēshon" (Negotiating the traps of language), *Gendai shisō*, 18(14): 212–224.
—— (1997a) "Gender representation in Japanese–English dictionaries used by Japanese-as-a-Foreign-Language (JFL) learners: a survey of basic verbs, basic adjectives and illustrations," in *The Tōhō Gakkai Transactions of the International Conference of Eastern Studies*, 42: 83–101.
—— (1997b) "Jendā no shihyō to jendā no imisei no henka: eiga 'Shinjuku Boizu' ni okeru onabe no bāi" (Gender indexicals and shifts in the meanings of gender in the case of the speech of *onabe* in the documentary *Shinjuku Boys*), *Gendai shisō*, 25(13): 263–275.
Marriott, H., J. V. Neustupny and R. Spence-Brown. (1994) *Unlocking Australia's Language Potential: Profile of 9 Key Languages in Australia*, Canberra: National Languages and Literacy Institute of Australia.
Matsumoto, Y. (2002) "Gender identity and the presentation of self in Japanese," in M. Rose, S. Benor, D. Sharma, J. Sweetland and Q. Shang (eds) *Gendered Practices in Language*, Stanford, CA: CSLI Publications.
Mishina, S. (1994) "A new perspective on women's language in Japanese: an interview with Sachiko Ide," *Issues in Applied Linguistics*, 5(2): 425–435.
Nagata, Y. (1998) "The study of culture in Japanese: towards a more meaningful engagement with Japanese language studies," *Australian Review of Applied Linguistics*, 15: 93–104.
—— (1995) "The culture of Japanese language teaching in Australia," *Japanese Studies*, 15(2): 34–47.
—— (1992) "A neglected issue: gender bias in Japanese language teaching," in V. Mackie (ed.) *Gendering Japanese Studies*, Melbourne: Japanese Studies Centre.
Ochs, E. (1992) "Indexing gender," in A. Duranti and C. Goodwin (eds) *Rethinking Context: Language as an Interactive Phenomenon*, Cambridge: Cambridge University Press.
Ogawa N. and J. (Shibamoto) Smith. (1997) "The gendering of the gay male sex class in Japan: a case study based on *Rasen no sobyō*," in A. Livia and K. Hall (eds) *Queerly Phrased*, New York: Oxford University Press.
Ohara, Y. (2001) "Finding one's voice in Japanese: a study of the pitch levels of L2 users," in A. Pavlenko and I. Piller (eds), *Multilingualism, Second Language Learning, and Gender*, Berlin, New York: Mouton de Gruyter.
Okamoto, S. (1997) "Social context, linguistic ideology, and indexical expressions in Japanese," *Journal of Pragmatics*, 28(6): 795–817.

—— (1996) "Representations of diverse female speech in styles in Japanese popular culture," in N. Warner et al. (eds) *Gender and Belief Systems: Proceedings of the Fourth Berkeley Women and Language Conference*, Berkeley, CA: Berkeley Women and Language Group, 575–587.

—— (1995) "'Tasteless' Japanese: less 'feminine' speech among young Japanese women," in K. Hall and M. Buchotz (eds) *Gender Articulated: Language and the Socially Constructed Self*, New York: Routledge.

Okamoto, S. and S. Sato. (1992) "Less feminine speech among young Japanese females," in K. Hall, M. Bucholtz and B. Moonwomon (eds) *Locating Power: Proceedings of the Second Berkeley Women and Language Conference*, Berkeley, CA: Berkeley Women and Language Group.

Pavlenko, A. and I. Piller. (2001) "New directions in the study of multilingualism, second language learning, and gender," in A. Pavlenko and I. Piller (eds) *Multilingualism, Second Language Learning, and Gender*, Berlin, New York: Mouton de Gruyter.

Rubin, G. (1984) "Thinking sex: notes for a radical theory of the politics of sexuality," in C. S. Vance (ed.) *Pleasure and Danger*, New York: Routledge.

Shibamoto, J. S. (1986). "Japanese women's language: as spoken by women, as spoken by men," in S. Bremner, N. Caskey and B. Moonwomon (eds) *Proceedings of the First Berkeley Women and Language Conference*, Berkeley, CA: Berkeley Women and Language Group.

—— (1985) *Japanese Women's Language*, Gainesville, FL: Academic Press, Inc.

Siegal, M. (1995) "Individual differences and study abroad: women learning Japanese in Japan," in B. F. Freed (ed.) *Second Language Acquisition in a Study Abroad Context*, Amsterdam/Philadelphia: John Benjamins Publishing Company.

Siegal, M. and S. Okamoto. (1996) "Imagined worlds: language, gender and sociocultural 'norms' in Japanese language textbooks," in N. Warner, J. Ahlers, L. Bilmes, M. Oliver, S. Wertheim and M. Chen (eds) *Gender and Belief Systems: Proceedings of the Fourth Berkeley Women and Language Conference*, Berkeley, CA: Berkeley Women and Language Group.

Silverstein, M. (1976) "Shifters, linguistic categories, and cultural description," in K. H. Basso and H. A. Selby (eds) *Meaning in Anthropology*, Albuquerque, NM: University of New Mexico Press.

Sturtz Streetharan, C. (2004) "Students, *sarariiman* (pl.), and seniors: Japanese men's use of 'manly' speech register," *Language in Society*, 33: 81–107.

—— (in press) "Japanese men's linguistic stereotypes and realities: conversations from the Kansai and Kanto regions," in J. S. (Shibamoto) Smith and S. Okamoto (eds) *Japanese Language, Gender, and Ideology: Cultural Models and Real People*, New York: Oxford University Press.

Summerhawk, B. (1998) "From closet to classroom: gay issues in ESL/EFL," *The Language Teacher Online*. Available online: <http://www.jalt-publications.org/tlt/files/98/may/summerhawk.html> (accessed 1 April 2003).

Takano, S. (2000) "The myth of a homogenous speech community: a sociolinguistic study of the speech of Japanese women in diverse gender roles," *International Journal of the Sociology of Language*, 146: 43–85.

Tsuruta, A. (2003) "Kyokkai ni motozuku jendā furī kyōiku e no kogeki" (The illogical counterargument against gender-free education), *Kodomo to kyōkasho zenkoku netto 21 News*, 31: 4–6.

Valentine, J. (1997a) "Pots and pans: identification of queer Japanese in terms of discrimination," in A. Livia and K. Hall (eds) *Queerly Phrased*, New York: Oxford University Press.

—— (1997b) "Skirting and suiting stereotypes: representations of marginalised sexualities in Japan," *Theory, Culture & Society*, 14(3): 57–85.

Yukawa, S. and K. Saito. (2002) "Ideorogii kenkyū toshite no 'nihongo to jendā' kenkyū" (Approaching Japanese and gender research from the viewpoint of ideology), *Gengo*, 31(2): 32–37.

3 The origins of "queer studies" in postwar Japan

Hitoshi Ishida, Mark McLelland and Takanori Murakami

Introduction

In a 1976 lecture at the Collège de France, Michel Foucault outlined how in the post-1960s world "all-encompassing and global theories" – from Marxism to psychoanalysis – have come under attack due to the emergence of "discontinuous, particular and local critiques" based on the (re)emergence of "subjugated knowledges" which he defines as:

> a whole series of knowledges that have been disqualified as nonconceptual knowledges, as insufficiently elaborated knowledges: naïve knowledges, hierarchically inferior knowledges, knowledges that are below the required level of erudition or scientificity ... it is a reappearance of what people know at a local level, of these disqualified knowledges, that make the critique possible.
>
> (Foucault 2003: 7)[1]

In recent decades it is not just totalizing theories that have been undermined but also the traditional holders of power and producers of meaning. Agents of the state, religious, judicial, medical and academic authorities have increasingly come under attack from a range of perspectives including feminism, postcolonial studies, and most recently, queer theory. These critiques have been enabled by the validation of previously disqualified knowledge systems, those typically produced by women and subjugated racial and sexual minorities. In English-speaking societies, at least, a considerable amount of effort has gone into recovering and documenting the experience of previously overlooked communities and these records are increasingly utilized in the production of more inclusive social and cultural histories. Lesbian and gay history, in particular, is now well established in English with the publication of numerous important works detailing the homosexual past of specific communities – (Newton 1979; Faderman 1981, 1991; Faderman and Eriksson 1990; Levine 1998), cities (Chauncey 1994; Kaiser 1997; Stein 2000) and even events such as the Second World War (Berube 1990). As well as pioneering specifically lesbian and gay histories, scholars in the Anglophone world have, via queer theory, sought to reclaim even mainstream "canonical" texts by giving them queer readings (see, for example, Sedgwick 1985).

In the case of Japan, it is only in the past decade that academic and activist communities have begun to seriously research the history of a range of *hentai*, that is, "queer" or "perverse," communities. Some of this work (see, for example, Kawaguchi *et al.* 1997) was influenced by trends in Anglophone scholarship and analyzed the prevalence of heterosexist structures in Japanese society. However, unlike much "queer studies" research in the USA which takes place in English Literature departments and is based on textual criticism, sexuality research in Japan, while hinting at queer theory, has tended to prefer sociological and historical research methods such as fieldwork, interviews and investigation of archival sources.

Two particular trends stand out among research being conducted by a new generation of academics, one focusing on the tension between the rather rigid categories of public sexual discourse and the lived experience of various sexual minority communities (see, for instance, Ino 1997a, 1997b, 2000, 2001; Kusayanagi 1998; Sugiura 1999; Takeda 2003; Tsuruta 2003) and another which aims to describe and analyze the everyday practices of these communities through participant observation and discourse analysis (see Ishida and Taniguchi 2001; Kaneta 2003; Mitsuhashi 2003; Sunagawa 2003).[2]

There are two reasons why queer studies in Japan tend to take place in the social sciences as opposed to Japanese Literature departments. First, researchers such as Ueno Chizuko and Ehara Yumiko, who in the 1980s brought feminist analysis into the mainstream, are sociologists. Many young queer researchers supervised by these two senior scholars have been influenced by social-science methodology. The second reason is that in Japan, literature study has tended to be seen as an aspect of literary history which is still largely concerned with the study of canonical texts (or "discovering" the literary merit of overlooked texts so that they can be admitted to the canon). As a result, there is little space within the mainstream for pioneering work offering alternative queer readings.

However, it would be a mistake to conclude that this recent upsurge in interest in a range of non-heterosexual identities and communities is a new development in Japan. Already in the 1920s there existed a range of publications which took as their focus the topic of *hentai seiyoku* or "perverse desire." While this genre was censored and disappeared during the long war years, it rapidly reemerged during the Occupation period following Japan's defeat at the end of the Second World War. So extensive is this literature that it would not be an exaggeration to say that during the 1950s, building upon the trajectory established in the 1920s, Japan had already developed a tradition of "queer studies" – albeit the genre has not, until recently, been acknowledged by "official" knowledge producers and the information contained there is a good example of Foucault's definition of "subjugated knowledge."

Fortunately, with recent changes in intellectual paradigms, the postwar "perverse press" is beginning to be investigated by Japanese and foreign researchers[3] and this chapter presents some of the main characteristics of the genre to an English-reading audience for the first time. It is our hope that by drawing attention to this material other researchers will be encouraged to help uncover the otherwise subjugated knowledges that are recorded in this literature – now our primary access to the "perverse" practices, fantasies and communities of the immediate postwar period.

Prewar sexual knowledge

Before looking at the postwar situation, it is necessary to give a brief outline of the changes in how non-heterosexual practices were codified in the preceding period. Discussion of non-heterosexual practices (particularly those between men) has a long history in Japan. Furukawa Makoto (1994) has outlined the shifts in understanding of homosexuality in Japan from the Meiji (1867–1912) until the early Showa (1926–89) period. He describes how the pre-modern *danshoku* (male eroticism) code was a form of pederasty based on the fixed roles of *chigo* (catamites), involving *wakashū* (male youths), and *nenja*, or their adult male lovers. However, as a result of a popular sexology boom which commenced in the early 1920s, this age-based model gradually shifted towards a modern pathological framework of interpretation, what Furukawa refers to as a "perverse sexual desire code." This new code turned attention away from sexual acts (which it had been supposed might be engaged in by men in general) towards internal, ontological factors which prompted specific types of individuals to express "perverse desires."

By the early Showa period, Japan had developed a significant publications industry devoted to the discussion of "perverse" sexuality. Journals published at this time included *Hentai shiryō* (Perverse material, 1926), *Kāma shasutora* (*Kāma shastra*, 1927), *Kisho* (Strange book, 1928) and *Gurotesuku* (Grotesque, 1928). These journals specializing in sexual knowledge, as well as articles and advice pages contributed to newspapers and magazines by a newly emerging class of sexual "experts," frequently discussed "perverse sexuality," albeit it was usually diagnosed as a problem. The result was that *hentai*, signifying sexual interests that were understood to be "queer" or "perverse," became a widely recognized term (Matsuzawa 1997: 55). The sexological journals offered readers the opportunity to write in and describe their own perverse desires in the hope that expert advice might remedy their condition. One unforeseen side-effect of this process was that the perverse themselves were given a voice.

Quite how this new, popular audience received and understood the sexological magazines is difficult to ascertain but Pflugfelder suggests that the readership was "clearly more attracted than repelled by the 'perverse' nature of their contents" (1999: 287). Pflugfelder describes how "the discourse on 'perversion' transformed the sexual behavior of others into a spectacle for consumption as well as a vehicle for self-understanding" (1999: 289) and provided both writers and readers with a new kind of narrative pleasure. Indeed, the perverse press is best understood in relation to the wider cultural phenomenon known as *ero-guro-nansensu* or "erotic grotesque nonsense" which was prominent in the popular culture of the late 1920s (Roden 1990; Furukawa 1994: 50; *Bessatsu Taiyō* 1997: 44–45, 132; Matsuzawa 1997: 55–56; Pflugfelder 1999: 311–317). This period saw considerable experimentation in sexual and gender roles, albeit among a narrow (and largely middle-class) urban elite. Institutions such as cafés and dance halls were sites for "foreign" or "French-style" modes of interaction between waitresses and clients (Garon 1997: 108) or more shockingly, between "modern boys" (*mobo*) and "modern girls" (*moga*) who socialized together away from the prying eyes of the family. This frivolous scene, one in which women participated with some autonomy, was considered a dangerous foreign development. The *moga* were one instance of the general category "problem women," that is women who failed to conform to a narrow, codified model of femaleness and who had caused consternation in Japan's press since the turn of the century (Robertson 1999: 2).

However, this brief efflorescence of popular sexual culture was to come to an end as Japan geared up for war in the early 1930s. Japan's 15-year war, as it is sometimes referred to by historians, was characterized by increasing state surveillance of and interference in the personal lives of the Japanese population. Igarashi points out how the wartime regime attempted to create obedient and patriotic bodies by forging ties between nationalist ideology and bodily functions, noting how Japanese bodies were "at the heart of nationalist discourse" (2000: 51). At this time, Japan shared with European nations, particularly Nazi Germany, an interest in "race improvement" and both the state and the media were proactively engaged in promulgating eugenicist policies (Fruhstuck 2003) which took an extremely functional view of human sexuality.

One result of this discourse was an increased polarity in gender roles resulting in women being cast as mothers whose purpose was to produce workers for the empire, and men being regarded as fighting machines, part of the "national body" (Low, 2003). Women, who had little political agency, were particularly constrained by this ideology. The most important role for women – that of "good wife, wise mother" (*ryōsai kenbo*) – was actively promoted by government policies, media reports and social pressure. Indeed, the government went so far as to introduce eugenic policies to ensure maximum reproduction, women being encouraged to "*umeyo fuyaseyo*" (bear children and multiply). Healthy baby contests were held across Japan and awards were made to families with more than ten children (Robertson 2002: 199; Fruhstuck 2003: 167). Given that reports on family-planning and the sale of contraceptives were illegal, sexual activity, for bourgeois women at least, came to be organized entirely around reproduction.

State surveillance of individual bodies was achieved through neighborhood and village associations, membership of which was necessary in order to receive rations of food and clothing. Also, as the war progressed and an increasing number of adult men were drafted and sent overseas, teenage children, particularly boys, were recruited to work in the factories where they were subject to a "protective guidance network" comprised of men and older boys who drilled them in both physical and mental hygiene. Young unmarried women, too, were sent to work in the factories where they also lived highly regimented lives under strict supervision. As the war progressed, many women and women's organizations were co-opted by the state to police the behavior of other women, children and those elderly men who remained at home.

Japan's sudden and shocking defeat, however, resulted in widespread disillusionment with the paradigms, practices and moral codes of the wartime era. As Dore comments, "the confusion which followed the defeat was catastrophic to the old morality. In some cases it was catastrophic to moral restraint of any kind" (1999: 162). It was in this context of widespread social confusion that new kinds of sexual culture rapidly emerged, including a range of new heterosexual practices and identities as well as a renewed interest in sexualities deemed to be *hentai* (perverse) and *abunōmaru* (abnormal) (Shimokawa 1995: 54).

Japan's postwar "perverse" press

Postwar intellectuals such as Sakaguchi Ango wrote about the sense of "liberation" (*kaihō*) from hegemonic gender and sexual norms that Japanese people experienced at the war's end. Jay Rubin points out that "the Japanese were sick to death of being preached at constantly to be good, frugal, hardworking, and self-sacrificing" and were consequently attracted to "a decadence that was simply the antithesis of prewar wholesomeness" (1985: 80). Many people were keen to forget the past and looked forward to the beginning of a new and newly private life in which eroticism was flaunted as an important symbol of "liberation."

The immediate postwar years saw the development of a *kasutori* (low-grade, pulp) culture which Dower describes as "a commercial world dominated by sexually oriented entertainments and a veritable cascade of pulp literature" (2000: 148). Japanese writers were now free to dispense with the "wholesome" preoccupations of earlier literature and instead explore more "decadent" themes (Rubin 1985: 72–73), including a whole genre of "carnal literature" (*nikutai bungaku*) in which the physicality of the body was emphasized over ideological concerns pivoting on official notions of purity. One had only to glance at the covers of the *kasutori* press to understand that there had been a radical break from the past. Women's naked bodies were prominently displayed in a manner that would have been inconceivable during the war. The covers alone of magazines such as *Venus*, *Sekai no onna* (World women), *Jitsuwa romansu* (True romance stories), *Wink*, *Lucky*, and *Happy* were testament to a new sexual regime that was challenging previous notions about the sanctity of Japanese womanhood and pioneering new Western trends in Japanese women's looks, dress and deportment. However, despite the frequent occurrence of terms such as *kaihō* (release, liberation) in the literature of the period, the "liberation" of Japanese women from traditional codes of feminine propriety was double-edged since female bodies were "immediately caught up in market forces that offered them to male desire at a price" (Igarashi 2000: 58). In the immediate postwar years, it was members of the Occupation forces who had privileged access to Japanese women's (and sometimes men's) bodies.

Nevertheless, Igarashi points out how, for some, "sexual enjoyment marked the postwar liberation of Japanese bodies and expressed defiance of the regulatory regime that demanded bodily sacrifices" (2000: 55). Indeed, the new visibility of kissing couples on the streets was humorously referred to as a symbol of the new democracy (Yamamoto and Ozawa 1975: 83). While in the prewar period, physical interaction between men and women in public had been extremely circumscribed and the modern custom of dating had been unknown in polite society, after the war a much more visible culture of heterosexual experimentation developed. The new visibility of "dating" couples on the streets of Japan's cities resulted in the popularization of a (significantly foreign) term describing the modern couple – *abekku* – from the French *avec* (or "with"). One magazine that pioneered this new mode of coupledom was itself entitled *Abekku*. Such *kasutori* magazines were replete with articles offering advice to the modern couple on the art of hand-holding, kissing and more *nikutaiteki* (carnal) pursuits such as petting and foreplay. The *kasutori* press commented on the popularity of sexual behaviors such as petting and "necking," noting how practices which had previously taken place as a prelude to intercourse within marriage were now being adopted as recreational activities by young people generally (Ōta and Kabiya 1954).

Marriage in Japan had long been viewed as an institution whose purpose was procreation and child rearing, but the new postwar environment saw a greater emphasis placed on fulfilling the emotional and sexual needs of the couple which resulted in a demand for information about sexual practice and pleasure. Dutch gynecologist Theodoor Van de Velde's international best-selling sex guide, *Ideal Marriage*, which had previously been banned, was translated into Japanese as early as 1946 under the title *Kanzen naru kekkon* (Perfecting marriage). The book, soon released in cheap pirated versions, placed great emphasis on foreplay and the role of oral-genital contact and was to have a major impact on sexual discourse over the next decade (Yamamoto and Ozawa 1975: 85–86). The extremely instrumental, eugenicist attitudes toward sexuality characteristic of wartime ideology were consequently challenged by new discourses stressing pleasure and conjugality.

While the new pulp magazines certainly contributed to the dissemination and popularization of new modes of heterosexual interaction and behavior – resulting in a new proliferation of heterosexualities, by the early 1950s a subgenre had developed focusing on *hentai seiyoku* or "perverse desire" which included both male and female homosexuality as well as a range of fetishistic behaviors. This genre was referred to as *ryōki* or "curiosity seeking" and had much in common with the 1920s' fad for publications specializing in erotic, grotesque nonsense which often featured stories of a homosexual nature. These magazines included titles such as *Ningen tankyū* (Human research; 1950–53),[4] *Amatoria* (1951–55), *Fūzoku kagaku* (Sex-customs science; 1953–55), *Fūzoku zōshi* (Sex-customs storybook; 1953–55), *Ura mado* (Rear window; 1956–65) and *Kitan kurabu* (Strange-talk club; 1952–75).

These *hentai* magazines had two common characteristics. First, they were all keen to stress that their goal was not mere titillation but "sex research." For instance *Ningen tankyū*, which was published by the sex researcher Takahashi Tetsu, referred to itself as a "Sexology magazine for intellectuals" and *Fūzoku kagaku* proclaimed the term "science" (*kagaku*) in its very title. While these magazines were commercial ventures that were for general sale, small subcultural magazines, too, adopted this strategy. For instance, a small society of lovers of

MtF transvestism in the mid-1950s referred to itself as the "Theater Research Group" and named its periodical *Theater Critique*, thus using "theatre research" as a cover for its activities (Mitsuhashi 2000: 9) and Japan's first homophile organization, founded in the early 1950s, referred to itself as the FKK – or Fūzoku Kagaku Kenkyūkai – that is the "study group for sexual morals science." The reason for stressing "research" and "science" in the titles of the magazines was to avoid police surveillance and possible prosecution for obscenity (*Kitan kurabu* 1956). However, apart from "academic" papers and columns by doctors and scientists, the genre also contained a great deal of real-life reports and pornographic fiction as well as sexual illustrations and photographs. Indeed, as the decade progressed the scientific material was overwhelmed by the more pornographic contents.

The second characteristic of the genre was the lively exchange which took place between specialist researchers, amateur hobbyists and readers themselves. The magazines frequently featured roundtable talks where medical doctors, writers, readers and editors came together to discuss specific issues such as male homosexuality, female same-sex desire or a range of fetishes. In these discussions, the discourse of modern medicine which rendered some sexual desires "abnormal" was represented alongside reports from actual people who self-defined as *abu* (or abnormal). Hence, this was a genre characterized by its hybridity. Various levels of discourse were blended – "expert" diagnoses stood alongside personal testimonies which at times modified or contradicted the opinions of the experts. The magazines functioned as a type of "contact zone" (Pratt 1992) in which a range of discourses seeking to position perverse sexuality competed in public. Importantly, *hentai* magazines such as *Kitan kurabu* created readers' columns to stimulate the critique of articles and encourage exchange of ideas between readers. These readers' columns not only functioned as personal advertisements which accorded people with the same interests opportunities to meet, but they also enabled the sharing of various sexual fantasies.

Despite the scientific stance of many of the articles, readers who saw themselves as subjects of perverse desires did not necessarily internalize the modern medical perspective that regarded such desires as abnormal and in need of treatment. For instance, issues of *Fūzoku kagaku* circulated during 1954 contained statements on the flap of each issue which proclaimed "Sodomites, you must have pride! You are definitely not abnormal!" or "Sodomites, you have allies! You are not alone!" Such affirmative statements are not far removed from the stance taken by early 1970s gay liberation in the West. While representing diverse readers' voices, the magazines also employed a wide range of "experts." They regularly contained columns by physicians such as Hiki Yūzō, who counselled readers, but also published work by Ōgiya Afu and Kabiya Kazuhiko who frequented "homosexual drinking places" and meeting spots. Hence, the perverse magazines facilitated interaction between men with homosexual interests by describing and even providing maps to find these places, as well as offering advice on how to understand the codes of behavior that applied there (see, for example, Kabiya 1954a, 1954b, 1955). This advice was often couched in terms of empirical observation, describing how "*dōshi*" – comrades or kindred souls – made themselves recognizable to each other. These descriptions were obviously useful to men hoping to seek out homosexual interactions and anticipated the *hattenba* (cruising spot) guides which were to become a staple of Japan's commercial gay press in the 1970s. It was therefore the writings of these "amateur" researchers rather than the opinions of the medical experts which had the most practical value for readers.

The "perverse studies" genre of the postwar period was characterized by the tendency to seek out relations between a wide range of non-normative sexual fantasies and desires. In this sense it has many parallels with contemporary queer studies in which a wide range of individuals whose sexual and gender identities are not sanctioned by the mainstream culture, come together in a variety of forums to consider the dynamics at play in the construction of some desires as normal and others as perverse. People who experienced perverse desires enjoyed sharing their experience and reading about the experience of others via readers' columns which functioned as spaces in which a variety of appropriations, connections and differentiations could be articulated. Let us give an example of how this worked. A contribution from one reader (*Fūzoku zōshi* 1953a) described how he had been awakened to a sense of his own masochism through appearing as an *onnagata* (female role-player in Kabuki) in a travelling theatre troupe. However, another man (*Kitan kurabu* 1958a) considered that masochism instead resulted from "that tight binding hobby" (i.e. fans of wearing *rokushaku* – a type of loincloth). The *hentai* magazines thus offered a space in which people who considered themselves *abu* offered diverse accounts of the origin of their own perverse desires.

There was also a sharing of fantasies between groups who experienced different sexual desires. For instance, many articles in the magazines focused on *seppuku* or the ritual disembowelment once practiced by samurai. One requirement of the ritual was the wearing of a loincloth which tightly wrapped both stomach and groin (to stop the intestines spilling out). A "male disembowelment maniac" (*Fūzoku kagaku* 1955b) recognized that articles and illustrations depicting his own sexual fetish were also appropriated by readers who were "loincloth maniacs" and "lovers of youths." In short, readers who experienced a range of perverse sexual desires treated the *hentai* magazines as broad resources for their sexual fantasies and this encouraged a sense of identification and solidarity beyond narrow identity categories.

This was particularly the case with the treatment of the "love of Lesbos."[5] While the main focus of the perverse press was upon the male subject and his desires, whether heterosexually oriented as in discussions of sadomasochism, fetishism and sex techniques or homosexually oriented as in the many articles on male homosexual meeting places, women's sexuality was not overlooked (McLelland 2004, 2005). Indeed, compared with prewar writing which tended to deny women's sexual agency, the postwar press recognized that women were as liable to sexual perversity as were men. Reports in the postwar magazines described a wide range of "Lesbos love" – from schoolgirl crushes to full sexual relationships between adult women. An unsigned article in *Fūzoku zōshi*, for instance, entitled "Various phases of Lesbos love," mentioned that "*resubosu*" (Lesbos) ranged from such "insignificant" things as the exchange of love letters between schoolgirls to more serious matters "which would make men blush," going on to describe the various ways in which women had historically pleasured themselves and each other, deriving examples from ancient Greece, Muromachi period Japan (1333–1568) and colonial Africa (*Fūzoku zōshi* 1953b).

Despite the fact that there were fewer articles discussing female same-sex sexuality, "Lesbos love" was a subgenre of considerable extent, created by writers using both male and female pen names, although it needs to be stressed that the framework within which women's same-sex love was discussed was unrelentingly "masculinist," that is, dependent upon categories derived from male same-sex paradigms. For instance, discussions of women's same-sex sexuality tended to be subsumed under the "active" and "passive" typology developed to describe male homosexual interaction and women were offered little opportunity to describe their own communities and practices without their testimony being framed by commentaries from male reporters, editors and other "experts" (McLelland 2004). Some of these writers, however, did attempt to approach the subject of women's same-sex love seriously, albeit within the narrow parameters available at the time. On the other hand, others produced works of fiction quite as prurient as those seen in the US genre of lesbian pulp which also sprang up after the war. In these graphically illustrated stories, the "sadistic" lesbian was a figure that evoked fascination in both men and women alike, and with titles such as "Under my elder sister's whip" (Narushima 1954) and "Inflamed skin" (Wada 1953), the purportedly female writers left little to the imagination.

If we can assume that the majority of readers of this genre were men, then the numerous articles published on the love of Lesbos might seem excessive, unless we assume that these articles were also of interest to males with a variety of perverse interests. An illustration from a roundtable discussion featuring four female practitioners of the love of Lesbos entitled "female homos here we go" in the March 1955 edition of *Fūzoku kagaku* (Saijō 1955), for instance, which features a bikini-clad Western woman, clearly seems to be inviting a male gaze. As for this illustration of a "human ashtray" from a 1959 edition of *Kitan kurabu*, it would obviously appeal to those with an interest in sadomasochism – both male and female (Figure 3.1).

Despite the diverse appropriations that were made of the *hentai* genre, there was general agreement as to the basic structure of perverse desire. All perverse desires tended to be organized around the binary principles of:

Active	Passive
Superior	Inferior
Sadistic	Masochistic
Male	Female
Male-attired	Female-attired
Elder	Younger

The rationale for this dualistic structure was that "if you look at the character of male and female, the male is a sadist . . . and the female a masochist." This "general

Figure 3.1 "Human ashtray" from *Kitan Kurabu*, January 1959

theory" was widely accepted by most readers and authors (see, for example, *Fūzoku kagaku* 1955a: preamble; Hanajiri 1953). All perverse desires and practices were aligned on one side or the other of the binary and one result of this categorization was that relations could be established between acts within both groups that were otherwise dissimilar. Hence, various perverse sexual desires were not viewed as being different *in kind*, but rather as reflecting different tastes. The personal narratives of perverse sexual desire in the *hentai* magazines were therefore eclectic, based on a process of bricolage, drawing comparisons between sexual acts and fetishes that today would be considered characteristic of separate "sexualities."

An example of the multivalent nature of these representations and the manner in which they were judged to correspond to "active" and "passive" or "sadistic" and "masochistic" tendencies is the image of the "horse-riding woman." In present-day Japan, no sexual meaning whatsoever is read into horse riding. However, in the *hentai* magazines, the "horse-riding woman" was associated with lesbianism due to the "active" nature of the pursuit as well as its unconventionality (*Kitan kurabu* 1961). It was also connected to FtM cross-dressing on account of the masculine nature of riding clothes (*Kitan kurabu* 1953a), and it was frequently discussed in terms of sadism due to its association with the "lashing of the whip" (*Kitan kurabu* 1954). Discussions of horse-riding women were thus available for diverse appropriation. Men who were intrigued by images of horse-riding women were thought to have masochist tendencies (*Kitan kurabu* 1953b). Indeed, "men who like working women" were commonly thought to be "masochist men" (*Fūzoku zōshi* 1953c). Thus, images of horse-riding women published in the magazines appealed to lesbians, FtM cross-dressers and sadists as well as male masochists who admired strong women.

The decline of the perverse paradigm – from hybridity to variety

So far we have discussed the 1950s' perverse press in terms of its hybridity and bricolage. The perverse press did not segregate their contents in terms of contemporary understandings of sexuality but, rather, the magazines were interested in discovering the relationships between practically all sexual activities other than "ordinary sex (*futsū no sekkusu*) between a man and a woman" (Shimokawa 1995: 53). However, as the 1950s progressed, these magazines began to change. Whereas early in the decade the readers' columns tended to place letters together irrespective of their theme, from mid-decade, letters' columns were increasingly divided according to specific tastes, such as "*Resubosu tsūshin*" (Lesbian mail), "*Homo no mado*" (Homo's window), "*Fetchi tsūshin*" (Fetishist mail) and "*Seppuku tsūshin*" (Disembowelment mail), thus reinforcing the idea that readers of these columns represented different constituencies.

This tendency toward increasing differentiation can also be seen in a 1958 controversy over the question "what is masochism?" (*Kitan kurabu* 1958b). This discussion ended by rejecting any necessary connection between "feminized men" and "masculinized women" with masochism and sadism. The interlocutors in the debate criticized the mixing up of various perverse sexual desires and were at pains to clarify discontinuities between sexual tastes which might be seen as having common denominators. As a result, fans of sadomasochism, which was treated as the central topic in most *hentai* magazines of the period, came to regard people who expressed same-sex sexual desires as well as lovers of disembowelment and other fetishes as marginal to the main agenda of the magazines and even as "impurities" (*Kitan kurabu rinji zōkan* 1959). The result was that the *hentai* magazines of the 1960s became increasingly organized around sadomasochism and other sexual interests were excluded from their pages.

Hence, whereas *hentai* magazines had once presented perverse sexuality as a network of related tastes and provided a forum for people with a wide range of perverse sexual interests to communicate with each other, the narrowing of their focus to sadomasochism meant that the magazines no longer served as a vehicle for a broader queer community. The *hentai* magazine genre, once referred to as a "comprehensive department store of perversity" finally came to an end when the most influential and long-lived magazines *Fūzoku kitan* and *Kitan kurabu* suspended publication in 1974 and 1975 respectively. From this time on it was the mainstream media that were to be most influential in spreading knowledge about perverse sexuality.

Conclusion

This chapter has introduced a group of magazines, referred to in Japanese as *hentai zasshi*, which during the 1950s were the primary medium for self-realization and community formation among people who experienced various non-standard sexual desires and gender identities. While ostensibly these magazines were aimed at the scientific study of "perverted" or exotic sexual desires, in reality they also served as fuel for pornographic fantasy as well as providing a "contact zone" for those who experienced marginalized sexualities to develop their own self-understanding. In the early years of the genre at least, the *hentai zasshi* regarded various marginal sexualities and genders as mutually adjacent by deploying a binary scheme which discovered relationships between different "active" and "passive" sexual desires that in later years would come to constitute distinct sexualities. The hybridity of the genre clearly has much in common with the recently emerged discipline of queer studies.

Japan's postwar perverse press, particularly in the 1950s, is important because of its breadth of reference and the fact that readers often wrote letters and contributed longer descriptive pieces about their own "perverse desires." This meant that pathologizing medical, criminal and psychoanalytic theories did not establish such a firm hold on popular discourse about transgenderism and homosexuality in Japan as was the case in Anglophone, particularly American popular writings, at this time. The voice of the experts was often muted, given that the magazines relied on contributions from readers for a substantial percentage of their copy and actively solicited confessional stories. The fact that the perverse magazines were published on a monthly basis and featured letters columns and other submissions by readers, gave those who experienced queer desires the opportunity to engage with and sometimes contest the theories of the experts, thus permitting the circulation of what Foucault refers to as previously "subjugated knowledges." For a long time this genre has been overlooked by researchers of sexuality in Japan and is still today practically untouched in the English-language literature on Japan. Although in this short chapter it has not been possible to give a detailed reading of the genre, we hope that we have been able to point out some of its salient features and that readers, particularly postgraduate students, will be encouraged to investigate this literature further.

Notes

1 Mark McLelland would like to thank transgender activist and academic Dr Susan Stryker for first bringing this passage from Foucault to his attention during a lecture at the University of Queensland in 2004.
2 In addition to research conducted by a new generation of academics, queer studies is being advanced by activists who are not aligned with any particular academic institution or community organization, but who address sexuality issues in their published works. The most prominent among these is the gay writer Fushimi Noriaki whose books *Puraibēto gei raifu* (Private gay life, 1991) and *Kuia paradaisu* (Queer paradise, 1996) as well as the magazine *Queer Japan* (1999–2001), of which he was the chief editor, built bridges between researchers and members of minority communities.
3 Material in this chapter draws on McLelland (2004, 2005) and Ishida and Murakami (forthcoming). Other sources are limited; however, Fushimi (2002) has made an initial analysis of the relationship between the gay community and *hentai* magazines in postwar Japan. For a brief historical outline of the development of male erotic art in postwar *hentai* magazines, see Tagame (2003).
4 Designating the exact dates at which these magazines began and ceased publication is difficult. These approximate dates are based on the collection held by Tokyo's Fūzoku Shiryōkan and our search of online databases provided by second-hand booksellers.
5 During the 1950s the term lesbian (transliterated into Japanese as *resubian* or *rezubian*) was not widely used. The most common designation for female same-sex sexuality in the magazines discussed was *resubosu ai* or "Lesbos love." See McLelland (2004) for a description of representations of female same-sex love in the genre.

References

Berube, A. (1990) *Coming Out Under Fire: The History of Gay Men and Women in World War Two*, New York: The Free Press.
Bessatsu Taiyō (ed.). (1997) *Hakkinbon* (Banned books), Tokyo: Heibonsha.
Chauncey, G. (1994) *Gay New York: The Making of the Gay Male World, 1890–1940*, London: Flamingo.
Dore, R. (1999) *City Life in Japan: Study of a Tokyo Ward*, Richmond, Surrey: The Japan Library.
Dower, J. (2000) *Embracing Defeat: Japan in the Wake of World War II*, New York: W.W. Norton.
Faderman, L. (1991) *Odd Girls and Twilight Lovers: A History of Lesbian Life in Twentieth Century America*, New York: Colombia University Press.
—— (1981). *Surpassing the Love of Men: Romantic Friendship and Love between Women from the Renaissance to the Present*, New York: Morrow.
Faderman, L. and B. Eriksson (eds). (1990) *Lesbians in Germany 1890–1920*, Tallahassee: Naiad Press.
Foucault, M. (2003) *"Society Must Be Defended" Lectures at the Collège de France, 1975–76*, New York: Picador.
Fruhstuck, S. (2003) *Colonizing Sex: Sexology and Social Control in Modern Japan*, Berkeley, CA: University of California Press.
Furukawa, M. (1994) "The changing nature of sexuality: the three codes framing homosexuality in modern Japan," *Nichibei Josei Journal* (U.S.-Japan Women's Journal), 17: 29–55; also published in (transl. A. Lockyer) *U.S.-Japan Women's Journal English Supplement*, 7: 98–127.
Fushimi, N. (2002) *Gei to iu keiken* (The experience of [being] gay), Tokyo: Potto Shuppan.

—— (ed.). (1996) *Kuia paradaisu* (Queer paradise), Tokyo: Shōeisha.
—— (1991) *Puraibēto gei raifu* (Private gay life), Tokyo: Gakuyōshobō.
Fūzoku kagaku. (1955a) "Abu kurabu no hitobito" (People of abnormal club), January, unpaginated preamble.
—— (1955b) "Seppuku tsūshin" (Self-disembowelment report), April, 31–33.
Fūzoku zōshi. (1953a) "Mazohisuto tsūshin" (Masochist report), October, 121.
—— (1953b) "Resubosu ai no shujusō" (Various aspects of Lesbos love), December, 299.
—— (1953c) "Donna otoko ga mazohisuto ka: Mazo dansei no hanbetsuhō" (What do masochist men look like?: Judgement test for masochist men), December, 79–81.
Garon, S. (1997) *Molding Japanese Minds: The State in Everyday Life*, Princeton, NJ: Princeton University Press.
Hanajiri, K. (1953) "Sadisuto to mazohisuto" (Sadists and masochists), *Kitan kurabu*, January, 1.
Igarashi, Y. (2000) *Narratives of War in Postwar Japanese Culture, 1945–1970*, Princeton, NJ: Princeton University Press.
Ino, S. (2001) "Kōchiku sareru sekusharitī: Kuia riron to kōchikushugi" (Constructed sexuality: queer theory and constructionism), in Ueno Chizuko (ed.) *Kōchikushugi towa nanika*, Tokyo: Keisō Shobō: 189–211.
—— (2000) "Shutai aidentitī eijenshī: Batorā riron no saikentō" (Subject, identity and agency: reviewing Butler's theory), *Gendai Shisō*, 28(14): 247–255.
—— (1997a) "Sekusharitī to jendā no atsureki: jendā konshasu na gei sutadīzu ni mukete" (Friction between sexuality and gender: pursuit of gender-conscious gay studies), *Soshiorogosu*, 21: 44–58.
—— (1997b) "Kuia sutadīzu no shatei" (The scope of queer studies), *Kuia Sutadīzu '97*, Tokyo: Nanatsumori Shokan.
Ishida, H. and T. Murakami. (forthcoming) "A history of queer studies in Japan," *Intersections: Gender, History and Culture in the Asian Context*, special "Queer Japan" issue, December 2005.
Ishida, H. and Y. Taniguchi. (2001) "Homo bā ni jūjisuru wakamono tachi" (Youths working in homo bars), in M. Yajima and H. Mimizuka (eds) *Kawaru wakamono to shokugyō sekai: transition no shakaigaku*, Tokyo: Gakubunsha.
Kabiya, K. (1955) "Geibā no seitai" (The gay bar mode of life), *Amatoria*, July, 38–46.
—— (1954a) "Danshoku kissaten" (Homosexual coffee shops), *Fūzoku zōshi*, January, 146–151.
—— (1954b) "Sodomiya kōsaijutsu" (Homosexual interaction techniques), *Fūzoku zōshi*, June, 236–241.
Kaiser, C. (1997) *The Gay Metropolis*, Boston: Faber and Faber.
Kaneta, T. (2003) "'Kamingu auto' no sentakusei wo meguru mondai ni tsuite" (Issues of choice concerning "coming out"), *Shakaigaku Ronkō*, 24: 61–81.
Kawaguchi, K., T. Kazama and K. Binsento. (1997) *Gei sutadīzu* (Gay studies), Tokyo: Seidosha.
Kusayanagi, C. (1998) "'Mondai keiken' no katararekata: kureimu moushitate kenkyū no rekishiteki seikaku to gendai" (How problematic experience is spoken: history and present circumstance of studies of claim-making), *Shakaigaku Nenshi*, 39: 9–36.
Kitan kurabu. (1961) "Bakakyō tsūshin sōkessan" (Wannabe horse-crazy report roundup), April, 164.
—— (1958a) "Dokusha tsūshin" (Readers' column), January, 164–176.
—— (1958b) "Mazohizumu e no izanai" (Invitation to masochism), May, 36.

—— (1956) "KK shi henshū hōshin ni tsuite hitokoto" (A word about the editorial policy of KK magazine), August, 46.
—— (1954) "Jin ya ba ya" (People and horses), February, 164.
—— (1953a) "Aru mazohisuto no techō kara: (1) Numa Shōzō" (From the notebook of a certain masochist, no. 1, Numa Shōzō), June, 164.
—— (1953b) "Dokusha tsūshin" (Readers' column), October, 105.
Kitan kurabu rinji zōkan. (1959) "Kinbaku foto to kinbaku moderu yobanashi" (Night tale about bondage photos and models), November, 164.
Levine, M. (1998) *Gay Macho: The Life and Death of the Homosexual Clone*, New York: New York University Press.
Low, M. (2003) "The Emperor's sons go to war: competing masculinities in modern Japan," in Kam Louie and Morris Low (eds) *Asian Masculinities: The Meaning and Practice of Manhood in China and Japan*, London: RoutledgeCurzon.
McLelland, M. (2005) *Queer Japan from the Pacific War to the Internet Age*, Lanham, MD: Rowman and Littlefield.
—— (2004) "From sailor-suits to sadists: 'Lesbos love' as reflected in Japan's postwar 'perverse press'," *U.S.-Japan Women's Journal*, 27: 27–50.
Matsuzawa, G. (1997) "Meiji, Taishō, Shōwa, kindai fūzoku shuppan no rekishi" (Meiji, Taisho, Showa, a history of modern sexual-customs publishing), in Wani no ana (ed.) *Ero no hon*, Tokyo: Wani no ana.
Mitsuhashi, J. (2003) "Genzai Nihon no toransujendā sekai: Tokyo Shinjuku no josō komyunitī wo chūshin ni" (Transgender world in modern Japan: focusing on the male transvestites' community in Shinjuku), *Shakai Kagaku Kenkyūjo Nenpō*, 7: 85–115.
—— (2000) "Sengo Nihon toransujendā shakai no rekishiteki hensen no sobyō" (Historical sketch of transgender society's transition in postwar Japan), in M. Yajima, J. Mitsuhashi, and I. Sugiura (eds) *Sengo Nihon toransugendā shakaishi I: kiso kenkyū shiryō*, Tokyo: Sengo Nihon Toransugendā Shakaishi Kenkyū Kai.
Narushima, Y. (1954) "Onēsama no muchi no shita" (Under my elder sister's whip), *Fūzoku zōshi*, March, 70–78.
Newton, E. (1979) *Mother Camp: Female Impersonators in America*, Chicago: University of Chicago Press.
Ōta, T. and K. Kabiya. (1954) "Petting wa ryūkō suru" (Petting is popular), *Fūzoku kagaku*, March, 79–83.
Pflugfelder, G. (1999) *Cartographies of Desire: Male-Male Sexuality in Japanese Discourse, 1600–1950*, Berkeley, CA: University of California Press.
Pratt, M. (1992) *Imperial Eyes: Travel Writing and Transculturation*, London: Routledge.
Robertson, J. (2002) "Blood talks: eugenic modernity and the creation of new Japanese," *History and Anthropology*, 13(3): 191–216.
—— (1999) "Dying to tell: sexuality and suicide in imperial Japan," *Signs*, Autumn, 25: 1–36.
Roden, D. (1990) "Taisho culture and the problem of gender ambivalence," in J. Rimer (ed.) *Japanese Intellectuals during the Inter-War Years*, Princeton, NJ: Princeton University Press.
Rubin, J. (1985) "From wholesomeness to decadence: the censorship of literature under the Allied Occupation," *Journal of Japanese Studies*, 11(1): 71–103.
Saijō, M. (chair). (1955) "Zadankai: josei no homo makari tōru" (Roundtable: female homos here we go), *Fūzoku kagaku*, March, 148–156.
Sedgwick, E. (1985) *Between Men: English Literature and Male Homosocial Desire*, New York: Columbia University Press.

Shimokawa, K. (1995) "Hentai no sōgō depāto *Kitan kurabu* kara *SM serekuto* ga ubugoe wo agerumade" (From *Kitan kurabu*, perversity's general department, to *SM serekuto*'s first cry), *Bessatsu Takarajima*, "Sei media 50 nen," 240: 48–55.

Stein, M. (2000) *City of Sisterly and Brotherly Loves: Lesbian and Gay Philadelphia, 1945–1972*, Chicago: University of Chicago Press.

Sugiura, I. (1999) "K san wa toransu ka: seiteki aidentitī no rikai kanōsei" (Can K be said to be a 'trans'?: The understandability of sexual identities), *Kaihō Shakaigaku Kenkyu*, 13: 53–73.

Sunagawa, H. (2003) "Shinjuku nichōme ga shōsha suru iseiai shakai" (Heterosexual world illuminated from Shinjuku nichōme), in M. Matsuzono (ed.) *Sei no bunmyaku: kurashi no bunka jinruigaku* 4, Tokyo: Yūzankaku.

Tagame, G. (ed.). (2003) *Nihon no gei erotikku āto: gei zasshi sōseiki no sakka tachi* (Japanese gay erotic art: artists at the dawn of gay magazines), Tokyo: Pot Shuppan.

Takeda, M. (2003) "Aidentitī kategorī ni taisuru 'gyappu' kara 'oriai' e: hi iseiaisha josei no sei ishiki chōsa oyobi intabyū yori" (From "gap" toward "compromising" with identity categories: from attitude surveys and interviews about sexuality with heterosexual women), *Sosiorojisuto*, 5(1): 67–115.

Tsuruta, S. (2003) "Kokoro no sei wo miru toiu jissen: 'sei dōitsusei shōgai' no 'seishin ryōhō' ni okeru seibetsu kategorī" (The practice of looking for distinction of sex in the mind: sexual categories used in the "psychotherapy" of "gender identity disorder"), *Nenpō Shakaigaku Ronshu*, 16: 114–125.

Wada, N. (1953) "Tadareta hadae" (Inflamed skin), *Fūzoku zōshi*, September, 52–57.

Yamamoto, A. and S. Ozawa (1975) "Kisu wo suru koto minshushūgi no shinboru da" (Kissing is a symbol of democracy), in Nippon Shuppansha (ed.) *Kasutori fukkokuhan*, Tokyo: Nippon Shuppansha.

4 Transgendering *shōjo shōsetsu*
Girls' inter-text/sex-uality

Tomoko Aoyama

Introduction

It is only relatively recently that female adolescence has begun to attract scholarly attention in the West. Dalsimer, for instance, notes the traditional neglect of female adolescence (as opposed to early childhood or womanhood) and points out that "theoretical formulations in the past have tended either to assimilate the experience of the girl to that of the boy, or alternatively, to cast its difference in terms that are stark and grim" (1986: 1). Similar remarks can be found in the introductory pages of a study on North American girls' series books:

> Girls' series books have been quadruple outcasts from critical circles because they are written for young readers, are targeted at girls, are popular reading, and, even worse, are series books, which often have been regarded with disdain by literary critics.
>
> (Inness 1997: 1)

The first three elements neatly overlap with those identified in Japanese *shōjo* (girls, young women) culture. Despite (or because of) their immense popularity, the all-women musical theatre Takarazuka,[1] *shōjo shōsetsu* (girls' fiction, fiction targeted at girl readers), and *shōjo manga* (girls' comics) were all "regarded with disdain" for decades by critics. As for the status of series books, however, one should note that there is no such negative connotation attached to this form of publication in Japan. This difference is a reminder that what is true in one culture may not necessarily be true in another.

Shōjo is, according to Orbaugh's concise exposition (2002: 458–459), a "cultural construct," which began to be circulated from about 1920 to recognize "a period in life when a female was neither naïve child nor sexually active woman," and which in contemporary society symbolizes "a state of being that is socially unanchored, free of responsibility and self-absorbed – the opposite of the ideal Japanese adult," and hence can be used "as a tool for the critique of contemporary society." Just as *shōjo*, a Japanese cultural construct, is not the same as the English category "girl," *shōsetsu* and *manga* are both quite different from "fiction" and "comics," which is precisely why I prefer using original Japanese terms in this chapter.

Thanks to a series of recent studies (e.g. Robertson 1998; McLelland 2000),

Japanese *shōjo* culture and some of its favorite themes such as *bishōnen* (beautiful boys), androgyny, transgender, transsexuality and male homosexuality have gained some recognition within Japanese cultural studies. Outside this discipline, however, they seem to be still more or less unknown. Germaine Greer's recent study of the depiction of male youth in art, *The Boy*, for instance, makes no reference to any Japanese example (*shōjo* culture or otherwise). Her advocacy of "women's reclamation of their capacity for and right to visual pleasure" (Greer 2003: 11) would be completely unnecessary in Japan, where men and women, and particularly *shōjo*, did and still do admire the beauty of androgynous boys and girls in the visual, performing and literary arts.

Closely connected with the peripheral position of key elements of Japanese culture in the West is the general tendency to rely on the highly selective material available in English (and other European languages) when representing Japanese culture. Discussions of the *shōjo* in Japanese literature thus tend to focus on well-circulated texts such as those by Yoshimoto Banana. This is true not only of primary texts but also of critical and theoretical works. Important and original studies of *shōjo* culture such as those by Takahara (1999), Kawasaki (1990) and Honda (1982, 1986) have hardly been mentioned outside Japan.

This chapter seeks to fill this cultural gap by providing a close reading of Kanai Mieko's novel entitled *Indian Summer* (1988).[2] The novel is not specifically targeted at the *shōjo* audience but it is deeply (and entertainingly) concerned with the *shōjo shōsetsu*, as the following passage from Kanai's Afterword indicates:

> As someone who grew up reading *shōjo shōsetsu*, it has been my wish for many years to write at least one *shōjo shōsetsu* myself, as a kind of *okaeshi* (return/revenge). I would hesitate to call this particular novel a *shōjo shōsetsu*, for it lacks some essential elements of the genre; nevertheless I might be allowed to say that the *shōjo* narrator of this novel, who does share some of my blood, lives, in a way quite bravely, representing certain feelings of *shōjo* of a certain period.
>
> (1999: 204)

What is shōjo shōsetsu?

The definition of the *shōjo shōsetsu* is not simple. In addition to *shōjo* being a complex cultural construct, the term *shōsetsu*, too, is notoriously difficult to define; it is not confined to novels and short stories but includes a much wider range of prose fiction which may also contain some dramatic and/or poetic elements, and may at times seem rather like an essay, a diary, or a documentary, etc.[3] For the time being, however, let us tentatively consider the *shōjo shōsetsu* in its broadest sense, that is, as prose fiction targeted (usually) at the *shōjo* reader, and (usually) with a *shōjo* protagonist. It includes a few different types such as:

1 stories for and about adolescent girls published in prewar girls' magazines, as represented by Yoshiya Nobuko's (1896–1973) *Hana monogatari* (Flower tales, 1916–24);

2   translated "classics" such as *A Little Princess* and *Anne of Green Gables*;
3   juvenile (or "junior") fiction of the 1960s and early 1970s written mostly by middle-aged men;
4   later juvenile fiction (or Cobalt *shōsetsu*, named after the series published by Shūeisha) written by young women writers such as Himuro Saeko, Arai Motoko, and Yuikawa Kei.

Depending on these subcategories and the associated periods, "essential elements" vary. Given that Kanai (b. 1947) belongs to the generation that is most familiar with the second type of the *shōjo shōsetsu*, it seems worth noting the following common elements of this genre, as observed by Hico Tanaka[4] (in Saitō 2002: 18–24):

1   that the protagonist is an orphan;
2   that she has an eccentric and/or obstinate guardian;
3   that the protagonist has a vivid imagination;
4   that her losing some of her imagination is compensated for by something else, such as marriage;
5   that masculinity is checked and modified by physical and mental/emotional illnesses and weaknesses;
6   that romantic heterosexual love is treated ultimately as the most important value.

In Kanai's novel some of these elements are retained with modification but others are dramatically changed. Neither the first-person narrator-protagonist, Momoko, nor her friend, Hanako, is an orphan, although each girl's parents are divorced or separated. At the beginning of the novel Momoko, who has just entered university, leaves her mother's house and moves into her aunt's flat in Tokyo. This aunt may be regarded as a modern version of the girl protagonist's guardian, and may seem slightly eccentric, but she is by no means obstinate. She is single and does not reflect the stereotypical image of a middle-aged woman in Japan. Most importantly, she is, like Kanai herself, an established writer of fiction and essays. Both Momoko and Hanako are avid readers (and cinema fans), but rather than dream about the stories they have read, they tend to criticize them. So the loss of imagination is not an issue in this novel, although the significance of reading/viewing is a key issue that will be discussed in detail below. Of the six elements, the fifth (checked/modified masculinity) seems to be the only one that is maintained, and it is not merely maintained but actually expanded into an acute and articulate criticism of gender in this novel. Heterosexual love or sexuality, on the other hand, is questioned and repeatedly denied.

The above common elements refer to one particular type of *shōjo shōsetsu*, that is, translated girls' fiction. As we shall see, Kanai's novel alludes to some other types, especially *Hana monogatari*. In other words, *Indian Summer* presents a parody of *shōjo shōsetsu* and a critique of gender constructions in contemporary Japanese culture and society. What I wish to show in the following is how the two issues, intertextuality and gender criticism, are inseparably connected in this novel. Needless to say, our prime interest is not in *shōjo* culture as such but in the power and possibility of the *shōjo* to function as "a tool for the critique of contemporary society," to repeat Orbaugh's words (2002), or what Takahara (1999) terms her "arrogance" and "freedom."

What is *shōjo*?

Before discussing transgender and intertextuality, however, let us look at the construct of *shōjo* in a little more detail. The term *shōjo* seems to have been used widely from the third decade of the Meiji period onwards, that is, since around 1900. As Kume (1997: 195) notes, the distinction between *shōjo* and *shōnen* (boys, male youths, underage) in Meiji signified "difference in power," whereas the older and official term *joshi* (girl, woman, womankind) and its male equivalent *danshi* merely indicated difference in sex. *Shōjo* is also different from another earlier and clearly gendered term *musume*, which tends to connote daughterly duties and obligations within the *ie* (patriarchal family) and within the community and the nation as an extension of the family. The notion of the *musume* who leaves the confines of home and has some sort of cross-cultural experience is represented by Madame Butterfly – exotic, powerless, and conveniently virtuous.

That women assigned to perform female roles in the Takarazuka are called *musume-yaku* rather than *onna-yaku* (female roles), even though their counterparts are called *otoko-yaku* (male roles), certainly shows the asymmetrical nature of gender, and seems to indicate, as Robertson suggests, the intentions of the theater's founder, Kobayashi Ichizō:

> More important, he relegated the players of women's roles to the status of daughter, with its attendant connotations of filial piety, youthfulness, pedigree, virginity, and being unmarried. These were precisely the characteristics that Kobayashi sought in the young recruits and that marked the makings of a Good Wife, Wise Mother.
>
> (1998: 16)

Perhaps we should also mention here that there are at least three other relevant and widely used terms. *Onna no ko* (lit. female child) is interchangeable in many situations with *shōjo*, but being already a phrase consisting of three native Japanese words, *onna no ko* is not generally used for making further compound nouns and phrases (as is the Chinese-character term *shōjo*). *Onna no ko* may also sound slightly younger or more childish and less poetic in some cases than *shōjo*. In contrast, *otome* (virgin, maiden, girl) has a narrower range of meaning and usage.[5] Because of its pure, innocent image, it was often used by Yoshiya Nobuko as the reading of the Chinese characters for *shōjo*. Finally, *ojōsan* and the more formal/high-class *ojōsama*, are honorific versions of *musume* and hence used for someone else's daughter and young ladies of high status.

There is another important point to make about the term *shōjo*: from the beginning of the twentieth century it has been closely and directly connected to consumer and popular culture targeted at young women. Notably these popular cultural products, ranging from girls' magazines to fashion products and stationery, were mostly created by men – with one important exception – namely Yoshiya's *Hana monogatari*, which became an extremely popular and influential girls' cultural icon. Closely connected with the *shōjo* as the consumer is the so-called "cute culture" which flourished in the postwar period and has continued right through to the present. Ribbons, frills, flowers, hearts, and cuddly animals appear from cover to cover in girls' magazines, some of which are named *Himawari* (Sunflower, 1947–52), *Ribon* (Ribbon, 1955–), *Māgaretto* (Margaret, 1963–), *Hana to yume* (Flowers and dreams, 1974–). Furthermore they also appear on various kinds of stationery, on handkerchiefs, bags, aprons, pajamas, and slippers, and so on.

One of the central figures in *shōjo* studies, Honda Masuko, identifies several important factors in *shōjo*, which she explains with reference to the keyword *hirahira* (1982: 135–170). This onomatopoeic term usually indicates flitting, fluttering movement; hence it symbolizes the fluttering of ribbons and frills, which may charm the observer but may also be taken, literally, lightly, that is not seriously. Honda further points out the ephemeral nature of this *hirahira* movement, the momentariness that can further be interpreted as indicating the capriciousness of *shōjo*-hood as well as implying its transient and transitional nature. *Hirahira* is an apt adverb to describe butterflies dancing or flower petals falling.

To what extent are these characteristics of *shōjo* applicable to the girl protagonists of *Indian Summer*? Momoko is 19 years old at the beginning of the novel and turns 20 halfway through. Hanako is the same age. In a sense the title of the novel may be interpreted as a mild, pleasant day before the onset of winter (that is, adulthood). Both women may be older than some *shōjo shōsetsu* protagonists, but they are definitely *shōjo*, free and arrogant, unlike meek and dutiful *musume* or pure and innocent *otome*. They consume urban culture, including some of the "cute" (and at times quite expensive) cultural products such as pajamas with Felix the Cat's prints (Kanai 1999: 67). Nevertheless, both Momoko and Hanako do revolt against the stereotypical image of cute and mindless material girls. In this revolt both transgender and intertextuality play crucial roles.

Transgender in *shōjo* culture

It is well known that the theme of transgender was already evident from the outset of the two most innovative and influential genres targeted at *shōjo*: Takarazuka and *shōjo manga*. Tezuka Osamu's *Ribon no kishi* (The ribbon knight, serialization began in 1953, translated as *Princess Knight*) is widely known as the first *shōjo manga* ever to appear. Its androgynous heroine, Princess Sapphire, is dressed and fights like a knight. Tezuka is reported to have said that he "tried to transfer the world of Takarazuka into girls' comics," which, in Fujimoto's view (1998: 132), signifies two important things: first, that from its outset *shōjo manga* was clearly marked by transgender elements and, second, that that these transgender elements are based on an imaginary world completely removed from ordinary life. Let us note here that this imaginary world corresponds to what we have already stated about *shōjo shōsetsu*. Although each was created by an adult man, these two genres and their transgendering aspects have appealed to generations of young women.

Needless to say, transgender, transsexuality, androgyny, etc. are all found in much earlier graphic, oral, and written texts and performing arts in Japan and elsewhere. But no other period, audience, or genre seems to be so preoccupied with such themes as the *shōjo manga* of the late 1970s onwards – produced, notably, by women artists. The preoccupation of the *shōjo* with these themes has been associated partly with the physical, sexual, and psychological developmental changes experienced by girls in adolescence. Kanai, for example, comments thus:

> Such yearning on the part of the *shōjo* for a neutral sex, however, is very much of a transitional nature. Shibusawa Tatsuhiko once said about Alice [in Wonderland] that she is a girl in a sexual safety zone, the interspace between sexual unconsciousness and consciousness. Why do girls want to be androgynous? Why do they admire Jeanne d'Arc? Alice's state of consciousness gives us an insight about these things. In their transition from sexual unconsciousness to consciousness, girls are torn into two different sexes, masculine and feminine. What used to be one and undivided, or something that could be either earlier in their childhood is starting to be torn asunder within themselves, in the form of a notion of sex that goes against themselves.
>
> (1981: 258)

Kanai's comments do not simply describe the transitional and ambivalent nature of *shōjo*'s sexuality but also suggest the fear and antagonism on the part of the *shōjo* who finds herself forced to become a female sexual being. In fact, as many critics have pointed out, the *shōjo*'s longing for androgyny is closely related to her questioning of, or rebellion against, conventional gender roles. The popular theme of male homosexuality in *shōjo manga* can be interpreted as "a safety device for the *shōjo* to handle such a dangerous substance as sexuality safely, away from her own body," and "as wings that would allow her to fly" (Ueno 1998: 131). Hatred for women expressed by some characters (typically a *bishōnen*) may well imply, as Fujimoto (1998: 140–141) points out, refusal on the part of the *shōjo* to comply with the expected gender role for women.

Many of these transgender themes are used in *Indian Summer*, though in many cases in a teasing, tongue-in-cheek way. The clearest example is Momoko's father and his partner. The father, divorced several years before, lives with a *furawā āchisuto* (flower artist), that is, someone who designs and makes bouquets and floral decorations. At the beginning of the novel Momoko is unaware of this new partner's existence. When she hears the voice of this person on the telephone for the first time, Momoko finds it very strange – "a curiously high-pitched, husky, and artificial kind of voice sounding neither like a man nor like a woman" (Kanai

1999: 38). Halfway through the novel the *shōjo* narrator realizes that the flower artist is in fact a man and that the divorce of her parents must have been caused by her father's sexuality – a shock for Momoko, though neither a devastating nor a lasting one.

In this rather *shōjo manga*-like situation we see multiple play. First of all, the homosexual partner is far from the *bishōnen* of typical *shōjo manga* stories; he is middle-aged, and his face looks like an earthenware pot. He speaks like a retired *geisha* (he calls Momoko "*ojō*," which is a very quaint way to address a young woman in contemporary Japan). We may also note the implications of his profession, which is not traditional *ikebana* flower arrangement but something more modern and we might say, more feminine than *ikebana*. Modern "flower artists" use not just flowers but ribbons, frills, tulle, and other objects that would fit the *hirahira* category. Momoko's father also seems to be having an affair with a younger man, which makes Momoko feel sympathy for the flower artist. Here homosexuality is not the romantic and aesthetic trope found in typical *shōjo manga*; rather it is given a comic, almost farcical twist.

It is not coincidental that the two *shōjo* in the novel are named Momoko (literally, peach child) and Hanako (flower child).[6] Despite her literally "flowery" name, Hanako, in particular, represents an alternative to the stereotypical *shōjo*, an alternative that involves transgender. She is short in height, and she favors an extremely short haircut, which makes her look like a schoolboy.[7] Her refusal to conform is obvious in her language, too – she usually refers to herself by the plain (and non-cute) masculine first person pronoun *ore*.[8] All these factors combined, some strangers take her for a boy. For instance, she and Momoko meet a group of young men at a cinema and start a heated discussion on film. After more than an hour these boys still believe that she is Momoko's younger brother, who is well informed for "his" age.

We are told that the name Hanako itself is an alternative to the one given by her father – Arisa, after the heroine Alissa of Gide's *La Porte Étroite*. This obviously concerns intertextuality, but the point to note here is that Hanako's rejection of her original given name represents the rebellion of a *shōjo* against her father's expectation that his daughter (*musume*) be as pure, innocent, and self-sacrificing as Gide's Alissa.

Gender reversal is also hinted at when Hanako brings a bunch of flowers – forget-me-nots and daisies – in her first visit to Momoko's aunt, whose writing she deeply admires. This is an obvious parody of Yoshiya's *Hana monogatari*, which consists of 52 stories, each of which, only several pages long, is given a specific flower title such as "Lily of the Valley," "Rose," "Gardenia," "Cosmos," etc. that would suit its girl protagonist. Furthermore, in many of the *Hana monogatari* stories a young woman yearns for another young woman. Hanako's admiration for her aunt occasions the following remarks from Momoko:

> I was impressed but at the same time thought it was a bit too much when she started to recite from memory a passage from Auntie's novel. To Auntie, the solitary novelist, this must be a very flattering, endearing thing. How lucky

that she is my aunt rather than my uncle! For it would be a bit of a problem if a 38-year-old bachelor uncle were to seduce a girl in my class.

(Kanai 1999: 89)

However, this does not develop into a lesbian love story; sexuality, hetero or homo, is not treated as centrally important in this novel. This in itself is a critique of the last element (i.e. the ultimate promulgation of heterosexual love) Tanaka identified in translated *shōjo shōsetsu*.

Intertextuality in *shōjo shōsetsu*

Unlike issues concerning gender, the significance of intertextuality in texts targeted at the girl reader and/or texts dealing with *shōjo* themes and protagonists, has attracted hardly any scholarly attention.[9] This is an area, however, that needs our special consideration, for the absorption and transformation of other texts are in fact central to *shōjo*-hood. The term intertextuality is used here in a broadly Kristevan sense, namely that "tout texte se construit comme mosaïque de citations, tout texte est absorption et transformation d'un autre texte" (Kristeva 1969: 85). The mosaic involves neither the simple imitation nor the repetition of preceding texts but absorption and transformation. We might also consider Genette's notion of transtextuality, which refers to "all that which puts one text in relation, whether manifest or secret, with other texts," and is divided into five types: intertextuality (effective co-presence of two texts), paratextuality (relation between the text proper and its title, preface, postface, epigraph, dedication, illustrations, etc.), metatextuality (critical relationship between one text and another), architextuality (generic taxonomies suggested or refused by the titles), and hypertextuality (relation between a hypertext and an anterior text, that is, hypotext) (summary of Genette 1982, based on Stam *et al.* 1992: 206–210).

As we have seen, Kanai, in her Afterword (that is, paratext), declares that she once was a reader of *shōjo shōsetsu* and that her text is her expression both of her gratitude towards, as well as the grudge she bears against the genre.[10] She certainly explores all types of transtextuality in her writing.[11] Before going into these examples, however, let us briefly discuss the long tradition of girls' intertexuality.

From the age of *The Tale of Genji* (eleventh century), the figure of a girl preoccupied with tales, stories, romance and fantasies – all of which have been regarded as belonging to "women and children" rather than to mature and respectable men – has appeared again and again in fiction, often with interesting meta-fictional debates and implications. The young Tamakazura, for instance, defends the "truthfulness" of tales as well as her own virtue against her seductive step-father, the Shining (if by then somewhat middle-aged) Prince Genji. Austen's young Catherine Morland, on the other hand, eventually learns the absurdity of the Gothic novels she has been absorbed in. It may not be appropriate to declare, as Reynolds (1990: xv) does, that "[g]irls have always read more, and read more widely than boys," for that certainly depends on the period, on the society and on class; many girls were/are not given opportunities to learn reading and writing or to spend time and money on reading, and today many girls, like many boys, have options – *manga*, games, mobile phones, *anime*, films, etc. – other than books. One can say at least, however, that a girl fantasizing about the story she has read or heard is just as commonly seen in literatures of many different periods and cultures as is a girl dreaming or making up a story. Perhaps the most celebrated example in Japanese literature is the author of the *Sarashina nikki* (The Sarashina Diary, translated by Ivan Morris as *As I Crossed a Bridge of Dreams*, 1971), known to us as the Daughter of Fujiwara no Takasue. Recalling her girlhood in remote provinces, she writes:

> Yet even shut away in the provinces I somehow came to hear that the world contained things known as Tales, and from that moment my greatest desire was to read them for myself. To idle away the time, my sister, my step-mother, and others in the household would tell me stories from the Tales, including episodes about Genji, the Shining Prince; but since they had to depend on their memories, they could not possibly tell me all I wanted to know and their stories only made me more curious than ever.
>
> (Morris 1971: 41)

The girl, not yet 12, is in love with tales, particularly *The Tale of Genji*, and longs to read the real thing – perhaps just as heroes of tales often fall in love with a lady by hearsay and yearn to see her in person. In other words, "[s]he craved," as Keene notes, "not the social life that actually existed at the court but the vicarious pleasure of reading about imaginary people who had once populated it" (1999: 384). Let us note the imaginary nature of the world she longs for. This corresponds well to the third element Hico Tanaka identified in translated *shōjo shōsetsu*. The narrator of the *Sarashina Diary* turns to religion in later life and regrets her earlier obsession with tales, but it is precisely this obsession that has charmed readers, particularly women, for centuries. For reading, hearing, thinking about, or making up a story is an integral and "real" part of a girl's life. It helps her not simply "to idle away the time" but to overcome various difficulties: solitude, poverty, illness, boredom, and social restrictions including gender-based ones. One of the most celebrated girl protagonists, Sara Crewe, consoling her friend Ermengarde, says: "*Everything's* a story. You are a story – I am a story. Miss Minchin is a story" (Burnett 2002: 89; emphasis in the original). Stories, read and imagined, are equally important to Anne Shirley (of Green Gables) and many other girls.

Absorption, however, is only one part of the intertextual mosaic: we need to acknowledge the other aspect, that is, transformation, as well. Parody, allusion, quotation, adaptation, and travesty play significant roles in *shōjo shōsetsu* as well as in *shōjo manga*, and in the new genre called *yaoi*.[12] The choice of these embedded texts and particularly their transformation strongly indicate the difference from, and often the antagonism towards, the non-*shōjo*, particularly adult male culture. Thus these texts within texts help to construct and define the exclusive *shōjo* world, within which the writer, the protagonist, and the reader share the same texts woven into the primary texts. Furthermore, the ambivalent relationship of a

58 Tomoko Aoyama

parody with its original – affectionate and respectful, on the one hand, and teasing and critical, on the other – corresponds well with the ambivalent representations of gender and sexuality.

The intertextuality of *Indian Summer*

One of the important features of the friendship and companionship between Momoko, Hanako, and the Aunt is that they enjoy sharing texts with each other. A book plays an important role in the first meeting of Momoko and Hanako – Hanako abruptly asks Momoko to give her the cover of the book she is reading because the cat in the cover photograph resembles one she used to have.[13] Furthermore, Hanako turns out to be a fan of the Aunt's writing, which clearly marks her difference from other young women at the university, "those innocent girls who never probably read any of Auntie's novels, and have absolutely no idea about what sort of life she has" (Kanai 1999: 8). The conversation with the boys Momoko and Hanako meet at a cinema, too, is prompted by a book, in fact a collection of critical essays on film written by Momoko's aunt. In other words, those who cannot share the same texts are excluded from the companionship of Momoko, Hanako and the Aunt (and vice versa).

Momoko's father, for example, is definitely disqualified. He is tall, well groomed, generous, and absent, which may remind us of some idealized fathers in *shōjo manga* or *shōsetsu*. As the manager of a hotel in Tokyo, he has the knowledge (or rather information), the contacts, and the money to take his daughter to the best restaurants and boutiques and offers her not only food and other presents but also his extensive knowledge about these things. Momoko does not refuse the gifts but she regards her father's efforts to keep up with the latest and the best merely as snobbish affectation. What offends Momoko about her father is that he is a poseur with no intellectual substance. This is what she says about him after one of their shopping excursions in the Ginza:

> Dear me! It makes you wonder. Being weak in the head, he's probably thinking of himself as the father in *Bonjour tristesse*. In other words he's a snob. I remembered the father in Mishima Yukio's popular novel *Megami* [Goddess] I read when I was a child. . . . Seeing his daughter choose a cocktail because it matched the color of her dress made him ecstatic about the fruits of his education. When we were back at home that evening, I had a good laugh with my aunt at the three of them, i.e. my old man, the father of the melodrama, and the author of the melodrama.
>
> (Kanai 1999: 46)

The mosaic of preceding texts makes the criticism sharper and more complex. The father in Sagan's novel is regarded as a fool by his daughter, and Momoko says that her own father is stupid enough to fancy himself as Cécile's father. Such a critical viewpoint is completely lacking in the daughter of Mishima's "melodrama." Unlike the young women in these two preceding texts, Momoko would never become an accomplice in her father's love affair or an object of his indulgence. Furthermore, while not totally rejecting fashion and consumerism, the daughter still despises her father's snobbery.

Momoko's criticism is directed not only toward her father but perhaps more severely toward her mother, especially her efforts to maintain traditional gender roles and respectability. Given the absence of the father (first because of work and then because of the divorce), the mother does seem to fit in with what Ueno (1996: 15) has called the "transvestite patriarch," that is, the mother acting as a substitute for the absent patriarch. Momoko firmly rejects her mother's view.

If Momoko's mother is repressive and her father shallow and unreliable, the heterosexual father of Hanako is worse; he is notorious for harassing women, exploiting his position as the editor of a magazine – a pretentious and trendy kind of health publication which Hanako and her circle of course despise. Just as Momoko was not yet aware of her father's sexuality, Hanako seems not to know the whole truth about her father, and yet she definitely rejects the patriarchal values he tries to maintain. As mentioned before, Hanako is her self-adopted name, but when there is a telephone call for her, her father insists that there is no one called Hanako in his house. To her the name Arisa is an embarrassment or a bad joke, whereas to him it is a beautiful name he himself chose from a famous literary work. In reporting to her father that she has failed an entrance examination for a national university, she says, "Arisa couldn't pass through the strait gate"[14] (Kanai 1999: 80), but the joke is completely lost on her father. Furthermore, his ignorance of *really* important books, such as Deleuze and Guattari's *Anti-Oedipus*, irritates Hanako beyond measure.

Equally pathetic, if not as positively objectionable as Hanako's father, is Momoko's admirer. This young man, the heir to a successful family business in Momoko's hometown, has (like Momoko's father) the wherewithal to wine and dine her in the expensive and trendy venues of Roppongi. He has carefully drawn up a future plan for himself and Momoko, which only bores her. She has no illusions about food, marriage, or any other lures this eligible young man has to offer. It is obvious that he cannot *share texts* with her. When they go to see Godard's *Prénom Carmen*, which is of course her choice, he falls asleep halfway through.

So these people cannot share textual pleasure with Momoko and her companions. Those who can, on the other hand, share not only reading of the preceding texts but their transformation which may result in new published texts. In fact, *Indian Summer* structurally depends on this notion of shared and transformed texts. It is not confined to the numerous books and films mentioned in the primary narrative; inserted into the narrative told in Momoko's voice are eight short pieces (two short stories and six essays) written by the Aunt for literary magazines and other publications. The Aunt is (as we have already noticed) very much like Kanai Mieko herself, and yet no reader would mistake this novel for an autobiographical text, for it is clearly about the adventures and experiments of the *shōjo* and ex-*shōjo* in reading and writing. Whether any of the events are based on the author's own experiences is irrelevant here. The Aunt's work is inserted because Momoko and

Hanako are its first readers and critics, often before it is faxed to the publishers. The two girls share with the Aunt not only the written texts but also preceding texts (which include not only literary or written texts but also oral and other types of texts as well) which are absorbed and transformed into them. And we as readers, in turn, can share their amusement and pleasure through reading *Indian Summer* and the texts within its text.

The most obvious example of intertextual amusement is a story entitled "Hana monogatari," an obvious takeoff of Yoshiya Nobuko's *Hana monogatari*, which, in turn, is (at least partly) Yoshiya's "absorption and transformation" of Louisa May Alcott's *A Garland for Girls*. As already mentioned, *Indian Summer* is full of flower motifs, which is both tribute to, and parody of, the *shōjo shōsetsu*. The Aunt's "Hana monogatari" looks like a typical Yoshiya story – the story of a girl admiring a beautiful young woman whom she calls "Onēsama" (the elegant and respectful term for an elder sister/woman). It is not only the obvious title and the theme of faintly homoerotic and yet platonic adolescent love but also the detailed description of clothes (color, texture, style), and use of props (a rose pink cashmere shawl which belongs to the beautiful woman) that all indicate that this story is an *okaeshi* (return/revenge), at once both an affectionate pastiche and a tongue-in-cheek parody of Yoshiya's *Hana monogatari*. That is if the text is read simply as a story published in a magazine – in this case we are told it is not for a literary magazine but for a company's PR magazine – without the primary narrative (or the context) of *Indian Summer*.

There is much more to be enjoyed in the Aunt's "Hana monogatari" than this: the beautiful Onēsama is an *ikebana* artist. The girl finds out that the object of her love and admiration is having an affair with her father. The reader cannot but smile at this radical transformation of the "real-life" gay flower artist into the "fictive" Onēsama. The Onēsama, despite her elegance and beauty, does have some masculine traits – almost like an *otoko-yaku* in the Takarazuka, with her 173 cm height (more than 10 centimeters taller than her lover) and her big strong hands and arms that enable her to clip with ease the thick and hard branches for her flower arrangement. The very first sentence of the "Hana monogatari" describes the *kimono* she is wearing as like a man's, with subdued colors and patterns. So in terms of gender, the Aunt's parody is intriguing indeed: presenting a stark contrast with Yoshiya's "pre-homosexual" *Hana monogatari*, which, as Kume Yoriko points out, ultimately "reinforces the existing gender system and women's evaluation rather than shakes heterosexism" (2003: 110–112).

Conclusion

In *Indian Summer* sexuality, hetero- or homo-, is not the source of *jouissance* or the object of yearning. What brings blissful moments seems to be the *shōjo*'s freedom and pride, to recapitulate Takahara's keywords, and those friendships in the context of which this freedom and pride can be shared. Auntie's essays and stories are entertaining and subversive in and of themselves, but when juxtaposed with the primary narrative, the intra-textual writer (the Aunt), her immediate readers (Momoko and Hanako), and the extra-textual readers can share the additional pleasure of identifying and musing about various connections between what is written and what has happened or has been talked about in the primary narrative. In addition to the examples seen above, for instance, the unsolicited confession of a girl at Momoko's university about her relationship with her boyfriend and her ordeal of having an abortion is transformed into a comic short story narrated by a young male student.[15]

The powerful and cheerful "*shōjo*" may be a young woman, like Momoko or Hanako, or she may be middle-aged, like the aunt, or she might even be a man, like the flower artist. In one of her tongue-in-cheek essays, Momoko's aunt, who is called throughout the novel "Obasan" (Aunt), insists that there is no real difference between *shōjo* and *obasan* (middle-aged women) except that the latter look older than the former. The immediate subjects of her essay are schoolgirls who walk like middle-aged women and middle-aged women whose favorite reading matter deals with virtually the same kinds of topics as those found in girls' magazines. So, the aunt concludes, "*obasan* are still very much *shōjo*," and "therefore there is no reason for the *obasan* to treat their own girlhood as something special or for the *shōjo* to despise the *obasan*" (Kanai 1999: 147). Obviously Momoko and her company are different from those *shōjo* and *obasan* teased in the essay, and yet while celebrating their freedom and pride, and their power of subversion, the novel also seems to suggest that that jubilation, too, can be, and may even need to be, subverted. Momoko's aunt concludes another essay, a piece on Barthes, with these words. "Am I, then, a reader (and at the same time a writer) with a detestable bourgeois complacency – a reader who reads in books only what I can understand?" (Kanai 1999: 158).

So while the jubilation is based on, or can lead to, subversion (particularly of gender stereotypes) and textual incorporation, there is a certain internal skepticism. And this skepticism is an essential part of the critical power of the *shōjo*.

Notes

1 Founded by Kobayashi Ichizō in 1913, the troupe was originally named Takarazuka Shōkatai but within months changed its name to Takarazuka Shōjo Kageki Yōseikai, commonly known as Takarazuka Shōjo Kagekidan. "Shōjo" was dropped from the name in 1940 (Robertson 1998: 5).
2 The novel was first serialized in a magazine called *Ansanburu* (Ensemble) between October 1985 and April 1987. It was then published in book form in November 1988. The text used here is the paperback edition. The original Japanese title of the novel is written in the Chinese characters for *koharu biyori*, which does mean Indian summer. Kanai specifies the reading of these characters by giving the *katakana* "*indian samā*."
3 See Noguchi (1996) for a concise and yet comprehensive treatment of the problem.
4 This is Tanaka's preferred name order and romanization. Hico is normally written in *hiragana*.
5 Honda (1986: 258–261) gives a brief but insightful etymological analysis of the word *otome*.
6 It may be worth noting that there are famous eponyms: the writer of children's stories, Ishii Momoko, and the translator of stories including *Anne of Green Gables*, Muraoka Hanako. Momoko may also be associated with the Girls' Festival (March 3), which is

also called the festival of peaches. Readers familiar with 1970s' popular culture might further associate the name with Hashimoto Osamu's *Momojiri musume* series or with the actress Momoi Kaori, who was regarded as the representative of the recalcitrant and impudent girl. Michael Ende's *Momo* is another possibility. Hanako, though itself a rather old-fashioned name, may sound fashionable and contemporary when it is associated with the eponymous magazine targeted at young women (slightly older than *shōjo*), which was first published in May 1988, several months before *Indian Summer* was published in book form.

7 In a sense this is an extreme case of the "manifesto of liberation from state sanctioned womanhood" that Robertson (2002: 162) sees in Yoshiya Nobuko's hairstyle.
8 Unlike the younger sounding *boku*, which was used by some girls as an obvious joke version of the first person pronoun, *ore* would normally be regarded as too rough and masculine to be used by young women in that way.
9 Some exceptions exist: Kawasaki (1990) and Foster and Simons (1995), for example, do include some discussions of intertextuality.
10 In her commentary included in the paperback edition of *Indian samā*, Saitō Minako poignantly notes this ambivalent nuance of *okaeshi* (Kanai 1999: 213). Interestingly, Ueno Chizuko also uses the same word in the same kind of ambivalent way in her review of Honda 1986 (included in Ueno 1988: 89–90).
11 In fact, *Indian Summer* includes a wonderful example of metatextuality involving Genette's work, whose penchant for taxonomies is gently teased by Momoko's Aunt. In her essay (within the novel) entitled "Text and Texture" she remarks that although Genette's *Narrative Discourse* is interesting, she cannot see much value in its lists and tables (Kanai 1999: 154).
12 As Mizoguchi explains, the term *yaoi* was coined in the early 1980s by amateur writers as a self-derogatory term. It was "an acronym for the Japanese phrases that mean 'no climax' (*yama nashi*), 'no punch line' (*ochi nashi*), and 'no meaning' (*imi nashi*)." Although it was "originally applied to pornographic parodies using the characters of popular animation shows," it has come to be widely used to refer to male homosexual romance fictions created by and for women" (Mizoguchi 2003: 49–50).
13 Here we have an interesting example of paratextuality: Kanai, a noted cat lover, has published a few books with pictures of a tabby. Readers familiar with other works of Kanai would also see that Kanai's portraits attached to various publications remind us not only of Momoko's aunt but also of Hanako with her short hair.
14 "*Semaki mon*" (strait gate) is a colloquialism denoting the competitiveness of entrance examinations.
15 The piece is entitled "Akachan kyōiku," which is identical to the Japanese title of Howard Hawks' 1938 film *Bringing Up Baby*. Kanai originally published this short story not as a story within a novel but as an independent story in the April 1983 issue of *Gunzō*.

References

Burnett, F. H. (2002) *A Little Princess*, New York: Penguin Books.
Dalsimer, K. (1986) *Female Adolescence: Psychoanalytic Reflections on Literature*, New Haven, CT: Yale University Press.
Dollase, H. T. (2003) "Early twentieth century Japanese girls' magazine stories: examining *shōjo* voice in *Hanamonogatari* (Flower tales)," *Journal of Popular Culture*, 36(4): 724–756.
Foster, S. and J. Simons. (1995) *What Katy Read: Feminist Readings of "Classic" Stories for Girls*, Iowa City: University of Iowa Press.
Fujimoto, Y. (1998) *Watashi no ibasho wa doko ni aru no?: shōjo manga ga utsusu kokoro*

no katachi (Where is my place?: the state of mind reflected in girls' comics), Tokyo: Gakuyō Shobō.
Genette, G. (1982) *Palimpsestes: la littérature au seconde degré*, Paris: Seuil.
Greer, G. (2003) *The Boy*, London: Thames and Hudson.
Honda, M. (1990) *Jogakusei no keifu* (The genealogy of girl students), Tokyo: Seidosha.
—— (1986) *Shōjo fuyū* (The floating girl), Tokyo: Seidosha.
—— (1982) *Ibunka to shite no kodomo* (The child as another culture), Tokyo: Kinokuniya Shoten.
Honda, M., K. Iizawa, Y. Kurabayashi, K. Fujisaki, I. Kohama, N. Horikiri, T. Taniguchi, S. Kanezuka, F. Seo, T. Watanabe, O. Hashimoto, S. Tanemura, and S. Yagawa. (1988) *Shōjo ron* (On the girl), Tokyo: Seikyūsha.
Inness, S. A. (ed.). (1997) *Nancy Drew and Company: Culture, Gender, and Girls' Series*, Bowling Green, OH: Bowling Green State University Popular Press.
Kanai, M. (1988) *Indian samā* (Indian summer), Tokyo: Kawade Shobō Shinsha, Kawade Bunko.
—— (1981) *Kaku koto no hajimari ni mukatte* (Toward the beginning of writing), Tokyo: Chūō Kōronsha, Chūkō Bunko.
Kawasaki, K. (1999) *Takarazuka: shōhi shakai no supekutakuru* (Takarazuka: A spectacle of consumer society), Tokyo: Kōdansha.
—— (1990) *Shōjo biyori* (A perfect day for the girl), Tokyo: Seikyūsha.
Keene, D. (1999) *Seeds in the Heart: Japanese Literature from Earliest Times to the Late Sixteenth Century*, New York: Columbia University Press.
Kristeva, J. (1969) *Séméiôtikè recherches pour une sémanalyse*, Paris: Seuil.
Kume, Y. (2003) "Shōjo no sekai: nijusseiki 'shōjo shōsetsu' no yukue" (Girls' world: the direction of twentieth-century "girls' fiction"), in Y. Komori, T. Tomiyama, M. Numano, H. Hyōdō and H. Matsunra (eds) *Kyokō no tanoshimi* (*Iwanami kōza bungaku*, vol. 6), Tokyo: Iwanami Shoten.
—— (1997) "Shōjo shōsetsu: sai to kihan no gensetsu sōchi" (Girls' fiction: the discursive devices of difference and norm), in Y. Komori, K. Kōno, and O. Takahashi (eds) *Media, hyōshō, ideorogii: Meiji sanjūnendai no bunka kenkyū*, Tokyo: Ozawa Shoten.
McLelland, M. (2000) *Male Homosexuality in Modern Japan: Cultural Myths and Social Realities*, London: RoutledgeCurzon.
Mizoguchi, A. (2003) "Male-male romance by and for women in Japan: a history and the subgenres of *Yaoi* fictions," *U.S.-Japan Women's Journal*, 25: 49–75.
Morris, I. (1971) *As I Crossed a Bridge of Dreams*, New York: Dial Press.
Noguchi, T. (1996) *Ichigo no jiten: shōsetsu* (A dictionary of one word: *shōsetsu*), Tokyo: Sanseidō.
Orbaugh, S. (2002) "Shōjo," in S. Buckley (ed.) *Encyclopedia of Contemporary Japanese Culture*, London and New York: Routledge.
Ralph, P. C. (1989) *Victorian Transformations: Fairy Tales, Adolescence, and the Novel of Female Development*, New York: Peter Lang.
Reynolds, K. (1990) *Girls Only?: Gender and Popular Children's Fiction in Britain, 1880–1910*, Philadelphia, PA: Temple University Press.
Robertson, J. (2002) "Yoshiya Nobuko: out and outspoken in practice and prose," in A. Walthall (ed.) *The Human Tradition in Modern Japan*, Wilmington, DE: Scholarly Resources Inc.
—— (1998) *Takarazuka: Sexual Politics and Popular Culture in Modern Japan*, Berkeley, CA: University of California Press.

Saitō, M. (ed.). (2002) *L bungaku kanzen dokuhon* (A complete reader of L literature), Tokyo: Magajin Hausu.
—— (ed.). (2001) *Danjo to iu seido* (The institution called men and women), Tokyo: Iwanami Shoten.
Stam, R., R. Burgoyne, and S. Flitterman-Lewis. (1992) *New Vocabularies in Film Semiotics: Structuralism, Post-Structuralism and Beyond*, London and New York: Routledge.
Takahara, E. (1999) *Shōjo ryōiki* (The territory of the girl), Tokyo: Kokusho Kankōkai.
Tsuchida, T. (2000) *Kantekusutosei no senryaku* (The strategy of intertextuality), Tokyo: Natsume Shobō.
Ueno, C. (1998) *Hatsujō sōchi: erosu no shinario* (The mating device: scenarios of eros), Tokyo: Chikuma Shobō.
—— (1996) "Collapse of 'Japanese mothers'," *US-Japan Women's Journal*, 10: 3–19.
—— (1988) *Onna asobi* (Woman's play), Tokyo: Gakuyō Shobō.

5 From *The Well of Loneliness* to the *akarui rezubian*
Western translations and Japanese lesbian identities

Beverley Curran and James Welker

> *Everything is borrowed, including our bodies.*
> (David La Chapelle)

Introduction

In his preface to the Mary Barnard translation, Dudley Fitts describes Sappho as

> [a] lyricist unparalleled, a great beauty, no great beauty, a rumor, a writer of cultist hymns, a scandal, a fame, a bitchy sister to a silly brother, headmistress, a mystic, a mistress of the poet Alkaios, a pervert, a suicide for love of a ferryman [*sic*], an androgyne, a bluestocking, a pretty mother of a prettier daughter, an avatar of Yellow Book neodiabolism, a Greek.
> (cited in Johnson 2003: 12)

Inexplicably missing from this list identifying Sappho as Oriental, literary and sexually unclassifiable, is the equally unstable term "lesbian." All the possible semantic dimensions of "Sappho" or "lesbian" make construction of a clear sexual subject impossible. This is certainly the case in Japan where the project of constructing individual and communal lesbian identities has used translation to introduce a shifting lexicon of borrowed terms, from "bluestocking" to "lesbian," to articulate a plurality of sexualities. In fact, the choices of the translator have become inextricable from the process of fashioning and performing lesbian identities. This chapter will trace the tension between the instability of the range of terms and the desire to render the lesbian both meaningful and visible in Japan.

In *The Apparitional Lesbian*, Terry Castle (1993) calls for the recognition of how fully, if invisibly, the lesbian has been a part of the Western literary imagination, and indeed, cultural life. The invisibility of the translator has been similarly remarked on by Lawrence Venuti, who suggests that its ubiquity, particularly in the Anglophone tradition, simultaneously occludes the power translation exerts in the construction of representations of foreign cultures. Venuti offers as an example English translations of modern Japanese fiction that conformed to domestic expectations and rendered Japan as "quintessentially *foreign*" (1998:

72) by selectively concentrating on three authors, namely Tanizaki Jun'ichirō, Kawabata Yasunari and Mishima Yukio. Foreignizing translation, on the other hand, which foregrounds the translator and the interference of her values "is a dissident cultural practice, maintaining a refusal of the dominant by developing affiliations with marginal linguistic and literary values" (1995: 148). Keith Harvey has applied Venuti's observations on domestic and foreignizing translations to consider the effects texts in translation have on the formation of gay identity and community building in a receiving culture. The activity of translation then operates as a "textual elaboration of this identity position either to introduce it as an innovative device in the target cultural polysystem or to modify (heighten or attenuate) it for the target reader" (2000a: 140). This chapter in turn will consider how the translation of lesbian texts into Japanese and the visibility of lesbian-identified translators contribute towards individual and communal constructions of a Japanese lesbian.

Literary borrowing is nothing new in Japan, where linguistic appropriation through translation has been going on for some time by "selectively adapting for domestic and often dominant purposes institutions and technologies that were first established and coined outside Japan" (Robertson 1999: 9). Early borrowings were from the Chinese, and, from the sixteenth century, Europe, where most early translations consisted of religious materials, and also included scientific translation from the Dutch (Howland 2002: 10). In the late nineteenth century, Euro-American loanwords started making their appearance with increasing frequency amid a "craze for Westernization" (Huang 2002: 32) taking place in Japan at the same time that *japonisme* was spreading through Europe and America. Translators were also attempting to express new literary forms and new ways of thought in Japanese as just one aspect of *bunmeikaika*, a national "translation" project intended to refashion a wealthier and more powerful Japan out of political, economic, and cultural ideas imported from the West.

Along with the borrowing, there has been modification. The lesbian in many Western literary representations is tinged and often saturated with a particular kind of melancholy; as the maxim of Colette's *Ces Plaisirs* sums it up, "We can never bring enough twilight, silence, and gravity to surround the embrace of two women" (Castle 1993: 45). Exemplary in plot and representation of the brooding lonely lesbian is Radclyffe Hall's *Well of Loneliness* (1928). While Japanese lesbians have borrowed words and translated texts from the West, they have often reconstructed "lesbianism" in the image of an *akarui rezubian*, a cheerful, eccentric lesbian identity with the imaginative energy and earnest devotion that typifies such translated literary icons as Anne Shirley and her "bosom friend" Diana Barry in the wildly popular *Anne of Green Gables* (1908),[1] with the dress sense of a dandy. This *akarui rezubian* is an aesthetic construction, in the sense that it is built on the literary, and while its contemporary representation may be a member of the lesbian *komyuniti*, membership is neither exclusive nor separate; that is, it acknowledges a desire for harmony within the larger community, as well. The shifting terms used to designate "lesbian" in Japanese have variously accented sexuality as essential or pathological, foreign or local, perverse or romantic, imaginative or real. For the purposes of this chapter, "lesbian" and *rezubian* are employed as aesthetic terms that escape determination (Johnson 2003: 11) and cannot be fixed. Keeping this in mind, we will selectively look at some of the lexical choices that have attempted to "contain" the lesbian in Japan, and some of the translations and translators that have been pivotal in foregrounding her presence.

Whether borrowing terms directly or localizing them through transgressive translation, Japanese looked westward for words and information in critical and creative writing to designate a *rezubian* that nevertheless was linguistically marked as a foreign pathological phenomenon, more than a little ironic given that the European literary lesbian is in part an Orientalist construct (Schultz 2001: 379). However, as we will argue, translation has also been put to use in imagining "local" Japanese lesbian identities and building community by making space for a lesbian to write (or read) herself in on her own terms that still allow "competing understandings" (Schuster 1999: 129) of what a lesbian self or community might mean. We will begin with a brief historical overview of translations of terms and texts about the lesbian. We will then focus on the early 1910s by looking at the appropriation of the term "bluestocking" to identify the seminal literary women's group Seitōsha and to consider the importance of the group's founder Hiratsuka Raichō a "lesbian" icon who links the role of the translator with sexual transgression, a performance which is repeated throughout the century. Finally, we will consider how the Western representations of the translator and the lesbian as solitary and lonely figures have been transformed in Japan by a communal praxis of "lesbian" translation into a dandy *akarui rezubian*.

A *rezubian* by any other name

One area where translation was particularly active in Japan was in the formation of gender and sexuality. In 1875, the first Japanese translation of a European scientific text on sexual difference was published and over the next 20 years, more than a hundred books and treatises on the subject appeared (Kano 2001: 28). Jennifer Robertson maintains that among the "loan words and Japanese social scientific neologisms that were household words in the early 1900s" was the term "*rezubian*" (1999: 9), but the extent of its use in the prewar period – indeed, prior to the 1970s – is debatable. Other terms seem to have been preferred. For example, in the wave of translations of sexological texts, including those by Havelock Ellis and Richard von Krafft-Ebing, which led to a shift in Japanese conceptions of sexuality, terms coined and used to represent homosexuality included *dōseiyoku* (same-sex desire), *hentai seiyoku* (abnormal desire), *dōsei no ai*, *dōsei no koi* (both meaning "love of same sex") and *dōseiai* (same-sex love) which were used concurrently in the early decades of the twentieth century before the latter term was settled on (Furukawa 1995, 1994; Hiruma 2003). In August 1911, for instance, *dōsei no ai* and *dōsei no koi*, rather than any loan word, are used in articles that mark the spark of interest in lesbian desire shown in the pages of the women's weekly *Fujo shinbun* (Women's newspaper). Further, while the invisible lesbian translator of Havelock Ellis's work on female homosexuality which appeared in the April 1914 issue of *Seitō* as "*Joseikan no dōsei ren'ai*" (Same-sex love among females),[2] employs Japanized loan words such as *passhōnātona furendoshippu* (passionate friendship) and *abunōmariti* (abnormality), she leaves the word "Lesbianism" (Ellis [1914] 1980: 4, 10) in English, refusing to render it in Japanese even by writing it in the *katakana* script usually used to identify foreign loan words.

More than 20 years later, an article for a general audience in *Chūō kōron* (Central review) offers Sappho as a "historical perspective on homosexuality" for lack of a history of female homosexuality in Japan. While it uses the Germanic loanword "*toransuvechichisumusu*" (*transvestitismus*, that is, transvestism), its preference for *dōseiai* rather than *rezubian* suggests that the latter term was still not in common usage (Yasuda 1935: 147, 149). By at least 1960, demonstrating the influence of translated literature in articles about but not necessarily by lesbians appearing in popular sexology magazines, *resubosu ai* (Lesbos love), *resubian* and *rezubian* were used, only to be outstripped a decade later by *rezu* (McLelland 2005), a term with a lasting pornographic residue (Chalmers 2002: 39). With the rise of lesbian activism in the 1970s, and *rezubian feminizumu* (lesbian feminism) as evidence of the contact with sisters abroad, *rezubian* finally became a "household word," although even the translators of lesbian historian Lillian Faderman, Tomioka Akemi and Hara Minako, prefer *resubian* to reflect the identity's Sapphic roots (see translators' notes in Faderman 1996: 392). Most dictionaries too have continued to privilege *resubian*.

Although the lexical shift between *resubian* and *rezubian* may appear subtle, it clearly indicates change in "discursive attitude" (Robyns 1994: 40). From the initial reluctance to admit "lesbian" even into *katakana*, the Japanese script purposefully designated to contain the foreign, it is eventually rendered as *resubian*, a literary and likely French import. *Rezubian*, on the other hand, which enters Japanese through American English, along with an American sense of a gay and lesbian identity and community, developed in the 1960s out of or alongside civil rights and women's liberation. It carries a more restricted sense of specific sexuality which marks a distinct group and it is structured around the centrality of "coming out" (Harvey 2003: 12). In short, traces of the source contexts adhere to translated words, such as *resubian* and *rezubian*, which complicate their meaning and usage. The general persistence of *resubian* in such hegemonic social texts as dictionaries suggests that in Japan, human rights are prioritized over special sexual interest groups. The choice of *rezubian* may implicitly link self-identity and sexual community more closely. The difficulty in settling on a term for "lesbian" is indicative of the way translation can "register an element of 'trouble' (however small) consequent upon the traces of difference borne by the foreign" (Harvey 2003: 99) and its potential for revealing systemic values in both source and target cultures.

The lesbian turn

In the early 1910s the *josei dōseiaisha* (female homosexual) was "discovered and quickly problematized" (Hiruma 2003: 9–10). It is no coincidence that Seitōsha (The Bluestocking Society) was established in September 1911, a year marked

Translation and Japanese lesbian identities 69

globally by the first celebration of International Women's Day, and in a more local context, by the first performance in Tokyo of *Ningyō no ie*, the Japanese production of Henrik Ibsen's *A Doll's House*, in which Matsui Sumako played Nora. That same year, there were also newspaper reports of at least two separate incidents of attempted love suicides in Japan involving women. One pair, a couple of maids living in Tokyo, were rescued, while the other couple, two graduates from women's schools, drowned themselves, but through these incidents the subject of lesbian love came to the attention of the media (Wu 2002: 65). While the press used variants of *dōsei no ai* and *dōsei no koi* (Furukawa 1995), other words were being employed in women's schools to discourage lesbian play among the students. As reported by Kuwaya Sadaitsu in a September 1911 interview, *netsu* (passion) was the term employed at Ochanomizu Women's School; *haikara* ("high collar," that is, fashionably Western) was used at Gakushūin Women's School, and *shin'yū* (friendship) described the situation at Atomi Women's School (Wu 2002: 69). The proliferation of the "relationship of S," friendships between girls as intimate as sisters, was part of "American school dormitory culture, in which girls became romantically involved with their same-sex friends and enjoyed the thrill of a 'crush'" (Dollase 2001: 160). In other words, lesbian love became more visible in Japan alongside a growing recognition of women in 1911, but it was identified or, rather, obscured by a number of terms chosen on the basis of perspective and desired effect.

It is important to remember here that not only new constructions of womanhood were being imported but, as Aoyama's chapter in this volume illustrates, the term *shōjo* (girl) was also being redefined as educational policies became more explicitly gendered. In 1879, the Education Ministry introduced separate women's schools at the post-elementary level, and in 1899, each prefecture was required to have at least one higher school for girls (Kano 2001: 30). By 1913, these *kōtō jogakkō* numbered 213, although their students were representative of just a sliver of society, being drawn from the upper-middle class which comprised about 2.3 percent of the population (Dollase 2001: 154). In the privileged space of girls' schools, students had a temporary reprise from the inevitable responsibilities of wife and mother that the curriculum was preparing them for. Local magazines fostered a *jogakusei* (girl student) culture, marked by melancholy and sentimental emotion, and visually supported by illustrations of sweet, mournful young women. Translations of Western girls' stories were popular, and works such as *Little Lord Fauntleroy* (1892), *Little Women* (1906) and *A Little Princess* (1910) excited readers and motivated Japanese writers to inscribe their own little lesbians, as well. For example, Louisa May Alcott's classic was an important influence on lesbian writer Yoshiya Nobuko whose stories, while "fantasy narratives," "embody tremendous issues of feminism and sexuality" (Dollase 2003: 724, 726–728). Dollase notes how:

> The Occidental atmosphere was quickly adapted into Japanese girls' stories ... New concepts and terms such as "piano," "organ," "church," "opera," and "mission school," written in katakana [script], were actively employed, [and]

such western ideas as sisterhood, romance, sentimentalism, and "home sweet home," became the basis of girl culture. The language of these stories – flowery, sentimental, and peppered with foreign terms – rejected the intrusion of the male code and was at variance with male literary conventions.

(2001: 157)

While girls and their passionate friendships became more distinct, these relationships were subject to explicit expiry: although they could be enjoyed as a rehearsal of heterosexual romantic love, they were not to be continued after schooling was over. And while "[a]ll women in public were problematic, the *shōjo* was perceived by some as a downright dangerous phase of unstructured social interaction" (Robertson 1998: 156; see also Aoyama, this volume). In short, although lesbian love was gaining visibility through borrowed language and imagery, it was also being constrained by age limit and location. The post-adolescent lesbian was still invisible.

Fashioning the lesbian

While melancholy schoolgirls were representing lesbian love in books and magazines targeting an emerging girl culture, Seitōsha was fashioning a self-affirming, "*akarui erochikkuna kūkan*" (cheerful erotic space) in which women were free to love each other, and, at the same time, love themselves (Watanabe M. 1998: 271). As graduates from women's universities, Seitōsha members had already experienced a form of female community, and also were part of an international *Zeitgeist* which involved women publicly voicing their dissatisfaction with their status and agitating for change. Among women's magazines, *Seitō* also occupied a specific space as "Japan's first 'women only' literary magazine" (Watanabe S. 1998: 514). Seitōsha's women-only membership consisted not only of graduates from the literature departments of women's universities, but others with experience studying overseas who brought with them a "global gaze" (Watanabe S. 1998: 515). This gaze looked particularly to foreign, that is, Western theater and literature as a way to raise the average woman's knowledge and interest in literature, and, in the process to cultivate literary production by and for women (Watanabe S. 1998: 516). At the same time, and as their intense interest in Ibsen's drama indicates, Seitōsha's literary goals were proto-political. With the Tokyo performance of Ibsen's *A Doll's House*, came a realization that "for the first time a woman succeeded in being a main character; theatre proclaimed the advent of a new age" (Kaneko 1998: 438), and Seitōsha's literary activity was explicitly based on the promotion of the principle that "women, too, are human beings" (Watanabe S. 1998: 514). At the same time, their literary activity promoted women developing their own identity in order to later participate with a more confident voice and greater effect in society at large. Seitōsha's primary interest in literature also involved a more specific sexual politics which concerned women's rights to sexual pleasure and control over their own bodies. Since sexual satisfaction for both sexes was rooted in the "eternal" conflict between men and women, Seitōsha, in literature and in life, aspired to representations and performances of "new kinds of love unrestricted by old conceptions and traditions" (Kaneko 1998: 441). This interest was initially more evident in transgressive sexual behavior, which contested "homosexuality" and flamboyance as exclusively male privileges. Later, private and political concerns overlap, and women's literary creations and women's liberation become twin concerns in *Seitō*, and social issues related to women's bodies, namely, virginity, abortion, and prostitution, are discussed.

Members of Seitōsha were simultaneously involved in the translation of sexologists who defined lesbian love as pathological, while, in their own lives, they were engaging in those very same-sex relationships which were being seen as increasingly transgressive. The society's literary activities also included translating plays, as well as responding with intense critical interest to translated stage productions that represented women and performed gender. The representations in these cultural productions had an effect on how they saw themselves, as well.

If it, on the one hand, helped cultivate "the relationship of S" among schoolgirls, translation also contributed to the Japanese public's anxiety about same-sex desire. Before looking at how *Seitō* paired sexology and literary texts in a juxtaposition still typical of "special lesbian issues" of contemporary journals in Japan, let us first consider how Seitōsha's founding members decided on a name for the literary society which from its onset was seen as an audacious affront to *ryōsai kenbo shugi*, the powerful concept of "good wife wise mother," sanctioned by the Meiji Civil Code and perceived as a "traditional" value, despite having originated in Germany (Robertson 1999: 2). Seitōsha's choice of "bluestocking" to name the women's group and literary journal, first of all, was based on the appeal of a borrowed English word used to describe "an intellectual or literary woman" that nevertheless was usually used in a derogatory sense to suggest a pedantic and "grim ... figure in lumpy tweeds" (Castle 1993: 16). The group's name was initially proposed by member Ikuta Chōkō, using the existing translation *kontabitō*, or navy-blue *tabi* socks. Dissatisfaction with this translation, and perhaps its image, led to its revision (Watanabe S. 1998: 521–522). The evocation of English blue worsted stockings, in lieu of Japanese *tabi*, had an impact on a burgeoning lesbian identity in Japan by taking a Western image to shape its own. At the same time, the "grim figure in tweeds" which Terry Castle has identified as the prototypical image of the Western lesbian was being translated and refashioned into a more cheerful (if not downright gay) *akarui rezubian*, a version of the clothes-conscious dandified aesthete.

With a piece of clothing as the signifier of Seitōsha's identity, it is not surprising that there was considerable attention being paid to appearance. As Ayako Kano observes, "The visibility of the [Seitōsha] feminists tempts us to call them theatrical. They incorporate the viewpoint of the audience as part of constructing their own roles" (2001: 127). For example, in her short story *Nikki* (Diary) ([1913] 1988), Seitōsha's founder, Raichō's[3] ex-lover Tamura Toshiko, recalls Raichō consistently wearing serge *hakama* (wide men's culottes) and, on the train, folding her arms and assuming a male posture (1988: 341), clearly both dressing and performing a trouser role. This transgressive transvestism calls much (critical) attention to itself at the opening of the Taisho Era (1912–1926). In the case of the

Yoshiwara Incident (1912), Raichō and Otake Kōkichi, fellow Seitōsha member, were censured not merely for physically entering male territory, that is, a brothel, and daring to act like men, but for wearing male clothing (Yoshikawa 1998: 79), thus attempting to embody male privilege.

Seitōsha's prop of borrowed hosiery serves to fashion an identity with the same play and self-consciousness that Emily Apter has noticed in French feminists of the same period, who defined the political in the salon and on stage by using "Oriental stereotypes . . . as a means of partially or semi covertly outing sapphic love" (1999: 135). In Japan, this practice of cultural cross-dressing allowed members of Seitōsha to merge recognizable stereotypes, such as the flamboyant Wildean aesthete, with their own stereotype in the making, the *atarashii onna* (new woman) who acts, and sometimes looks, like a man. The theatricality, with its "excessive affect, function[s] to create politically strategic points of semantic commentary among the blurred procedures of *acting, outing, being, doing, passing*, and *meaning*" (Apter 1999: 147). Borrowing clothes, like borrowing texts, was a gesture of appropriation that declared a new identity and a range of sexual and political choices for women as well as men.

Raichō's sexuality was as unstable as the meaning of "lesbian." Although Raichō performed the lesbian in print and in life, she also took on other roles, particularly under the influence of her translations of Ellen Key, who advocated the liberation of women in all areas but motherhood. In her introduction to the translation of Havelock Ellis's article on female homosexuality, Raichō coyly professes curiosity about "*dōsei ren'ai*" (same-sex love) between women and in "*sententeki no seiteki tentōsha*" (inborn sexual inverts) but denies having first-hand experience, at least of school-girl romance (Hiratsuka [1914] 1980: 1). It is necessary to read this as tongue-in-cheek, given her previous profession of desire towards Kōkichi in the pages of *Seitō*.

Perhaps a more consistent model for the lesbian translator is the figure of Yuasa Yoshiko, who never married and indeed was greatly disappointed that Raichō herself got married and had children (Sawabe 1996: 156). Yuasa, in her seventies, reflecting back on her life agrees that the word "*rezubian*" applies to her own experience (Hirosawa 1987: 69). While not attracting the same scandalous media attention as Raichō, Yuasa's life was shaped in various ways by the women of Seitōsha, and has in turn served as a role model for contemporary Japanese lesbians.[4] In addition to Senuma's translations, which helped inspire Yuasa to study the Russian language and literature (Sawabe 1996: 133), Yuasa's life course seems clearly modeled after the *atarashii onna* she found in the pages of *Seitō*. A dandy who rejected the trappings of femininity as well as the *ryōsai kenbo* model, Yuasa lived with the great love of her life, writer Miyamoto Yuriko, in both Tokyo and Moscow. Though romantically linked to other women, including Seitōsha member and writer Tamura Toshiko, Yuasa ultimately lived much of her life on her own (Sawabe 1996), a dapper figure in well-cut tweeds.

Complex identity issues

The connection between the psychological and the literary found in *Seitō*'s pages finds a parallel in the pairing of psychological discussion and literary representation of the lesbian, which continues in contemporary journals in Japan, although the borrowing is increasingly from English, and drawn from American writing and feminist journals.[5] The entanglement of sexual identities, readers, and texts can get tied up in knots. Witness the presence of a lesbian section in a guide to fiction about male homosexuality, edited by women who translate foreign gay fiction for an audience of ostensibly heterosexual women obsessed with men who love men (Kakinuma and Kurihara 1993). There is a blurring of the representations of *bishōnen* (beautiful boys), particularly gay ones, and of lesbians. Gay Wachman (2001) has identified lesbian crosswriting as "transpos[ing] otherwise unrepresentable lives of invisible or silenced or simply closeted lesbians into narratives about gay men." While Wachman describes crosswriting as "a strategy of ambivalence as well as disguise" (2001: 1), it can also function as a readable code of connections.

Similar to the ways in which male-authored "lesbian" texts have occupied a space in lesbian discourse in countries such as France and the US (e.g., the Daughters of Bilitis; Schultz 2001), and the fact that such lesbian classics as *The Well of Loneliness* (Hall [1928] 1952), and *Nightwood* (Barnes [1936] 1983) were translated by men, translations of male-authored "lesbian" fiction have found their way into the Japanese lesbian imagination. LeFanu's lesbian vampire tale *Carmilla* ([1872] 1948), for example, has inspired Japanese lesbian criticism (Takeda 1999a, 1999b) and become the title of a recent periodic lesbian sex guide. References to Baudelaire's *Les fleurs du mal* (1861) (published initially under the title of *Les fleurs du mal – les lesbiennes*) have likewise found their way into lowbrow discourse on lesbian bar culture and the title of the first commercial lesbian magazine, *Phryné*.[6] There clearly continues to be a direct link between the act of translating and promulgating Western lesbian literature and lesbian cultural production in Japan.

Translated works may also serve as a link between the psychological and the literary in personal quests for clarification about sexual identity. In his discussions of gay community and identity and the translated text, Keith Harvey (2000a) offers a possible explanation for the pairing of the psychological with the literary representation by seeing them as variations of the fundamental question of identity formation: that is, "Who am I?" Harvey suggests that "Am I different?" and "Where do I belong?" merge personal and community identification, and that this "twofold understanding of identity allows . . . a perception of the linkages with the posited concrete and imagined components of community" (2000a: 146–147). He makes a further connection with translated texts as crucial, in their subject matter and their very existence, to the formation of "both internal identity formation and imagined community projection." Harvey writes:

> Such texts may well be the result of . . . the introduction into a target cultural polysystem of representations of selfhood and community organisation that

have not been articulated or, alternatively, that have been proscribed in the receiving culture. In short, the space of literature – including, crucially, translated literature – is one in which a (gay [or lesbian]) community can be imagined by the reader.

(2000a: 147)

Karen Kelsky has argued that foreign languages do indeed offer Japanese women the opportunity to "enter bodily into alternative systems of thought and value" (2001: 101). However, many of the increasing number of translations of and borrowing from lesbian writers, theorists and historians, such as Adrienne Rich, Lillian Faderman, Monique Wittig, and Bonnie Zimmerman, still seem aimed at introducing Western lesbian criticism to Japanese readers. The translators' notes have often largely or completely ignored the situation of the intended Japanese readers of the translation (e.g., Takeda 1999a, 1999b; Tomioka 1994). Nevertheless, there have been efforts to apply what is borrowed to the situation of the Japanese lesbian, and certainly these translations have provided concepts, such as Rich's notions of a "lesbian continuum" and "compulsory heterosexuality" or Faderman's use of "romantic friendship," which have been employed by scholars and translators such as Iwabuchi Hiroko (1995), Watanabe Mieko (1998) and Yoshikawa Toyoko (1998) to re-visit Japanese literary works and writers from the early twentieth century and re-claim them as part of their lesbian history. An awareness of the diverse female experiences that Western lesbian critics have placed within the lesbian continuum has given Japanese women the freedom to re-position a variety of female experiences in Japanese history within that same continuum (e.g., Ōsawa 1990).

Bibliographic surveys of lesbian writing found in books and magazines have until recently positioned writings in translation ahead of local works in both number and prominence. Only a fifth of the fiction and non-fiction mentioned in *Onna wo ai suru onnatachi no monogatari* (Stories of women who love women; Bessatsu Takarajima 1987) are about the local lesbian experience (Nishihara *et al.* 1987). The positioning of articles on the Japanese lesbian experience in *Tanbi shōsetsu gei bungaku bukkugaido* (A guide to aesthete novels and gay literature; Kakinuma and Kurihara 1993), as well as the listing of local lesbian writing after Western works implies that the Japanese lesbian tradition is a descendant of a broader lesbian heritage. Certainly overt parallels with Western experiences are not rare: Yoshiya Nobuko and her partner Monma Chiyo, for example, have been described as "the Japanese Gertrude Stein and Alice B. Toklas" (Izumo and Maree 2000: 79; see also *Imago* 1991: 122–123). The guide also seems to prioritize the Western lesbian by offering a lengthy introduction that begins with a discussion of Sappho and features literary and cultural figures such as Natalie Barney, Radclyffe Hall, and Gertrude Stein. The Japanese lesbian literary tradition, on the other hand, is given no formal introduction save short articles on Raichō, and lesbian couples Yuasa Yoshiko and Miyamoto Yuriko, and Yoshiya Nobuko and Monma Chiyo. From this very short list of Japanese lesbian icons, however, we can still see that the indigenous version of the highly visible lesbian is often a translator.

Communal translation

The choice for translation and adaptation of Western lesbian representations into Japanese suggest much about the construction of lesbian identity in Japan. The name of the first lesbian group, Wakakusa no Kai (literally, "new grass club"), which was active for 15 years following its 1971 inception, echoes with deliberation or coincidence *Wakakusa monogatari*, the title of the 1941 Japanese translation of Alcott's *Little Women* by Suga Ryōgen. As Harvey has pointed out, the specifics of translation not only emerge from community building but contribute toward its elaboration. Along with imported language and representations, the very process of translation itself has had an impact on building Japanese lesbian identity. The past several decades have seen women collaborating in translation and lesbians gathering in collective groups, obviating the many levels on which translation works as a community-shaping process. The Rezubian Shōsetsu Hon'yaku Wākushoppu (Lesbian novel translation workshop) at the Tokyo lesbian space LOUD (Lesbians Of Undeniable Drive), organized by staff member Mizoguchi Akiko in 1995, is currently guided by prolific translator Kakinuma Eiko, a noted scholar of gay (male) literature and Japanese translator of Edmund White and Anne Rice. The lesbian translation project also includes Edmund White's essay, "Straight Women and Gay Men," another indication of the ways the gay male continues to interact with the Japanese lesbian identity.

The current project (2003) is the translation of Patricia Highsmith's novel *Carol*. Several of the members of the workshop are middle-aged and perhaps this has a bearing on the translation choices. The works of Jane Rule, for example, as well as Highsmith's *Carol*, offer representations of older lesbians. These translation projects, then, let the lesbian see herself and her desire as ongoing, representing women-loving women's bodies not just at their sexual prime, but as they weaken and age, thus expanding the representation of "lesbian" beyond dreamy or experimental adolescence. It is not just the body image that is being constructed in the communal practice of translation. When a member of the LOUD workshop was asked if the Japanese image of the lesbian/translator, as neither lonely nor solitary, was an attempt to create lesbian community, she answered, "For sure, I think that is precisely why translating lesbian literature as a group is so significant" (personal communication). Moreover, this project is not limited to the small community of readers who engage in the actual process of translating together. As the workshop's manifesto states, "More than just being motivated participants in the workshop, absorb all you can and give it back to the *komyuniti* (community)." The translated term *komyuniti*, like *rezubian*, comes out of American English and retains the residue of that specific cultural context. However, the appeal of identification with a group on the basis of sexuality is tempered in Japanese translation by powerful social imperatives to locate *komyuniti* within the larger community and acknowledge other bonds and obligations. Thus, the milieu of the *akarui rezubian* is a community where difference locates itself in the heart of Japanese society and not outside it.

Conclusion

As we have seen, a number of terms have been borrowed and translated into Japanese to fashion lesbian identity as an aesthetic construct. The English term "bluestocking" was borrowed and translated into Japanese to identify Seitōsha, an important group of literary women who continue to have cultural resonance for lesbians as flamboyant mentors, especially in the figure of Raichō. "*Rezubian*" is another example of the ongoing linguistic and cultural translation of the term "lesbian" and the possibilities of it being read in a variety of ways that may place the accent on the literary, the political, or somatic pleasure. From untranslated "Lesbianism" to *resubosu* to *resubian* to *rezubian*, a shifting lexicon insists on undecidability and resists fixing lesbian identity. "*Rezubian*" has been shortened to both the widely used and often pejorative *rezu* and to *bian*, a more specific usage grounding itself in community values.[7] Examining the translated text and lesbian identities in Japan "makes explicit the imbrication of texts and contexts" (Harvey 2000b: 466); and in the choice of text and linguistic terms, the text under translation reflects much in its domestic reinscription. Rather than "a complete domestication of the text" (Harvey 2000a: 150), translated terms and texts make space for a personal sense of sexual otherness to be articulated; "the presence of translatedness in a target culture provides readers who are working at a skew with dominant culture norms the space in which their difference can be worked out as a positive cultural attribute" (ibid.: 159). The lesbian in Japanese society comes into view through the visibility of the lesbian-identified translator, regardless of her translation choices, as well as translations of lesbian texts. Influenced by gay role models and inspired by bonds of cheerful and passionate friendship that imply bonds of lesbian community, the *akarui rezubian* succeeds in re-appropriating diverse lesbian representations from abroad and re-constituting them "into something closer in spirit to their own lives" (ibid.: 386). And that's just dandy.

Notes

1 The translated novel is in its hundredth printing since it was first published in 1952, demonstrating its continuing popularity. For an extended discussion of lesbian desire in *Anne of Green Gables*, see Robinson (2004).
2 The translator of this work is cryptically identified only by the surname Nomo, and in her preface, Raichō teases readers who might try to guess Nomo's real identity (Hiratsuka [1914] 1980: 1).
3 Hiratsuka Raichō, who founded Seitōsha and bankrolled Seitō with her dowry, is widely referred to as, simply, Raichō. We use the term to acknowledge her role as an iconic figure.
4 Her status as a lesbian icon is evidenced by the interview with Yuasa (Hirosawa 1987) featured in the seminal lesbian book *Onna wo ai suru onnatachi no monogatari* (Bessatsu Takarajima 1987) and an article on her romance with writer Miyamoto Yuriko in *Tanbishōsetsu gei bungaku bukkugaido* (Higuchi 1993). In both books, the only other Japanese lesbian fore-sisters mentioned are Hiratsuka Raichō and Yoshiya Nobuko, along with their lovers Otake Kōkichi and Monma Chiyo.
5 See, for example, the special 1991 lesbian issue of *Imago* (Rezubian).
6 The analogy between lesbian bar culture and *Les fleurs du mal* comes from a 1969 panel

discussion with two lesbian couples (*Aien* 1969: 188). Phryné appears in a quote from *Les fleurs du mal* in the lesbian literature section of *Tanbi shōsetsu* (Kakinuma and Kurihara 1993: 237), a book contributed to by some of the same women active in the production of *Phryné*. Editor Hagiwara Mami, who, incidentally, worked on *Tanbi shōsetsu* under a different name, seems unaware of this association, however (personal correspondence, 6 August 2002).

7 The term *bian*, derived from *rezubian*, is both a code word and a proactive effort to reclaim *rezubian* from its pornographic implications by "put[ting] the *bian* back into lezu!" (Izumo and Maree 2000: 108).

References

Aien. (1969) "Taiyō no shita no rezubian" (Lesbians under the sun), 1: 183–189.
Alcott, L. M. ([1868–1869] 1941) *Wakakusa no monogatari* (*Little Women*), Vols 1–2, trans. R. Suga, Tokyo: Suginami Shoten.
Apter, E. (1999) *Continental Drift: From National Characters to Virtual Subjects*, Chicago: University of Chicago Press.
Barnes, D. (1983 [1936]). *Yoru no mori* (*Nightwood*), trans. H. Nojima, Tokyo: Kokushokankōkai.
Bessatsu Takarajima, No. 64. (1987) *Onna wo ai suru onnatachi no monogatari*, Tokyo: JICC Shuppankyoku.
Castle, T. (1993) *The Apparitional Lesbian: Female Homosexuality and Modern Culture*, New York: Columbia University Press.
Chalmers, S. (2002) *Emerging Lesbian Voices from Japan*, London: RoutledgeCurzon.
Coyote, I. E. (2004) "The good book," *Little Sister's Book Review*, February 2004, Issue 001, available online: LittleSistersBookStore.com (accessed 2 February 2004).
Dollase, H. T. (2003) "Early twentieth century Japanese girls' magazine stories: examining *shōjo* voice in *Hanamonogatari* (Flower tales)," *Journal of Popular Culture* 36(4): 724–755.
—— (2001) "Yoshiya Nobuko's 'Yaneura no nishojo': in search of literary possibilities in *shōjo* narratives," *US-Japan Women's Journal, English Supplement* 20: 151–178.
Ellis, H. ([1914] 1980) *Josei no dōseiaisha* (translation of *Sexual Inversion of Women*), Nomo (trans.), *Seitō*, 4(4) February, n.p. (Special supplement), reprint, Tokyo: Ryōkei Shosha.
Faderman, L. ([1991] 1996) *Resubian no rekishi* (*Odd Girls and Twilight Lovers: A History of Lesbian Life in Twentieth Century America*), trans. A. Tomioka and M. Hara, Tokyo: Chikuma Shobō.
Fujo Shinbun 586 ([1911] 1983) "Dōsei no ai" (Same-sex love), (original 11 August 1911: 1), reprint vol. 12: 265, Tokyo: Fuji Shuppan.
Fujo Shinbun 586 ([1911] 1983) "Dōsei no ai no kenkyū" (Research on same-sex love), (original 11 August 1911: 4), reprint vol. 12: 268, Tokyo: Fuji Shuppan.
Furukawa, M. (1995) "Dōsei 'ai' kō" (Thoughts on same-sex "love"), *Imago* 6(12): 201–207.
—— (1994) "Sekushuariti no kindai no hen'yū: kindai Nihon no dōseiai wo meguru mitsu no kōdo" (The changing nature of sexuality: three codes for framing homosexuality in modern Japan), *Nichibei josei jānaru*, 17: 29–55.
Hall, R. ([1928] 1951) *Sabishisa no izumi* (*The Well of Loneliness*), vols 1–2, trans. Y. Ōkubo, Tokyo: Shinchōsha.
Harvey, K. (2003) *Intercultural Movements:* American Gay *in French Translation*, Manchester: St Jerome Publishing.

—— (2000a) "Gay community, gay identity, and the translated text," *TTR*, 12 (1): 137–165.

—— (2000b) "Translating camp talk: gay identities and cultural transfer," in L. Venuti (ed.) *The Translation Studies Reader*, London and New York: Routledge.

Higuchi, A. (1993) "Jinbutsu retsuden 3: Yuasa Yoshiko to Chūyō (Miyamoto) Yuriko" (Human lives 3: Yuasa Yoshiko and Chūyō [Miyamoto] Yuriko), in E. Kakinuma and C. Kurihara (eds) *Tanbi shōsetsu, gei bungaku bukkugaido* (A guide to aesthete novels and gay literature), Tokyo: Byakuya Shobō.

Hiratsuka, R. ([1913] 1983). "Ichinenkan" (One year), *Hiratsuka Raichō chosakushū* (Hiratsuka Raichō's collected works), Vol. 1, Tokyo: Ōtsuki Shoten.

—— ([1914] 1980) "Introduction to Havelock Ellis's Joseikan no dōsei ren'ai" (*Sexual Inversion of Women*), *Seitō*, 4(4): 1–2, (Special supplement), reprint, Tokyo: Ryūkei Shosha.

Hirosawa, Y. (1987) "Dandi na Roshia bungakusha Yuasa Yoshiko hōmonki" (A visit with dandy scholar of Russian literature Yuasa Yoshiko), *Bessatsu Takarajima*, No. 64: 67–73, *Onna wo ai suru onnatachi no monogatari* (Stories of women who love women), Tokyo: JICC Shuppankyoku.

Hiruma, Y. (2003) "Kindai Nihon ni okeru josei dōseiai no 'hakken'" (The "discovery" of female homosexuality in modern Japan), *Kaihō shakaigaku kenkyū*, 17: 9–32.

Honda, M. (1991) "'S' – Ta'ainaku, shikamo kongenteki na ai no katachi" ("S" – the shape of essential yet frivolous love),' *Imago*, 2(8): 68–73.

Howland, D. R. (2002) *Translating the West: Language and Political Reason in Nineteenth Century Japan*, Honolulu: University of Hawai'i Press.

Huang, Y. (2002) *Transpacific Displacement: Ethnography, Translation, and Intertextual Travel in Twentieth-Century American Literature*, Berkeley, CA: University of California Press.

Imago. (1991) [Special issue] "Rezubian" (Lesbian), 2(8), August.

Iwabuchi, H. (1995) "Rezubianizumu no yuragi: Miyamoto Yuriko no 'Ippon no hana,'" (The swaying of lesbianism: Miyamoto Yuriko's "Ippon no hana") in H. Iwabuchi, S. Kitada and R. Kōra (eds) *Feminizumu hihyō e no shōtai: kindai josei bungaku wo yomu* (An invitation to feminist criticism: reading modern women's literature), Tokyo: Gakugei Shorin.

Izumo, M. and C. Maree. (2000) *Love upon the Chopping Board*, North Melbourne, Australia: Spinifex.

Johnson, B. (2003) *Mother Tongue: Sexuality, Trial, Motherhood, Translation*, Cambridge, MA: Harvard University Press.

Kakinuma, E. and C. Kurihara (eds). (1993) *Tanbi shōsetsu, gei bungaku bukkugaido* (A guide to aesthete novels and gay literature), Tokyo: Byakuya Shobō.

Kaneko, S. (1998) "Seitō no yōran" (The cradle of Seitō), in Shin feminizumu hihyō no kai (eds) *Seitō wo yomu* (Reading Bluestocking), Tokyo: Gakugei Shorin.

Kano, A. (2001) *Acting Like a Woman in Modern Japan: Theater, Gender, and Nationalism*, New York: Palgrave.

Kelsky, K. (2001) *Women on the Verge: Japanese Women, Western Dreams*, Durham, NC: Duke University Press.

McLelland, M. (2005) *Queer Japan from the Pacific War to the Internet Age*, Lanham, MD: Rowman and Littlefield.

Mizuzaki, N. (1998) "Gaikoku bunka no juyō to hyōka: hon'yaku" (The reception and review of foreign literatures: translation), in Shin feminizumu hihyō no kai (eds) *Seitō wo yomu* (Reading Bluestocking), Tokyo: Gakugei Shorin.

Nishihara, R. and Bukkurisuto Han. (1987) "Bukkurisuto 35: rezubian no suimyaku wo tadoru" (Booklist 35: following the stream of lesbians), *Bessatsu Takarajima, no. 64, Onna wo ai suru onnatachi no monogatari* (Stories of women who love women), Tokyo: JICC Shuppankyoku.

Ōsawa, M. (1990) "Subarashii ūman ravingu no sekai" (The wonderful world of woman-loving), in M. Watanabe, E. Ōniwa, M. Hara, R. Kimura, M. Ōsawa (eds) *Ūman ravingu* (Woman loving), Tokyo: Gendai Shokan.

Robertson, J. (1999) "Dying to tell: sexuality and suicide in imperial Japan," *Signs*, 25(1): 1–35.

—— (1998) *Takarazuka: Sexual Politics and Popular Culture in Modern Japan*, Berkeley, CA: University of California Press.

Robinson, L. (2004) "Bosom friends: lesbian desire in LM Montgomery's Anne Books," *Canadian Literature*, 180: 12–28.

Robyns, C. (1994) "Translation and discursive identity," *Poetics Today: International Journal for Theory and Analysis of Literature and Communication*, 15(3): 405–428.

Sawabe, H. ([1990] 1996): *Yuriko, dasuvidāniya: Yuasa Yoshiko no seishun* (Yuriko, *do svidanya*: Yuasa Yoshiko's youth), Tokyo: Josei Bunko.

Schultz, G. (2001) "Daughters of Bilitis: lesbian genealogy and lesbian authenticity," *GLQ: A Journal of Lesbian and Gay Studies*, 7(3): 377–389.

Schuster, M. (1999) *Passionate Communities: Reading Lesbian Resistance in Jane Rule's Fiction*, New York: New York University Press.

Shimanaka, Y. ([1911] 1983) "Dōsei no koi to sono jitsurei" (Same-sex love with an example), *Fujo Shinbun*, 587 (original 18 August 1911: 6), reprint, vol. 12: 276, Tokyo: Fuji Shuppan.

Takeda, M. (1999a) "Hisuterii/merankorii: Rezubian kyūketsuki shōsetsu *Kāmira* I" (Hysteria/melancholy: the lesbian vampire novel *Carmilla* pt. I), *Eigo seinen*, 144(10): 23–26.

—— (1999b) "Hisuterii/merankorii: Rezubian kyūketsuki shōsetsu *Kāmira* II" (Hysteria/melancholy: the lesbian vampire novel *Carmilla* pt. II), *Eigo seinen*, 144(11): 25–27, 31.

Tamura, T. ([1913] 1988) "Nikki" (Diary), *Tamura Toshiko sakuhin zenshū* (Tamura Toshiko collected works). Tokyo: Orijinshuppan.

Tomioka, A. (1994) "Amerika ni okeru rezubian hihyō no nagare: Bonii Jimaman wo chūshin ni" (Lesbian criticism in the works of Bonnie Zimmerman), *Nichibei Josei jānaru* (*US-Japan Women's Journal*), 16: 62–68.

Venuti, L. (1995) *The Translator's Invisibility: A History of Translation*, London and New York: Routledge.

—— (1998) *The Scandals of Translation: Towards an Ethics of Difference*, London and New York: Routledge.

Wachman, G. (2001) *Lesbian Empire: Radical Crosswriting in the Twenties*, New Brunswick, NJ: Rutgers University Press.

Wakabayashi, J. (1996) "An alternative tradition: translation theory in Japan," *IIAS Newsletter*, 10 (Autumn), available online: <http://www.iias.nl/kreeft/IIASNONLINE/Newsletters/Newsletter10/Regional/10CECD03.html> (accessed 10 August 2003).

Watanabe, M. (1998) "Seitō ni okeru rezubianizumu" (Lesbianism in Seitō), in Shin feminizumu hihyō no kai (eds) *Seitō wo yomu* (Reading Bluestocking), Tokyo: Gakugei Shorin.

Watanabe, S. (1998) "Seitō undō reki" (The history of the Bluestocking movement), in Shin feminizumu hihyō no kai (eds) *Seitō wo yomu* (Reading Bluestocking), Tokyo: Gakugei Shorin.

White, E. (1997) "AIDS awareness and gay culture in France," in J. Oppenheimer and H. Reckitt (eds) *Acting on AIDS: Sex, Drugs and Politics*, London and New York: Serpent's Tail.

Wu, P. (2002) "Performing gender along the lesbian continuum: the politics of sexual identity in the Seitō Society," *US-Japan Women's Journal English Supplement*, 22: 64–86.

Yasuda, T. (1935) "Dōseiai no rekishikikan" (A historical perspective on same-sex love), *Chūō kōron*, (March): 146–152.

Yoshikawa, T. (1998) "Kindai Nihon 'rezubianizumu': senkyūhyakujūnendai no shōsetsu ni egakareta rezubian-tachi" (Lesbianism in modern Japan: images of lesbians in novels in the 1910s), in K. Kondō (ed.) *Sei gensō wo kataru, kindai wo yomikaeru* (Narrating the phantasm of sex: rereading modernity), vol. 2, Tokyo: San'ichi Shobō.

6 The politics of *okama* and *onabe*

Uses and abuses of terminology regarding homosexuality and transgender

Wim Lunsing

Introduction

Although Japan has a long tradition of plurality of queer categories, many speakers of Japanese are not sure about the meanings of the various terms in relation to homosexuality and transgender phenomena. This is not surprising, given the fact that the meanings vary according to the speaker, regardless whether the speaker is using terms to refer to categories of people other than him- or herself or in self-reference. Some gay activists have branded some terms politically incorrect, arguing that they must be avoided, while recommending other terms as "proper" usage. These interventions, however, have tended to increase the confusion. From time to time heated discussions about terminology take place in the media, on the internet and in gay bars. In all these contexts the term *"okama,"* which is the main focus of this chapter, is without doubt the most problematic.

"Okama," which used to be written with the character for *"kama"* (cooking pot), originally referred to the anus and eventually, by implication, to men whose rear is penetrated during sex. It has been suggested that *"okama"* is related to the *"kagema"* of the *"kagemajaya,"* the male brothels of the Edo period, which would explain the connotation of male prostitute often attached to *"okama."* When referring to the anus, *"okama"* can also be seen as stressing the supposed "feminine" aspect of being penetrated (Pflugfelder 1999: 322–323). Thus, it may be seen to incorporate the double whammy of effeminacy and prostitution, both of which are images associated with homosexuality that those attacking the usage of *"okama"* wish to avoid, as they see them as derogatory.

"Okama" recently became the focus of a heated discussion between the two major streams of Japanese gay organizations, which I have referred to as *"katai"* (rigid, hard) and *"yawarakai"* (flexible, soft) following wording used by my informants (Lunsing 1999a, 1998). This discussion is central to my investigation of terminology, which focuses on the questions of how terms regarding homosexuality and transgender may be understood and used and why the term *"okama"* is more problematic than other terms, including its other-sex counterpart *"onabe"* (applied to non-gender-normative women). Originally designating a "maid servant," and written with the character for a shallow type of pot, *"onabe"* came to be used as a female counterpart for *"okama"* during the 1970s (Valentine 1997).

82 Wim Lunsing

This chapter looks at the contemporary debate over queer categories in Japan. The majority of data was acquired through intensive fieldwork carried out during eight periods ranging from five weeks to 18 months and spanning the period from 1986 to 2003. Initially contacts were established with all gay and lesbian activist organizations in Japan, as well as with a number of non-activist organizations and these contacts have been maintained throughout as far as possible[1] while others have developed since. Initially I spent more time in the Kansai area and later I lived in Tokyo. As an anthropologist engaging in fieldwork, I value data from primary sources more than secondary sources, which in Japan, where there is little tradition of academic research on queer topics, remain highly fragmented. While not in Japan, contacts have been maintained by email, chat, phone, correspondence and meeting people visiting Europe.[2]

Preceding discussion

The Japanese gay activist group Occur has been the most concerned with changing official definitions of terms relating to homosexuality in Japan and, through participating in international lesbian and gay conferences and events, has been influential in shaping the view of Japan in international contexts. However, despite these activities, their following is very limited among Japanese gay and lesbian people. Occur split off from the now defunct JILGA (Japan International Lesbian and Gay Association) in 1986 because they felt that the older members of JILGA were keeping them from engaging in political activism (Lunsing 1998). Occur has pointed to the use of "*okama*" to address and speak about gay men as proof of a deeply rooted yet largely latent homophobia particular to Japanese culture (e.g. Binsento *et al.* 1997: 173). They argue that once homosexuality is made openly visible, this homophobia becomes clearly visible also, mostly based on their one experience of staying as an openly gay group at the Fuchū Seinen no Ie, a youth hostel facility on the outskirts of Tokyo. Indeed, during their stay at the center, they were called "*okama*" and "*homo*" by other residents. The Seinen no Ie management later refused Occur accommodation on the grounds that the center had a sex-segregation policy in sleeping arrangements which gay men were considered to contravene, being attracted to each other. Occur then filed a discrimination suit against the Tokyo Metropolitan Government, the Seinen no Ie's administrative body; it won both the original trial and the government appeal (Lunsing 1998, 1999a; McLelland 2000: 40). Nevertheless, Occur has continued to use this incident as proof of Japan's supposedly deeply rooted homophobia.

One of Occur's first and most highly successful activities was to lobby the editing staff of dictionaries and encyclopedias to change the definitions of terms pertaining to homosexuality to exclude any allusions to prostitution and femininity in men. By making these distinctions, though important in their own right, a hierarchy was created in which gender-normative gay men were presented as somehow better than those gay men who engage in prostitution or who appear feminine. Yet, their easy success in this matter, as in the court case, has not altered their view of Japanese society as being immensely homophobic. Occur's rhetoric, which is explicitly borrowed from the US (Binsento et al. 1997: 48), remains unchanged and has not been adapted to the Japanese situation, no matter how particular Occur argues that it is.

My own research has led me to believe that Japanese society's homophobia is mostly of an implicit nature. Rather than being aimed at homosexuality in particular, Japanese disquiet over non-normative sexuality is aimed at anything that deviates from a highly limited common-sense discourse (Lunsing 2001a: 2–14), which is inclusive of the heterosexual matrix (Butler 1990: 35–78), and consequently, homosexuality as such is often not even considered (see also McLelland, Chapter 7, this volume). As Occur's court case and its lobbying of dictionary editors illustrate, however, when homosexuality is explicitly considered, the outcome is not necessarily one of homophobic resistance. On the contrary, it usually is not. I found a number of gay and lesbian informants who maintained or had previously internalized homophobia. They had or used to have negative feelings about being gay or lesbian and dared not talk about it to people in their surroundings for fear of their reactions. However, among those who did speak out, negative reactions were uncommon, whether in work situations or at home (Lunsing 2001a: 229–58; McLelland, Chapter 7, this volume).

This internalization of homophobia can be related to a tendency in Japanese culture to individualize problems people may have, instead of dealing with them on a social level. This is even evident in particular forms of psychotherapy which stress that people should not burden their environment with "weird" behavior but should swallow their problems and act "normally" (Lebra 1976; Murase 1986). At least until the early 1990s, Japanese education used sanctions such as ostracism to discourage people from standing out or being too different (Hendry 1986; Tobin 1992), which puts pressure on people who feel different to deal with it privately. Obviously, this implies that it was somehow unadvisable to be gay, thus promoting the internalization of homophobia by those directly concerned (Lunsing 1999b; 2001c) and this as a matter of course leads to the silencing of homosexuality, as it does to any deviation from a "common-sense" standard of what is normal. Even victims of industrial pollution and rape alike have typically adhered to the practice of *nakineiri* (crying [themselves] to sleep, e.g. Kawamura 1994), thereby not upsetting the social order. In order to break out of this situation where it concerns the silencing of homosexuality, Occur felt the need to attack society for being homophobic, even though their main proof of widespread homophobia was limited to the usage of the term "*okama*."[3]

Occur have mobilized the concept of the *tōjisha*, literally "those concerned" (see also McLelland, Chapter 7, this volume), depicting gay men as victims of a homophobic straight society. However, even some of my informants who were members of Occur felt unhappy at this focus on victimization. From the early 1990s the education system has begun to promote individuality and difference, stressing that everybody needs to find a "*jibunrashii*" (self-like) way of life, which can easily be interpreted as including homosexuality, if that is perceived to be self-like. Indeed, members of the gay organization associated with the Sōka Gakkai, Japan's largest Buddhist lay movement, had in 1992 already pointed out to me that their ideology stressed individuality and developing what comes from inside. They felt that homosexuality was compatible with this (Lunsing 2001a: 300).

During the 1990s, Japan saw what is called the "gay boom" followed by a "lesbian boom" and a "transgender boom" during which all mass media gave major attention to sex and gender difference, making it possible for gay, lesbian and transgender people to write about their experiences (Lunsing 1997).[4] During fieldwork in the late 1990s, I found some young gay and lesbian people who had been out at high-school without having given much thought to their "coming out." It seems that the Ministry of Education's move towards promoting individuality, combined with the media booms, had some effect, which was further intensified by the spread of the internet, where young people can and do come out on line (see McLelland, Chapter 7, this volume). However, increased discussion of homosexuality and sex and gender difference in the media, particularly by "those concerned," has brought disagreements over appropriate terminology to the fore.

Occur's official line is that not only is "*okama*" derogatory but so too is the widely used "*homo*" (an abbreviation of *homosekushuaru*). Instead, they support the use of the medical-sounding "*dōseiaisha*," literally "homophile" but generally accepted as the Japanese rendering of "homosexual,"[5] and "*gei*," stemming from the English "gay." However, when I used the term "*gei*" in an essay for a composition class at Osaka University of Foreign Studies in 1991, my teacher, a Buddhist priest, thought it was derogatory because to him "*gei*" implied effeminacy. According to him, I should have used "*homo*." In fact, this is quite logical, as in postwar Japan "*gei*" was widely used in combination with "*bōi*," the term "*gei bōi*" referring specifically to transvestite performers (McLelland 2004; Lunsing and Maree in press). As a result, some Japanese gay men report that they have similar reservations about using the term "*gei*" to those expressed by Occur in relation to "*okama*," rendering problematic Occur's preference for *gei*.

The "*okama*" controversy

In 2001, the progressive magazine *Shūkan Kinyōbi* (Weekly Friday) published a series of interviews with the gay activist/politician/theater performer/publisher/bar owner/pornography producer Tōgō Ken beginning with the words "*Densetsu no 'okama'*" (The legendary "*okama*").[6] The 70-year-old Tōgō had been using the term *okama* as a self-referent consistently from the early 1970s when he began running in parliamentary elections. Most Japanese above the age of 30 are aware of Tōgō as his television broadcasts as a political candidate were (in)famous – he spoke of penises and other topics that were unheard of on Japanese television at the time. Claiming to have aristocratic roots, Tōgō said that he was ostracized by his family upon his coming out in the late 1960s. He became a cult figure partaking in the underground culture movement (*angura*) of the 1970s as well as in the anti-Vietnam War movement, until he was ostracized for stressing his regret over the loss of the lives of young male soldiers which was seen as neglectful of the loss of lives of Vietnamese women and children. The series of interviews marks a revival of interest in Tōgō, also demonstrated by an invitation to speak at Waseda University in February 2000.

The gay activist/high-school teacher/writer Itō Satoru, founding member of Sukotan Kikaku, a group that strives for the promulgation of "proper" knowledge about homosexuality and the development of new lifestyles for gay and lesbian people,[7] subsequently attacked *Shūkan Kinyōbi* for using discriminatory language – namely the word "*okama*." He maintained that the usage of the term in the title and on the cover of the magazine, where it was not placed in context, was harmful to gay men (Itō and Yanase 2001b). He also wrote that the Japanese Ministry of Justice was moving towards prohibiting discrimination against homosexuality (Itō and Yanase 2001c), which in this context seemed like a warning to the magazine. Itō, the author of several books on gay issues, two of which have been translated into English under the title *Coming Out in Japan* (Ito and Yanase 2001a), maintains an essentialist political stance which stresses that gay men are just like any other men apart from their objects of love and sexual desire and that they are "innocent victims" of a homophobic society, since being gay is a characteristic present at birth. Like Occur, his reasoning is firmly located in the US minority community discourse, which the gay civil rights movement borrowed from the black civil rights movement and which has remained the dominant stream within the US gay movement until today (Epstein 1999).

Despite the rhetoric of homophobia in Itō's books, he describes hardly any actual instances of discrimination. The only real instance is a threat of blackmail which he claims made him lose his job as a school teacher, though his description of events gives ground to believe that his publication of a book criticizing absurd school rules (Itō 1984) was the actual reason (Itō 1993: 46–48; Ito and Yanase 2001a: 33–34). Apart from this, in *Coming Out in Japan* all his lengthily exposed fears – of being dismissed from his job or losing his mother's affection as a consequence of coming out – prove unfounded, as he might have expected if he had taken into account other people's experiences.[8] Itō's actual experience of having his homosexuality widely accepted by others has not altered his basic mindset that Japanese society is tremendously homophobic,[9] and his critique of *Shūkan Kinyōbi* should be understood in this context. With his insistence on being a victim, Itō appears to have an extreme case of internalized homophobia, which is also suggested by his disdain for aspects of the gay scene which he finds unpalatable (Itō 1993: 119–120; Ito and Yanase 2001a: 86–87).

When *Shūkan Kinyōbi* printed Itō's critique, other gay intellectuals were upset because they felt misrepresented by Itō whose writings are more popular among *straight* left-wing and feminist Japanese, who find in them welcome proposals on how to deal with yet another suppressed minority group (see Itō and Ochiai 1998). Itō's view of Japanese society as very oppressive towards gay men fits neatly with their own negative view of Japanese power structures. They appear keen to use issues of homosexuality for their own purpose of criticizing Japanese society, as they do with other minority issues, such as those involving Koreans in Japan and *burakumin*, the Japanese outcaste group.[10] It is no surprise that Itō, being a personal acquaintance of some of the staff of *Shūkan Kinyōbi*, was given the space for his critique, nor that other gay men were upset by this selection.[11]

As the straight journalist specializing in sex, Matsuzawa Kureichi explained to me, *Shūkan Kinyōbi* places much stress on correct terminology, even writing "*baibaishun*" (sell and buy spring [= sex]) to render "prostitution." "*Baibaishun*" was originally concocted following the existing term "*baishun*" (selling spring) to stress that without buyers sex cannot be sold, but by *Shūkan Kinyōbi* it is written in the unusual order of the character "*bai*" for "buying" preceding the "*bai*" for "selling," thus stressing even more that the clients are the problem. This order of writing the characters of "*baibai*" is contrary to the term "*baibai*" signifying "trade" in all other contexts. It minimizes recognition of sex workers and the choices they make. As in the case of gay men, sex workers' voices are usually ignored by Japanese self-appointed left-wing advocates of their rights, unless, like Itō in the case of gay men, they follow the left-wing rhetoric of oppression, which, to my knowledge, no sex workers do, apart from in contexts where this may be good for business.[12] In this way, sex workers are treated as hapless victims rather than as humans in charge of their own affairs (Lunsing 2002, 2004), which is also a point criticized in recent publications by sex workers themselves (e.g. Matsuzawa 2000). Hence, *Shūkan Kinyōbi*'s airing of Itō's complaint about "*okama*" is another example of the magazine running a politically correct line on terminology.

A symposium on "*okama*"

After Itō's articles were published, the gay writer and critic Fushimi Noriaki, whose work is very popular among gay and lesbian people, decided to organize a symposium about the use of the term "*okama*," which I attended. Both Itō and Tōgō were absent. Itō refused to appear without explaining why but I surmise that he did not relish a confrontation with Tōgō which he probably realized would not turn out to be to his advantage. Tōgō refused because he was outraged by Fushimi sending him a mere fax instead of a proper hand-written letter of invitation and because he was not consulted about the date, which was set on a Sunday, his only free day of the week, when he likes to indulge in betting at the horse races (personal communication). Due to the absence of Itō, Kurokawa Nobuyuki, the chief editor of *Shūkan Kinyōbi*, who participated in the panel, became the major focus of critique. Almost everything he said came under fire and in particular his effort to establish some general decision on what is correct terminology, excluding the term "*okama*," met with great disapproval.

Kurokawa's insistence that his magazine had been wrong to use "*okama*" and that apologies must be made was generally regarded as patronizing. He stressed that the people in the audience criticizing him were "strong" gay people but that the "weakest" should be the basis for decisions; if they felt hurt, then the wording was reprehensible. He had gained this view from study meetings on sexuality and human rights in which, again, Itō had been the major gay representative. At the symposium, this view was countered by the opinion that it was odd to make this distinction between "strong" and "weak," and that even if some people were "strong" now, they had not always been so. After all, everyone had their "weak" past, when first discovering their homosexuality and looking for ways to deal with it. Apart from that, if not hurting the feelings of the "weakest" was to be the norm, then any word referring to homosexuality would probably have to be banned, as any mention of it, whether derogatory or not, could be felt as unsettling by those in the middle of such struggles, as Fushimi and the actor Usui Yukio (lately performing as an openly gay actor under the stage name Yara Asatomo) stressed.

Kurokawa's defense for printing only Itō's critique and providing no room for other gay (or lesbian or transgender) voices was that he did not want to divide the gay movement. His proposition that not letting voices other than Itō's be heard was somehow good for unity met with ridicule and anger. Forms of cooperation do exist among the majority of people involved in gay activism. The audience felt that it was not up to a magazine editor to determine which gay man was to represent the immense variety of gay voices in Japan. The paternalism of Kurokawa towards gay people mirrors that of Itō, who displays similar behavior with his almost sermon-like writings on how gay men should live, that is in monogamous relationships based on equality (Itō 1993: 76–99; Ito and Yanase 2001a: 55–72).

Taking up Fushimi's express invitation for people who disagreed with the usage of "*okama*" to speak their mind, the office worker Nakamura Setsuo stated that generally he disliked the term but in this specific instance he had not felt offended. Even a member of Itō's own advocacy group, Sukotan Kikaku, added that in this case he felt that Itō had gone too far. Depending on the context, it was felt that "*okama*" was an acceptable term to refer not only to gay men, as Fushimi Noriaki himself sometimes uses it, but also to refer to MtF transgender people, represented in the audience by the MtF transgender school teacher and author Miyazaki Rumiko.

Miyazaki was, like Itō, a member of the human rights and sexuality study meeting mentioned above, and had at the time felt unease about Itō's insistence that mentioning "*okama*" must always be avoided. She felt that, rather than ignoring it, it would be better to discuss the term in, for instance, school classrooms since simply eliminating use of the term "*okama*" would not eliminate discrimination against gay people. Miyazaki also stressed that among MtF transgender people there were many who disliked alternative terms such as "*josōsha*" (literally, "female dresser," a little-used term for MtF cross-dressers), because they felt that their femininity was expressed by more than dressing in women's clothes and they therefore preferred to be known as "*okama*."[13]

Meanings of "*okama*"

The positive evaluation of the usage of "*okama*" at the seminar reflects sentiments I found present among people from the Kansai area in the first half of the 1990s. Some of Tokyo's gay movement people seem to be lagging behind as a result of their efforts to be accepted by straight intellectuals and their failure to consider the Japanese cultural context. Over ten years ago Osaka-based gay activist Morita

Shinichi, for instance, stressed the importance of cooperation between the various categories of people that are confronted with the term "*okama*" (Morita 1993). Furthermore, the Osaka-based drag queen/singer/HIV activist Shimōnu Fukayuki said to me in 1998 that while she had felt uneasy about the term "*okama*" when a female friend constantly used it, when questioning her friend about it, she replied that she thought it was a wonderful term. This made Shimōnu herself rethink the term and she says she realized that embracing "*okama*" as a self-reference was conditional on accepting one's homosexuality in the Japanese cultural context.[14] Indeed, some people may refer to themselves as "*okama*" precisely because embracing the term can help them overcome feelings of awkwardness in relation to their homosexuality (Fukayuki 1996; Lunsing 2003a). This attitude relates obviously to queer politics, of which Fushimi Noriaki, with his inclusion of all sorts of sexualities and genders in his published works and discussions, is the most public proponent (e.g. Fushimi 1991, 1996; Fushimi et al. 2002).[15]

"*Okama*" is given varying meanings by various people. Most eclectic is Tōgō Ken who maintains that it stems from the Sanskrit "*karma*" or "*kamāla*" and that this means "love." Therefore he believes that it is a beautiful term (Tōgō and Oikawa 2002: 202).[16] Itō, in his schoolmasterly fashion, criticized Tōgō's view as being incorrect and showing a lack of research (Itō 2001b). While Itō's critique of Tōgō may be correct in that Tōgō, rather then investigating the literature, came up with an explanation for the term he personally likes, it is also indicative of Itō's rigidity. Ironically, it appears that Itō, an advocate of the "*tōjisha*" movement which stresses the importance of self-determination on the part of minorities, denies "*tōjisha*" who do not agree with him their freedom of expression.

Among children "*okama*" is much used and usually understood as a term of abuse. However, this is not necessarily the case; I witnessed a boy explain to his mother that it referred to men or boys with long hair, including himself (Lunsing 2001a: 266–267). Likewise, children were quick to shout "*okama*" at drag queen Onan Spermermaid when she performed for them in Watariumu, an exhibition space in trendy Aoyama, Tokyo, in 2001. One of the boys decided to follow Onan's example and was later spotted in drag at various club events, accompanied by his parents. The transvestite manager of a transvestite bar also felt that the manner in which "*okama*" has lately come to be used by children and young people is not derogatory, often hearing them add the suffix "*san*" or "*chan*." She felt that "*okama-chan*" is an endearing term. On other occasions she felt less sure what to think of people's use of "*okama*." When she worked at a company as a male, for instance, a colleague asked him[17] whether another colleague was an "*okama*." She thought the other colleague might be gay but did not venture to explain the various usages of the term.

Japanese gay men may use "*okama*" in a manner similar to American gay men calling each other "faggot"[18] or simply as a term interchangeable with "*gei*" and/or "*homo*" (for instance, Takada 2001). However, when visiting Virgin, a bar in the gay area of Ni-chōme in Shinjuku in Tokyo frequented by MtF transvestites, I was asked whether I fancied "*okama*" or men (*otoko*). It appeared that in this context, "*otoko*" referred to gay (or non-gay but nevertheless available) men, while "*okama*" referred exclusively to MtF transvestites. This usage is similar to the usage of both "*okama*" and "*onabe*" in a semi-fictional book based on the life-histories of an MtF and an FtM transgender individual situated in the Kansai area, one of whom is the author, who calls himself "*onabe*" and uses both terms in the title of the book, evidently as these are the terms he is used to (Uchida 2001).

The less controversial nature of "*onabe*"

Understanding of the meaning of the female counterpart of "*okama*," "*onabe*" also varies. While some women I interviewed thought cross-dressing and loving women made them "*onabe*," others regarded it more as an occupation, as with the people working in New Marilyn, Tokyo's most famous "*onabe*" club, where FtM transvestites work as hosts and staff. The staff of another club, Apollo, however, maintained that New Marilyn was not a real "*onabe*" place, as, unlike themselves, Marilyn's staff did not all desire a full sex change. In order to work in Apollo it was obligatory to use male hormones to induce growth of facial hair, a lower voice and the like and half of the staff had actually had breast removal surgery, which was proudly demonstrated during the shows. The Apollo staff stressed their difference from other "*onabe*" places where dressing up as men was the norm. Some of them said that in Osaka there were no real "*onabe*" places, but only places where women merely dressed up for the job, and that they therefore preferred Tokyo, where they could be proper "*onabe*."

In some progressive and academic circles these days such women would not be called "*onabe*" but "*seidōitsusei shōgaisha*" ("sexual identity handicapped," a translation for gender identity disorder), a term invented to replace transsexuality, which until recently was rendered by terms like "*toransusekushuariti*" or "*seitenkan shujutsu*" (sex-change surgery). However, unlike transsexuality, the new term highlights that it is a "*shōgai*," a disability. Again, this implies the victimization – in this case victims of nature – of a category of people without necessarily reflecting their own views. Indeed, to be recognized and legally eligible for sex-change surgery, Japanese transsexuals, who have their own "*tōjisha*" movement which obscures the existence of other transgender phenomena, now have to make so many promises about their behavior in their future lives, that many prefer other ways of obtaining surgery or decide not to have surgery.[19] The "*onabe*" of Apollo, however, do not criticize Japanese society like Itō. All of them had previously been able to work as men in regular occupations for people with low educational backgrounds, simply by dressing up and behaving like men. The fact that they were now working in the *mizu shōbai* (lit. the water trade; the entertainment industry), which is widely regarded as marginal despite its enormous size, was not directly related to their transsexuality but rather to their desire to perform on stage.

Another informant, well known in the Ni-chōme bar scene in Shinjuku, referred to herself as "*rezubian*" but turned out to conflate this term with transgender meanings given to the term "*onabe*." Regarding herself as an older lesbian, she criticized younger ones for not being properly lesbian like herself and merely playing at being lesbian. By this she meant that they looked and behaved in too feminine a manner. This stands in direct opposition to women of Occur who stressed on television that they are just as feminine as other women and for instance feel attracted to women's long hair (Lunsing 2001a: 275). Nevertheless, my informant did make a distinction between herself as lesbian and transsexuals. When she had breast removal surgery to eliminate cancer, she was full of jokes about getting breast removal free of charge, while FtM transsexuals paid large sums for it. She maintained that lesbian women should have transgender qualities but still made a distinction between lesbianism and transsexuality, stressing that it was a matter of degree.

Among lesbian women it is common in some circles to refer to each other as "*onabe*." This, however, appears to be different from the usage of "*okama*" by gay men, as "*onabe*" is not perceived to have one or more negative connotation(s). Indeed, on the contrary, "*rezubian*" is often seen as having the negative connotation of pornographic model (Kakefuda 1992; Lunsing 1999, 2001a). In this scene, women have fewer problems with appearing masculine than some gay men have with appearing or being seen as feminine. This may be related to the sexism and misogyny present in Japanese society, which causes masculinity to be evaluated more positively than femininity. For women to make a career in contexts other than those typically regarded as feminine, some degree of masculinity may be deemed desirable, whereas femininity in men is only desirable if they want to work in transgender occupations in the entertainment industry or to become Kabuki or Nō actors. Even in the latter case, however, as several amateur *onnagata* (female impersonators in Kabuki) said, they should avoid being effeminate – they must be convincing as women. Finally, the uncontroversial nature of "*onabe*" in comparison to the controversial nature of "*okama*" is likely to be related to the sexist practice of women's issues being taken less seriously in general.

Conclusion: what's in a name?

Among young gay Japanese men the trend has not been to follow the lines set out by "hard" groups like Occur or activists like Itō. Although throughout the 1990s it seemed that their advocacy of the use of "*geī*" as the "correct" term to refer to gay men was working, lately "*homo*" is again gaining ground. This may be because the younger generation feels little connection with the political rhetoric of Occur and Itō, and it may also be that they feel "*homo*" is a more explicit term as it is the clear opposite of "*hetero*."[20] Whatever the reason for the growing popularity of the term, it appears that younger gay people have in general experienced less difficulty embracing themselves as gay or lesbian and using explicit terms of self-reference than some preceding generations have.

One of the most important points that came out of the seminar on "*okama*" was that it was useless to focus on particular terms as indicative of discrimination since all terms are used and understood differently by different people. Efforts by "*tōjisha*" movements to establish fixed meanings are doomed to fail when these meanings are not accepted by other "*tōjisha*" not affiliated with these groups.

Matsuzawa Kureichi stressed that proposals to outlaw words put freedom of expression at stake and had already led to some very undesirable effects, such as a television show using "*mōhō*" instead of the outlawed "*homo*," in an effort to be funny.[21] Obviously, outlawing terms does not promote discussion about them and, more importantly, their underlying issues.

Much of the disquiet about use of the term "*okama*" is related to its connotations of prostitution and effeminacy. Obviously there is a hierarchy at work here with sex workers placed lowest in the ranking. It also appears to be accepted as common sense that the more masculine a gay man is, the better. Itō's dislike of the term "*okama*" seems based on his fear of not being accepted as "normal" and his response is a good example of the internalization of homophobia. The normalcy he desires makes him want to draw a clear line between himself and male sex workers and MtF transgender people and this line is obfuscated by the term "*okama*."

As Oikawa Kenji, who authored the articles on Tōgō, pointed out at the symposium, the minority/majority, victim/society binaries adhered to by Itō and Occur occlude the fact that there is a broad variety in people's sexualities, within both the categories of homosexuality and heterosexuality as well as within the context of transgender phenomena. As outlined earlier, Itō and Occur represent the *katai* or "hard" faction within Japan's lesbian and gay movement but their approach has not gained popular support. Already, in 1997 a major proponent of the "*katai*" stream, Japan International Lesbian and Gay Association (JILGA), brought about its own demise due to its authoritarian attitude towards other groups and its disdain for women (Lunsing 1999a). The "hard" side was always more strongly represented in Tokyo than elsewhere in Japan but now, as the seminar on the use of "*okama*" demonstrates, it is becoming marginal even in Tokyo. I am confident that the more flexible "soft" stream will continue to thrive, as its proponents relate well to a wide range of gay, lesbian and transgender people out there in the bar scene and beyond – the very "*tōjisha*" that the "hard" activists and groups say they represent.

Acknowledgements

I wish to express my gratitude to my many informants and to Wim Boot, Jan van Bremen, David Groth, Joy Hendry, Roger Goodman and Ueno Chizuko for their support. Fieldwork leading to data used in this chapter has been funded by the Japanese Ministry of Education (1991–1993), the Japan Society for the Promotion of Science (1996) and the Japan Foundation (2001–2002).

Notes

1. In the case of Occur, official contacts largely ceased in 1993 due to their unresponsiveness but personal contacts with individual members continue today.
2. My research methods and ethical positions have been outlined elsewhere (Lunsing 1999b, 2001a).
3. Interestingly, Occur have many times announced an "Iceberg project" (originally an initiative of ILGA), to uncover the supposedly huge amount of invisible discrimination

against homosexuality in Japan but no report ever surfaced. Of course, discrimination against gay people does exist; I found evidence in particular when it comes to housing and employment, but discrimination in these areas applies as much to single straight men as it does to gay men (Lunsing 2001a: 210–217).
4 Leading figures of Occur dismiss the boom as having had only a local impact in Tokyo and some other major cities (Kazama and Kawaguchi 2003). However, my informants from rural areas read magazines and books and watched television programs springing from the boom and through the boom found ways of making contact with other gay and lesbian people, in particular thanks to publications like *Bessatsu Takarajima*'s gay issues (Ōtsuka *et al.* 1992; Ōtsuka and Ogura 1993, 1994).
5 The lesbian writer Kakefuda Hiroko pointed out to me that homosexuality should properly be rendered as "*dōseiseiai*" (same-sex-sexual-love); *dōseiai* means literally "same-sex love."
6 This series led eventually to production of a book (Tōgō and Oikawa 2002).
7 Their homepage can be found at: http://www.sukotan.com/index.html (accessed 10 October 2004).
8 Itō's coming out in 1993 was, among others, preceded by that of Osaka-based high school teacher Hirano Hiroaki and Fushimi Noriaki who encountered no problems.
9 See Lunsing (2001b) or McLelland (2004) for reviews and discussions of *Coming Out in Japan*.
10 The use of homosexuality for other political purposes is not particular to Japan only. In the Netherlands, for instance, it is used to attack Islam (Lunsing 2003b).
11 Kohashi Noriko (2003) points out that Itō is also the only gay man whose writings are printed in the *Asahi Shinbun*, Japan's largest progressive newspaper.
12 Several female sex workers pointed out that clients often want to believe that they engage in prostitution because of financial distress or otherwise sad life-histories and that they may play along with this when it suits them.
13 This discussion led to a booklet reflecting the contents of the symposium (Fushimi *et al.* 2002).
14 Also discussed in Lunsing (2003a).
15 As discussed in Lunsing (2003a), Fushimi's first publication using the terminology of queer preceded the introduction to Japan of the concept of "queer" from the US.
16 Tōgō came up with "*kamāla*" after being told that "*karma*" did not mean love – but it may well be that he actually meant "*kāma*" (sensual desire).
17 I use "him" here, as in this context "she" performed as "he."
18 However, the meaning of faggot is more unequivocally pejorative.
19 For instance, in order to have legal sex change surgery, one must declare that one will not work in the entertainment industry afterwards, which clashes with the Apollo staff's wishes.
20 This is the reason a member of Sōka Gakkai voiced when indicating his preference for the term "*homo*" (Lunsing 2001a).
21 Turning around and/or lengthening syllables is a common joke in Japan.

References

Binsento (Vincent), K., T. Kawaguchi and K. Kazama. (1997) *Gei sutadiizu* (Gay studies), Tokyo: Seidosha.

Butler, J. (1990) *Gender Trouble: Feminism and the Subversion of Identity*, London: Routledge.

Epstein, S. (1999) "Gay and lesbian movements in the United States: dilemmas of identity, diversity and political strategy," in B. Adam, J. W. Duyvendak and A. Krouwel (eds) *The Global Emergence of Gay and Lesbian Politics: National Imprints of a Worldwide Movement*, Philadelphia, PA: Temple University Press.

Fukayuki, S. (1996) untitled, in Kuia Sutadiizu Henshū Iinkai (ed.) *Kuia Sutadiizu '96* (Queer studies 1996), Tokyo: Nanatsu Mori Shokan.
Fukuoka, Y. (2000) *Lives of Young Koreans in Japan*, Melbourne: Trans Pacific Press.
Fushimi, N. (2002) *Gei to iu "keiken"* (The "experience" of being gay), Tokyo: Potto Shuppan.
—— (1996) *Kuia paradaisu: "sei" no meikyū e yōkoso* (Queer paradise: welcome to the labyrinth of sex, gender and sexuality), Tokyo: Shōheisha.
—— (1991) *Puraibēto gei raifu, posuto renairon* (Private gay life: post-love theory), Tokyo: Gakuyō Shobō.
Fushimi, N., K. Oikawa, K. Noguchi, K. Matsuzawa, N. Kurokawa and T. Yamanaka. (2002) *"Okama" wa sabetsu ka: "Shūkan Kinyōbi" no "sabetsu hyōgen" jiken* (Is *"okama"* discriminatory?: The affair of "discriminatory expressions" in *"Shūkan Kinyōbi"*), Tokyo: Potto Shuppan.
Hendry, J. (1986) *Becoming Japanese: The World of the Pre-school Child*, Manchester: Manchester University Press.
Itō, S. (1993) *Otoko futarigurashi: boku no gei puraido sengen* (Two men living together: my gay pride declaration), Tokyo: Tarō Jirōsha.
—— (1984) *Sensei! Binta ga mukatsuku ze!* (Sir! Slapping is disgusting!), Tokyo: Sanichi Shobō.
Itō, S. and K. Ochiai. (1998) *Jibunrashiku ikiru: dōseiai to feminizumu* (Living self-like: homosexuality and feminism), Tokyo: Kamogawa Shuppan.
Ito, S. and R. Yanese. (2001a) *Coming Out in Japan: The Story of Satoru and Ryuta*, trans. F. Conlan, Melbourne: Trans Pacific Press.
—— (2001b) "Watakushitachi ga koe wo ageta wake" (We raised our voices), *Shūkan Kinyōbi* (Weekly Friday) no. 376: 10–12.
—— (2001c) "Sekushuariti no kisō chishiki" (Basic knowledge on sexuality), *Shūkan Kinyōbi* (Weekly Friday) no. 376: 16–20.
Kakefuda, H. (1992) *"Rezubian" de aru, to iu koto* (On being "lesbian"), Tokyo: Kawade Shobō Shinsha.
Kawamura, N. (1994) *Sociology and Society of Japan*, London and New York: Kegan Paul International.
Kazama, T. and K. Kawaguchi. (2003) "HIV risk and the (im)permeability of the male body: representations and realities of gay men in Japan," in J. Roberson and N. Suzuki (eds) *Men and Masculinities in Contemporary Japan: Dislocating the Salaryman Doxa*, London and New York: RoutledgeCurzon.
Kohashi, N. (2003) "Tolerance towards gay people, especially lesbians, in Japanese society," paper presented at International Convention of Asia Scholars 3, Singapore, August.
Lebra, T. S. (1976) *Japanese Patterns of Behavior*, Honolulu: University of Hawaii Press.
Lunsing, W. (2004) "Japanese sex workers: between choice and coercion," in E. Micollier (ed.) *Sexual Cultures in East Asia: The Social Construction of Sexuality and Sexual Risk in a Time of AIDS*, London and New York: RoutledgeCurzon.
—— (2003a) "What masculinity?: Transgender practices among Japanese 'men,'" in J. Roberson and N. Suzuki (eds) *Men and Masculinities in Contemporary Japan: Dislocating the Salaryman Doxa*, London and New York: RoutledgeCurzon.
—— (2003b) "Islam versus homosexuality?: Some reflections on the assassination of Pim Fortuyn," *Anthropology Today*, 19(2): 19–21.
—— (2002) "The contemporary sex work (non-)debate in Japan," *Informationen des*

akademischen Arbeitskreises Japan – Minikomi (Information of the academic field work in Japan), 65: 27–33.

—— (2001a) *Beyond Common Sense: Sexuality and Gender in Contemporary Japan*, London, New York and Bahrain: Kegan Paul.

—— (2001b) "Pride and prejudice," *Japan: People, Power & Opinion*, 1: 108–109.

—— (2001c) "Between margin and center: researching 'non-standard' Japanese," *The Copenhagen Journal of Asian Studies*, 15: 81–113.

—— (1999a) "Japan: finding its way?," in B. Adam, J. W. Duyvendak and A. Krouwel (eds) *The Global Emergence of Gay and Lesbian Politics: National Imprints of a Worldwide Movement*, Philadelphia, PA: Temple University Press.

—— (1999b) "Life on Mars: love and sex in fieldwork on sexuality and gender in urban Japan," in F. Markowitz and M. Ashkenazi (eds) *Sex, Sexuality and the Anthropologist*, Urbana, IL: University of Illinois Press.

—— (1998) "Lesbian and gay movements: between hard and soft," in C. Derichs and A. Osiander (eds) *Soziale Bewegungen in Japan: Mitteilungen der Gesellschaft für Natur- und Völkerkunde Ostasiens*, Vol. 128, Hamburg: Ostasien Gesellschaft.

—— (1997) "'Gay boom' in Japan: changing views of homosexuality?," *Thamyris: Mythmaking from Past to Present*, 4(2): 267–293.

Lunsing, W. and C. Maree. (in press) "Shifting selves: negotiating reference in relation to sexuality and gender," in J. (Shibamoto) Smith and S. Okamoto (eds) *Japanese Language, Gender, and Ideology: Cultural Models and Real People*, Oxford: Oxford University Press.

McLelland, M. (2004) "From the stage to the clinic: changing transgender identities in post-war Japan," *Japan Forum*, 16(1): 1–20.

—— (2003) "Interpretation and Orientalism: outing Japan's sexual minorities to the English-speaking world," in Inge Boer (ed.) *After Orientalism: Critical Engagements, Productive Looks*, Amsterdam: Rodopi.

—— (2000) *Male Homosexuality in Modern Japan: Cultural Myths and Social Realities*, London: Curzon.

Matsuzawa, K. (ed.). (2000) *Baishun kōtei sengen: uru uranai watashi ga kimeru* (Declarations in support of prostitution: I decide whether I sell or not), Tokyo: Potto Shuppan.

Miyazaki, R. (2000) *Watakushi wa toransujendā* (I am transgender), Tokyo: Neoraifu.

Morita, S. (1993) "Nikushimi wo koete: tokushū: gei sabetsu" (Beyond hate: special: gay discrimination), *Poko a poko*, 1: 62–73.

Murase, T. (1986) "Naikan therapy," in T. S. Lebra and W. Lebra (eds) *Japanese Culture and Behavior: Selected Readings*, Honolulu: University of Hawaii Press.

Oikawa, K. (2001) "Densetsu no okama: aiyoku to hangyaku ni moetagiru" (The legendary *okama*: ablaze and seething with passion and treason), *Shūkan Kinyōbi*, 367: 34–39.

Ōtsuka, T., F. Noriaki and M. Ueda (eds). (1992) *Gei no okurimono* (A gay gift), Bessatsu Takarajima no. 159, Tokyo: JICC Shuppan.

Ōtsuka, T. and T. Ogura (eds). (1993) *Gei no omochabako* (A gay toy box), Bessatu Takarajima, January, Tokyo: JICC Shuppan.

—— (1994) *Gei no gakuen tengoku* (A gay campus heaven), Bessatsu Takarajima, February, Tokyo: JICC Shuppan.

Pflugfelder, G. (1999) *Cartographies of Desire: Male-Male Sexuality in Japanese Discourse, 1600–1950*, Berkeley, CA: University of California Press.

Takada, M. (2001) *Juku kama ga yuku!: jinsei wo yori yoku ikiru tame no Nichōme*

tetsugaku (There goes a ripe *kama*!: Nichōme philosophy to live a better life), Tokyo: Kōsaidō.
Tobin, J. (1992) "Japanese preschool and the pedagogy of selfhood," in N. Rosenberger (ed.) *Japanese Sense of Self*, Cambridge: Cambridge University Press.
Tōgō, K. and K. Oikawa. (2002) *Jōshiki wo koete: okama no michi 70nen* (Beyond common sense: 70 years of the way of *okama*), Tokyo: Potto Shuppan.
Uchida, Y. (2001) *Okama desse, onabe desse* (I am *okama*, I am *onabe*), Tokyo: Tōyō Shuppan.
Ueno, C. (1998) *Nashonarizumu to jendā* (Nationalism and gender), Tokyo: Seidosha.
Valentine, J. (1997) "Pots and pans: identification of queer Japanese in terms of discrimination," in A. Livia and K. Hall (eds) *Queerly Phrased*, New York and Oxford: Oxford University Press.

7 Salarymen doing queer
Gay men and the heterosexual public sphere

Mark McLelland

Introduction

As various chapters in this collection show, many Japanese people have adopted a wide range of sexual and gender identities and space has always existed for the performance of non-hegemonic sex and gender roles in Japanese society. Yet, as Itō and Dasgupta point out, hegemonic notions of how men and women *should* behave have been and remain strong in Japan. Much earlier work on Japanese gender has focused on the particular constraints felt by women in Japan, for, as Vera Mackie has observed "[Japanese] models of citizenship implicitly privilege the male, white-collar 'citizen in a suit'" (2000: 246). Indeed, for many Western people the image conjured up during talk about Japanese people is often that of the dutiful, suited and bespectacled salaryman – hard-working and dour – rather like the character of Tachibana in the recent movie *Japanese Story*. Although the lives of women in Japan have been well researched it is only recently that sustained attention has been paid to the lives of men and sexual minorities. The focus of this chapter is therefore on the gay salaryman – how does he negotiate his relationship with mainstream norms and expectations of how men should be?

While the salaryman often functions as a synecdoche for Japanese men in general, there are many more varied lifestyle patterns available, although they are not accorded the same status. As Connell's (1995, 2000) work has shown, "masculinities" are always plural, constructed as they are through forces such as class, generation, education, race, ethnicity, religion and sexuality. Central to Connell's argument is the idea that "masculinity" has a history and it is not only expressed differently in various societies and eras but is expressed in many different ways within one society – that masculinity is, in fact, plural, albeit certain forms of masculinity become established as particularly privileged – the dominant paradigm being referred to as "hegemonic masculinity." Despite the privileging of one mode of masculinity over others, Connell argues that "the hegemonic form need not be the most common form of masculinity, let alone the most comfortable" (2000: 11). This observation is as relevant for the situation in Japan as in Australia where the bulk of Connell's research was undertaken.

This chapter outlines some of the features of the hegemonic masculine ideal of the salaryman, focusing particularly upon the roles he is expected to play in the workplace and at home. One component of hegemonic masculinity in Japan, as elsewhere, has been heterosexuality. As Dasgupta (Chapter 12 in this volume) illustrates, the *shakaijin* (literally "social person") is expected to be both *productive* in the workplace and *reproductive* at home, since Japanese cultural factors place a higher premium on the continuation of the family line than is done in Anglophone societies. As Roberson and Suzuki point out, becoming a *daikokubashira* (that is, the large black pillar that is the main support for a traditional Japanese house) – an image which assumes a man will be both father and provider – is still an important index of mature manhood in Japan (2003: 8).

Yet, as Itō and Taga (Chapters 10 and 11 in this volume) argue, the hegemonic ideal of the heterosexually married and gainfully employed salaryman is under attack from a variety of forces. Some of these are economic as Japanese companies find that they can no longer guarantee the incentives of the boom years, resulting in widespread restructuring, early retirements and layoffs. Consequently, as men's role as the sole breadwinner becomes less feasible, more women are deciding to stay in the workforce after marriage and childbirth, resulting in a rapid rise in the number of dual-income families (Ishii-Kuntz 2003: 200). Other factors are social as a new post-boom generation of men (and women) begins to question the values and sacrifices that made Japan's postwar reconstruction possible. In this uncertain environment Japanese gay men are becoming increasingly vocal and organized in expressing their discontent with the status quo (McLelland 2003).

The number of gay men who have made a conscious decision not to conform to society's demands by getting married is growing and gay media, particularly on the Internet, are increasingly giving voice to the need to create and validate lifestyle choices outside the traditional heterosexual family (McLelland 2001, 2003). One important forum in which the need for new gay lifestyles has been debated was the magazine *Queer Japan*, edited by prominent gay critic and author Fushimi Noriaki.[1] *Queer Japan*, which, like other lifestyle-oriented gay publications in Japan, has unfortunately gone under (McLelland 2003: 65–66), saw five editions between 1999 and 2002. Unlike other gay magazines, *Queer Japan* eschewed pornography and was sold alongside regular publications (in one bookstore I visited it was in the "hobbies" section!) and reached a wider audience than regular gay publications. Issue two was dedicated to "salarymen doing queer" (*hentai suru sarariiman*) and contained several articles, a roundtable discussion and a questionnaire survey on problems that gay men face in the workplace.

Fushimi, in "salarymen doing queer," employs the notion of a "heterosexual code" (*iseiaisha no kōdo*) in arguing that certain spaces, in this instance the workplace, are also imbricated in largely invisible (to hetersosexual people) structures of (hetero)sexuality. As work by Bell (1995), McDowell (1995) and others has also shown in the case of Anglophone societies, sexuality, whether of a hetero or homo inflection, is defined as a "private" issue and yet in effect heterosexuality is allowed a level of visibility in the public sphere that is forbidden to homosexuality. Japan is much the same, and this chapter looks at the constraints some Japanese gay men experience in relation to the heterosexual public sphere as well as at attempts they are making to negotiate a role as full "sexual citizens" in a changing Japan.

The road to maturity: becoming *shakaijin*

As discussed by Taga and Dasgupta (Chapters 11 and 12 in this volume), Japanese notions of masculinity have been closely tied up with the roles men play in marriage and the workplace. A man's transition from the status of student (*gakusei*) to "social person" (*shakaijin*) does not take place at his coming-of-age ceremony held, along with his peers, on *seijin no hi* (adults' day) in the year of his twentieth birthday, but when he starts his first full-time job. The process is only finally completed when he marries, and just as importantly, fathers a child. A married man who does not work, for instance staying home to mind the children, would be considered odd by many Japanese people. As Allison, citing a Japanese sociologist, points out, "A husband who doesn't work has 'no meaning' in Japan" (1994: 91).

Sawazaki notes that, when faced with pressure from colleagues at work, many gay men choose to conform and get married since "Japanese society dictates that those who do not marry and have children are failing to do their part in society" (1997: S48). To an extent, this has been an easier choice for gay men in Japan than in Anglophone societies since romantic love has not traditionally been regarded as a necessary component of the marriage relationship and many marriage introductions are still arranged by intermediaries (McLelland 2000: 90–98). Indeed, as Lunsing (1995) points out, *Barazoku*, Japan's oldest gay magazine, has long had a "marriage corner" where gay men advertise for female partners. Work and marriage thus remain fundamental sites for both social- and self-definition for a vast majority of Japanese men.

Furthermore, a job is not just a job. The literature on corporate masculinity in Japan stresses how workers are "crafted" (Dasgupta 2000: 193) through a variety of disciplinary techniques that include dress and hair-style regulations, learning correct politeness levels, how to bow, what to read and even what to eat. For the salaryman, the workplace is not a venue in which to demonstrate individuality, flair or creativity but a situation in which individual desires and aptitudes should be suppressed – at work a man becomes a *kaisha no ningen*, or a "company person" (Allison 1994: 98–101). Smith (1987: 3) points out how this process of crafting males to fit in with the salaryman discourse actually starts in boyhood when, as students, boys are disciplined to study hard so as to be able to compete in the "examination war." If they succeed in this system, which stresses mastery of vast amounts of information rather than creative thinking, entrance to elite universities and the top jobs will be made easier for them. Girls, too, are frequently pressured to work hard at school but it is often assumed that a woman's role is to devote herself to family life and not a career. As Roberson argues, "work remains a more permanent source of social identification [for Japanese men] than it typically does for Japanese women, for whom eventual roles as wives and mothers generally provide more central sources of social and self definition" (1995: 293).

Once a fresh graduate enters a company, he is subjected to a new disciplinary regime. This disciplining is enabled by the fact that most new recruits join at the same time, in the April after their graduation. At this time, depending on the size and prestige of the company, they can be subjected to "almost military-like training practices" (Dasgupta 2000: 195) so as to transform them from students to ideal workers who are both responsible social persons (*shakaijin*) and respectable representatives of the company (*kaisha no kanban*). Even male staff recruited straight from high school (and thereby excluded from the promotion track), are required to engage with the discourse of social personhood. Roberson (1995: 307), for instance, notes that in the metal-parts factory where he conducted his fieldwork, new recruits had to write essays on such topics as "My thoughts on becoming a *shakaijin*" as part of the interview procedure.

Japanese men who, for whatever reason, either fail at or decide not to attempt to reach for the salaryman goal can face a variety of social pressures, not least from family and friends. "Social respectability" (*sekentei*) is, for many men, purchased through putting aside individual desires and conforming to social expectations as this statement from a young Japanese man who failed to enter university makes clear:

> I just hate this word [*sekentei*]. You can't do anything when you are stuck with social respectability . . . I made a mistake in my entrance exams for university . . . I spent two years trying to pass entrance exams. I was so concerned about my parents' reputation and I thought it would be a shame for my parents if I didn't go to university. I wanted to tell them that I didn't want to go . . . but I didn't have the guts to say it . . . Finally I had to betray them . . . I knew I liked cooking and wanted to become a cook . . . however, my parents expected me to go to a respectable university . . . I tried to fit in but everything they thought good for me was what the society [*seken*] would think good . . . I don't buy the idea of social respectability as the only way to make my life meaningful.
>
> (Cited in McLelland 2000: 246, note 5)

The above extract shows how accepting anything "less" than the salaryman ideal can be perceived as a failure that reflects badly not only upon the individual but upon his parents. This extract illustrates the strong social sense of self that many Japanese men experience, a sense of self which is not atomistic but is constructed in relation to a wide-ranging network of obligations and responsibilities. Mathews refers to the "*shikata ga nai* imperative" (2000: 55) that results in many men in Japan making extreme personal sacrifices so as to conform to society's expectations. *Shikata ga nai* is a commonly heard expression that means "it can't be helped" and expresses the kind of fatalism that many individuals feel when confronted with strong group expectations. Until recently many gay men felt similar resignation toward living as *kakure homo* (Fushimi 2000: 8), that is "hidden homosexuals," a term deriving from *kakure kirishitan*, or "hidden Christians" who secretly maintained their faith for centuries after the prohibition of Christianity in the Tokugawa period (1600–1857).

For many men, then, one way in which to establish their masculine credentials is to persevere and succeed in the workplace, but success at the office alone is not sufficient to establish their status as responsible "social persons." Men must also marry at the "correct marriageable age" (*kekkon tekireiki*) which is generally understood to be between ages 25 and 30. An individual's decision to remain single past the "scheduled" age (Brinton 1992) for marriage is somewhat over-determined in Japan since "the failure to [get married] carries the severe implications of immaturity and lack of moral responsibility" (Edwards 1989: 124).

Work by a new generation of men's studies researchers in Japan, such as that by Murata (2000, 2002), demonstrates some of the problems that can arise when a man "fails" to get married at the proper age. To be "single" (*shinguru*) after the age of 30 can have negative connotations both for the individual concerned and for his family and can result in a sense of alienation from peers, family and workmates. Murata's research is important as it shows the extent to which a great deal of social interaction in Japan is predicated on being part of a heterosexual family unit. Even ostensibly heterosexual single men living in rural areas, where long-standing ties between local families are important, point out how the connotation of immaturity that is attached to single status make it difficult to represent the family in village affairs. A story related by one of Murata's informants, a single man in his early fifties, highlights the sense of shame that can accompany an individual's "failure" to live up to the hegemonic ideal:

> Until some years ago, I could not go to my parents' home without apologizing. My mother also asked me not to visit her house in the daytime when it was still light outside as she is ashamed of having a middle-aged single son. Therefore, I visit their home discreetly at night.
>
> (Murata 2000)

As Murata shows, renting a city apartment, too, can be a problem because of the stereotype that single men are incapable of creating and maintaining a home, which will soon become "dirty." It is, however, in the workplace that many middle-aged single men feel out of sync with their colleagues and can be excluded from promotion because of their "suspicious" single status (McLelland 2000: 51). As one of Murata's (2000) informants relates, he was informed that a colleague would not be promoted because he was not married. Because of this widespread suspicion of the single status, in some instances, bosses who see themselves as "stakeholders" (Brinton 1990) in their subordinates' careers, may put pressure on them to hurry up and find a bride or even try to act as marriage brokers (Fushimi 2000: 15; McLelland 2001: 109–113).

Gay men in the workplace

Not surprisingly, gay men often report problems in the workplace due to their reluctance to get married. However, because of the largely pornographic interests of Japanese gay media, and the relative lack of community centers for lesbians and gay men, articulating identity and lifestyle issues has been difficult for many gay people who have not had access to forums in which such discussion is encouraged. As one of my informants wrote to me in 1998:

> Recently there seem to be more gay-related books being published than before but still I think there are not yet enough ... I can say that books that discuss the issue "Why am I gay?" [*naze jibun ga gei*] are very important to me. Somehow, even with my gay friends I'm not able to discuss questions like "What do you think about being gay?" or "How are you going to live as a gay from now on?" I have no idea what other Japanese gays think about these things.
>
> (Cited in McLelland 2000: 233)

Fortunately, the development of the Internet has provided a new interactive space for the discussion of issues surrounding gay identity and lifestyle. In the early 1990s, there existed only a handful of books and a few pages in specialty magazines that offered information on these topics. Today, only a decade later, there are many thousands of websites[2] that feature links to chat rooms, bulletin boards and special "consultation" spaces where men can discuss such topics as how to "live as [a] gay" (*gei toshite ikiru*) and the meaning of "gay life" (*gei no jinsei*).[3] This plurality is now being reflected in an increased diversity in the number of print media available for gay men and other sexual minorities such as lesbians and transgender individuals (McLelland 2003, 2004). As mentioned above, Fushimi's *Queer Japan* is typical of this trend, offering sophisticated essays, analyses and interviews on a variety of topics concerning sexual minorities.

As discussed, a man's single status can cause problems at work. Yet, in addition to problems of remaining single, gay men also experience the added burden of being unable to participate wholeheartedly in the homosocial bonding that underlies Japanese work practices. Allison's (1994) study of a hostess bar, where many salarymen retire with their colleagues after work, shows that the "male bonding" that takes place in these contexts is relentlessly heteronormative in nature. Although prostitution is not normally a part of hostessing, the men will bond together through flirting with the hostesses and joking about their own and each other's sexual prowess in a manner that Allison describes as "ritualistic" (ibid.: 156–164). In exceptional circumstances, sex may be involved and, as Allison points out, among some men there is the belief that "finding sex together would further strengthen their friendship" (ibid.: 152).

Testimony from gay men supports Allison's findings. For instance, in *Queer Japan*, Raku, a 34-year-old man formerly employed in the information industry, describes how he felt alienated at work because the only topics of discussion were "women, cars and sports" (Fushimi 2000: 14–40). More seriously, however, twice a year after the payment of the half-yearly bonus, he was required to visit a "soapland" with his colleagues.[4] Raku found this ritual to be particularly unpleasant since he had to wait several hours in the parlor while each man, in order of seniority, had sex with the same woman. As Fushimi, who was chairing this discussion put it, "so you had to stick your thing in the same place as your seniors?" As Allison points out, the nature of male bonding that takes place in such situations can be "coercive" (1994: 159) and is frequently orchestrated by the most senior member of the party, whose requests those more junior cannot refuse without fear of recrimination. While this particularly unpleasant male-bonding ritual may not be very common, situations in which new recruits to university sports clubs as well as junior members in office parties have been taken to strip joints or hostess bars where they have been forced to engage in heterosexual banter and flirtation are commonly reported by gay men (Fushimi 2000: 6).

The relentlessly heteronormative nature of male bonding in which desire for and discussion of women and their attributes are central, is often mentioned as a cause of stress on gay Internet sites. "A. K.," a man in his twenties, writes into gay activist Itō Satoru's *Sukotan* problem page:[5]

> I'm afraid of talking with my straight friends. When the topic of women comes up, I don't know what to reply . . . It's not just the topic of women but there are people who are extremely prejudiced against gays . . . of course if I argued against them it would seem suspicious so I go along with it. It's really tormenting me.

As Yanase, fellow activist and Itō's former partner, writes in his reply to A. K.'s concern, "This is a real problem reported by a large number of gay men and there is no easy answer." Yanase mentions that he himself worked in a factory where, apart from the office staff, all the employees were young men and the conversation was consequently nothing but "women, women, women."

The constraints felt by Japanese gay men are not, of course, unusual; gay invisibility in Anglophone societies, too, is perpetuated by men who fear they will stand out if they challenge heterosexist or homophobic practices. McDowell, drawing on her research into the UK's finance industry, points out that "a number of male respondents indicated that they had decided to conceal their sexual preference while at work and participate in the construction of an overwhelmingly heterosexist atmosphere" (1995: 84). Yet, while many gay men feel that to come out in such a relentlessly heteronormative sphere as the workplace would have a detrimental effect upon their careers and may even lead to loss of their jobs or worse, an increasing number do seem prepared to at least ponder the consequences of coming out.

Although the topic of whether to come out or not has been widely debated on gay websites and in recent publications such as *Queer Japan*, it has been difficult to get a sense of what regular, heterosexual workers in Japan think about this topic. However, as well as boosting opportunities for contact between gay men, the Internet has also provided a useful forum for the exchange of views between homosexual and heterosexual people. To take just one example, the website *Kaisha no tomo* (Office friend),[6] a site for the discussion of a variety of work-related issues and concerns, provided a forum for the airing of views about homosexuality and the workplace.[7] The views offered by the (supposed) heterosexual majority of posters on this board reveal the blindness that members of the majority have in relation to the problems experienced by subaltern groups. Often, it is only when an individual transgresses the unspoken codes of behavior that the coercive nature of what Lunsing (2001) refers to as "common-sense" values become apparent.

In December 1999 this query was posted to the website's advice column and by January 2004 had received 109 replies:

> I am a 23-year-old new employee. To put it bluntly, I am a homosexual [*dōseiaisha*], or in other words, I'm the kind of guy called gay [*gei'tte yatsu*]. I expect that almost all the people reading this will be heterosexuals [*iseiaisha*], but if your colleague or your boss came out [*kamingu auto*] to you (confessed that he was gay) in the workplace, what kind of a reaction would you have? Also, would coming out cause trouble [*meiwaku*] for others? Please let me know. 23 years old. Finance and securities business.[8]

The replies to this young man's query offer a fascinating glimpse into the attitudes held toward homosexuality by a wide range of Japanese workers of both sexes who would otherwise probably not have thought much about the topic. What is particularly interesting (and encouraging) is the very small number of homophobic comments about the young man's dilemma. Only a handful of responses evince negative attitudes toward homosexuality *per se* and only two are virulently homophobic. Of these, one (no. 90), reproduces a passage from the Bible stating that same-sex love is a sin whereas the other (no. 63) states "Since you are so disgusting why don't you go ahead and take rat poison?" The Bible citation is ignored by other commentators whereas the rat-poison poster is challenged in the very next post by the retort "I think there are some people who would think the same thing about you." While a few posters speculate as to why the young man should have become gay in the first place or suggest steps that he might take to "recover," most contributors take his dilemma seriously and are frank in their advice. However, lack of homophobic rhetoric does not mean that the majority of posters are sympathetic to the young man's dilemma. As the original poster seems to anticipate in his inquiry, a majority of respondents agree that to come out about one's homosexual preference in the workplace would prove "troublesome" (*meiwaku*) for others.

Most responses are negative about the need to come out as gay in the office and the reasons given are remarkably similar – sexuality, it is stated, is a purely "private" (*puraibēto*) or "personal" (*kōjinteki*) aspect of life which should play no role in "public" spaces such as the workplace. Consequently, to make this kind of personal statement would be seen as spoiled or selfish by others who would find the announcement unwelcome. A few examples will serve to give a flavor of these responses:

> If you were to come out to your colleagues, I'd just say this "Well, that's just fine, now just get on with your work." If you confess that sort of thing, you would be like a spoiled child [*amaete yarō*] . . . Who on earth says things like "I like women" in the company. It's got nothing to do with (work). (no. 6)

> I'm a woman but I don't go out of my way in the workplace to say "I like men!" (no. 13)

> It doesn't matter whether you are gay, lesbian or have some other fetish, I'd like you not to bring up that kind of topic in the workplace. (no. 36)
>
> You ought to distinguish between public [*kō*] and private [*shi*]. Since the workplace is a public [*ōyake*] environment I don't think it's necessary for you to come out. (no. 40)
>
> Whether you are homosexual or heterosexual, I think either is fine but . . . so long as you are a new employee, rather than talking about yourself, learning to do the job should come first! (no. 50)
>
> That would be troublesome. I think that for you personally the issue of whether you are gay or whatever is important but to say it in conversation would be extremely troublesome [*chō meiwaku*] . . . Isn't it the case that there really is no reason to say to other people "I'm this kind of person" . . . aren't you seeking to be indulged? (no. 55)

These comments, and many others like them, evince a strong feeling of separation between the public space of work (which is assumed to be a neutral space, devoid of issues to do with sexuality) and the private realm where one's "tastes" (*shumi*) can be expressed with one's fellow in-group members. However, in the light of comments made earlier by many gay men who have pointed to the fact that public space is always assumed to be heterosexual, the heterosexual people writing into the list seem totally unaware of the pressures faced by gay men in this environment. Poster number 13, for instance, who says "I'm a woman but I don't go out of my way in the workplace to say 'I like men!'" seems unaware that this confession would be unnecessary since heterosexuality is the assumed default position in the workplace. Consequently, it is primarily gay employees who, as McDowell points out, must respect "implicit rules about sexual identity, or at least its transfer into workplace performances" (1995: 77).

Oddly, no-one on the list seems to acknowledge that the workplace is never just about work. Although, given Japan's current economic woes, many gay salarymen may be spared the necessity of after-work socializing on the company account, end-of-year parties, business trips and company trips to hot springs and other resorts are a common enough experience for many. During these events, it is impossible to avoid discussing the kind of personal details that most posters seem to feel should play no part in office life. But such socializing is also part of the day-to-day routine of office life – during the lunch hour, over coffee breaks and as part of the chit-chat that takes place while working. As Fushimi points out, a person's sexuality is always implicit in any kind of personal conversation, whether the topic is about one's favorite media personalities, films or television programs, speculation on inter-office romances or discussion of future life plans. He argues that gay men, so long as they remain in the closet, are constantly "having to refract their personal position through a heterosexual code" (2000: 8) and that they do this not simply out of fear of the consequences of coming out but also because of the widespread assumption that "you should not bring up the sort of issues that might prove troublesome [*meiwaku*] for others" (ibid.: 7).

Hence, the notion that the workplace is a public sphere devoid of personal issues results in gay men's concerns being seen as purely personal and selfish, a "common-sense" notion that many gay men, until recently, also accepted. However, there is a strong sense that this situation is changing rapidly in Japan as new communications media such as the Internet make it possible for a wide variety of gay men to network and organize around issues such as their invisibility in the workplace and, perhaps more importantly, offer a safe space in which to "come out" and communicate with others from the speaking-position of a gay man, a position frequently denied them in their public work lives.

The rise of the *tōjisha*

The early 1990s were characterized by what turned out to be hyped-up claims about the revolutionary potential of the Internet for gay men and other minorities but in the case of Japan, there are reasons to suppose that the Internet has indeed had a very significant, one might even argue revolutionary, impact upon gay consciousness. Kadoya, for instance, points out that "For gay people, the most revolutionary event of the twentieth century wasn't Stonewall or the Mardi Gras Parade but ... the birth of the Internet" (2003: 65). Writing about the influence of the Internet on gay men in Japan, Sunagawa (2003: 30–31) notes a striking difference in the life stories of gay men under 25 and those, like himself, who are over 30. He finds that compared with more senior men, fewer young men are troubled by their "sexual orientation" (*seiteki shikō*), putting this down to the fact that they came of age during the early 1990s – which saw Japan's so-called "gay boom" – a time when discussion of homosexuality was no longer limited to a niche audience but had become a topic of general interest in the media (McLelland 2000: 32–37). However, he points out that another significant factor has been the manner in which many young men's "debut" on the gay scene occurs not via the bars but via the Internet, a medium which not only gives access to an unlimited amount of information about the gay world but, equally as important, allows individuals to voice (or, alternatively, construct) their own identities. On the Internet, young men are able to encounter the gay world and begin to communicate with others *as gay men* while still in their teens – something that was almost impossible previously. What the Internet offers, as Miller and Slater point out, is "*expansive potential*" (their emphasis), that is, "the encounter with the expansive connections and possibilities of the Internet may allow one to envisage a quite novel vision of what one could be" (2001: 11) and, importantly, to begin to act on that vision, initially online and then as one's confidence increases, in real life too.

Gay activist and author Ishikawa Taiga reflects on the nature of the Internet on the entrance page of his website.[9]

> How did you come upon this page? Through a search engine? By Net surfing? Or ... Anyway, of all the home pages that you could have visited, I'm grateful for this unexpected opportunity to meet you. As you know, countless information exists in the world of the Internet. No doubt there are

many people who discover completely fresh and surprising knowledge and information that they previously knew nothing about. I think that the Internet can be spoken of as a place where "new knowledge" can be encountered easily. When one encounters various sites with an open mind, from that point on one's life will doubtless become richer.

Ishikawa goes on to describe the contents of his site and to talk about his positionality as a *tōjisha* – that is, as a "person [directly] concerned" with the topic of homosexuality. Originally a legal term meaning "concerned party," the notion of the *tōjisha*, that is, an individual who speaks directly from a position of first-hand knowledge and experience, has now emerged as an important speaking position for a variety of minority communities – especially on the Internet. Despite the fact that Japanese media have, since the end of the war, offered a range of information about both male and female homosexuality as well as numerous transgender categories (McLelland 2004), they were never adequate for the lived realities experienced by same-sex desiring or transgender men or women since these images were essentially stereotypes. While stereotypes can be harmful and negative or harmless and positive, they always function by reducing diverse groups of people into easily communicated and culturally intelligible images, thus stemming the flow of signification and constraining the possibilities for diverse subjective performances. The importance of the Internet lies in the manner in which it allows individuals and communities to challenge the power of the media industries to control representation, particularly the representation of minoritized or abject persons and groups.

One effect of the Internet has been to facilitate the production and dissemination of a particular kind of story telling, that produced by a first-person narrator who, taking his or her most intimate thoughts and experiences as a theme, addresses the reader directly in their own "voice." Given the paternalistic manner with which Japanese authorities have dealt with individuals who did not fit into "normal" society (Nakanishi and Ueno 2003: 13; Stibbe 2004: 22), the notion of listening to the "people concerned" became a focus, particularly among feminist organizations fighting for women's rights and citizens' groups supporting the disabled and the mentally ill in the early 1980s (Nakanishi and Ueno 2003: 23–29; Stibbe 2004: 22). In the 1990s the notion of the *tōjisha* or "person [directly] concerned" emerged as an important authenticating device for stories about personal trauma, victimization, marginalization or disability.

The primacy of the *tōjisha*, that is, that the persons directly concerned and not third party "experts" are those who are most informed about their needs (Nakanishi and Ueno 2003: 12), is a point frequently stressed by minority rights' groups. The tenth anniversary meeting of the Asia-Pacific Disabled Persons' Seminar, held in Osaka in 2003, for instance, highlighted how "an important theme of this seminar is to put the viewpoints of disabled persons themselves (*shōgai tōjisha*) first."[10] This might seem an obvious stance to take, but given previous social attitudes in Japan which constructed disability as a "disease" requiring the intervention of both medical and psychiatric experts whose role was to help the sufferer adjust toward a "normal" life (Stibbe 2004: 22), the acknowledgement of the rights of those disabled to speak for themselves was radical. This trend has been gathering pace and in 2003 disabled activist Nakanishi Masamori and influential feminist writer Ueno Chizuko published *Tōjisha shūken* (The sovereignty of the *tōjisha*) outlining the ethical dimensions of interaction with disadvantaged communities and stressing the centrality of individuals' own accounts of their experience and needs. This collection was important in its inclusion of sexual minorities (*seiteki mainoriti*) as a category of discriminated persons in Japan (Nakanishi and Ueno 2003: 190–191).

The *tōjisha* is now an established speaking position for a variety of narratives about the self, closely inscribed in a discourse of rights, citizenship and belonging. This new association between one's most personal life experiences and one's public persona has helped raise the profile of numerous minority groups and conferred on them greater authority to talk about their experience in their own terms. The effect of this new speaking position can be seen in the founding of such groups as AGP (Association of Gay Professionals) in the late 1990s. AGP is an association for "homosexuals themselves (*dōseiaisha tōjisha*) with professional skills," and includes doctors, social workers, lawyers and teachers. Functions of the organization include representing the concerns of homosexuals working within these professions to the professions' representative bodies as well as offering advice to gay men and lesbians on how to acknowledge their sexuality in the context of their professional lives.

As one participant in an AGP roundtable discussion on current trends affecting minority sexualities commented, the situation in Japan is about thirty years behind the US in terms of professionals helping "general society" (*ippan shakai*) understand the problems facing members of sexual minority groups.[11] This has in large part been due to the reluctance of gay men working in the professions to publicly identify themselves as such. This issue was also highlighted by Fushimi Noriaki who attended a "gay business exhibition" in New York in 1998 where he was struck by the extent to which some mainstream businesses in the US had taken steps to accommodate the specific needs of sexual minorities (such as recognition of their domestic partners on company insurance policies). At the exhibition he met a lesbian lobbyist who worked with US companies to ensure their overseas branches extended the same rights to lesbians and gays in other countries as were guaranteed in the US, but as she pointed out to Fushimi, before she and other activists could do anything in regard to Japan, "Japanese homosexuals themselves must first raise their voices and say that discrimination is a problem" (2000: 10).

Although not itself a product of Internet communication, the rise in prominence of the subject position of the *tōjisha* can be related to the increased opportunities offered by this new communications medium for networking among social minorities and the sharing of "personal" experiences which turn out to be common to many. Plummer, in his book *Telling Sexual Stories*, points out that there is a reflexive relationship between social communities and the kinds of stories that are told by and about members of those communities. As he argues:

Stories need communities to be heard, but communities themselves are also built through story tellings. Stories gather people around them: they have to attract audiences, and these audiences may then start to build a common perception, a common language, a commonality.

(1995: 174)

This process is clearly taking place in Japan's gay community and gay perspectives, like the perspectives of married men who wish to take a more active role in parenthood and those of single men who want their lifestyle choice to be respected, are part of the on-going renegotiation of masculine roles and values in contemporary Japan.

Conclusion

As my discussion of heterosexual people's comments on sexual identity and the workplace showed, there is still a great deal of blindness in Japan about the needs and requirements of those who do not conform to hegemonic codes of behavior. Yet, there is a discernible movement away from the notion that sexual identity is a purely personal issue, something that can be likened to a hobby, play or fetish, and more toward the notion that sexuality is a fundamental organizing principle which makes an important statement about the kind of person one is. On the whole, gay magazines have not been venues for this kind of self-analysis and expression. Rather, it has been the Internet which has opened up a forum for exploring and narrating new versions of the self. However, despite the important impact that this kind of storytelling has had on the way in which gay, lesbian and transgender individuals conceive of themselves and communicate themselves to others, the importance of sexuality or of sharing one's experience of being sexually different is still not widely appreciated in Japanese society.

Yet, despite the fact that hegemonic attitudes and roles remain strong, that a young company employee in such a conservative environment as the finance industry can even *conceive of* the possibility of coming out so early in his career is evidence of a shift in social attitudes. While the responses to his query show that most heterosexual people remain blind to the heteronormativity of the public sphere, there is evidence that this perception is now being challenged. This challenge is not specific to gay men, lesbians or transgender individuals but represents a more widespread social movement in which previously silenced or disregarded groups of people are raising their voices in order to claim their place in society and be regarded as full citizens of Japan.

Notes

1 Details of Fushimi's publications and activities can be found on his home page: http://www.pot.co.jp/gay/fushimi/profile.html (accessed 3 February 2004).
2 In February 2004, the site *SindBad bookmarks*, just one of many Japanese links sites, had links to over 40,000 Japanese and overseas gay-related sites and was adding new ones at a rate of about 500 per week: Statistics available online: http://www.sindbad

bookmarks.com (accessed 1 February 2004). LOUD (Lesbians of Undeniable Drive) runs a small drop-in center but also provides opportunities for women to communicate online: http://www.space-loud.org/pc/index.html (accessed 1 February 2004).
3 See, for example, the gay information pages on the general lifestyle site *All About Japan* available online: http://allabout.co.jp/relationship/homosexual/closeup/CU20030720A/ (accessed 1 February 2004).
4 Although technically illegal in Japan, prostitution flourishes in various establishments known as soapland, pink salon and health massage parlors where women, often brought in from South-East Asian countries, offer a variety of sexual services at affordable prices.
5 Available online: http://www.sukotan.com/yukitosatoru/minnade.html (accessed 1 February 2004).
6 Available online: http://www.waw.ne.jp/kaisha/ (accessed 1 February 2004).
7 Another site where issues to do with homosexuality are fiercely debated by people identifying as both homo- and heterosexual is Japan's notorious Channel 2 which receives more than one-million posts per day and over 600-million page views every month. On 23 August 2004, there were three boards dedicated to the topic of "homosexuality" (*dōseiai*) containing a total of 899 separate threads. Online: http://2ch.net/ (accessed 23 August 2004).
8 Available online: http://www.waw.ne.jp/cgi-bin/kaisha2/board_r.cgi?type=kaisha_nayami9912 (accessed 1 February 2004).
9 Available online: http://www.taigaweb.jp/hajimete.htm (accessed 26 September 2003).
10 Available online: http://www.jdnet.gr.jp/ (accessed 11 November 2003).
11 See the article "Zadankai: sekushuarumainoriti no atarashii chōryū" (Roundtable: new trends in sexual minorities) in the *Medical Tribune*'s online journal *Sexual Science*, available online at: http://www.medical-tribune.co.jp/ss/2001-2-25/ssJan01.htm (accessed 4 February 2004).

References

Allison, A. (1994) *Nightwork: Sexuality, Pleasure and Corporate Masculinity in a Tokyo Hostess Club*, Chicago: Chicago University Press.
Bell, D. (1995) "Pleasure and danger: the paradoxical spaces of sexual citizenship," *Political Geography*, 14(2): 139–153.
Brinton, M. (1992) "Christmas cakes and wedding cakes: the social organization of Japanese women's life course," in T. S. Lebra (ed.) *Japanese Social Organization*, Honolulu: University of Hawaii Press.
Connell, R. W. (2000) *The Men and the Boys*, St. Leonards, NSW: Allen & Unwin.
—— (1995) *Masculinities*, Cambridge: Polity Press.
Dasgupta, R. (2000) "Performing masculinites? The 'salaryman' at work and play," *Japanese Studies*, 20(2): 189–200.
Edwards, W. (1989) *Modern Japan through its Weddings: Gender, Person and Society in Ritual Portrayal*, Stanford, CA: Stanford University Press.
Fushimi, N. (ed.). (2000) "Hentai suru sarariiman" (Salarymen doing queer), *Queer Japan*, 2, Tokyo: Keisō shobō.
Ishii-Kuntz, M. (2003) "Balancing fatherhood and work: emergence of diverse masculinities in contemporary Japan," in J. Roberson and N. Suzuki (eds) *Men and Masculinities in Contemporary Japan: Dislocating the Salaryman Doxa*, London: RoutledgeCurzon.
Kadoya, M. (2003) "Nettoraifu" (Net life), in N. Fushimi (ed.) *Dōseiai nyūmon* (Introduction to homosexuality), Tokyo: Potto Shuppan.

Lunsing, W. (2001) *Beyond Common Sense: Sexuality and Gender in Contemporary Japan*, London: Kegan Paul International.

—— (1995) "Japanese gay magazines and marriage advertisements," in G. Sullivan (ed.) *Gays and Lesbians in the Asia Pacific: Social and Human Services*, Binghampton, NY: Haworth Press.

McDowell, L. (1995) "Body work: heterosexual gender performances in city workplaces," in D. Bell and G. Valentine (eds) *Mapping Desire: Geographies of Sexualities*, London and New York: Routledge.

Mackie, V. (2000) "The dimensions of citizenship in modern Japan: gender, class, ethnicity and sexuality," in A. Vandenberg (ed.) *Citizenship and Democracy in a Global Era*, London: Macmillan.

McLelland, M. (2004) "From the stage to the clinic: changing transgender identities in postwar Japan," *Japan Forum*, 16(1): 1–20.

—— (2003) "Gay men, masculinity and the media in Japan," in K. Louie and M. Low (eds) *Asian Masculinities: The Meaning and Practice of Masculinity in China and Japan*, London: RoutledgeCurzon.

—— (2001) "'Live life more selfishly:' an on-line gay advice column in Japan," *Continuum: Journal of Media and Cultural Studies*, 15(1): 103–116.

—— (2000) *Male Homosexuality in Modern Japan: Cultural Myths and Social Realities*, London: RoutledgeCurzon.

Mathews, G. (2000) *Global Culture/Individual Identity: Searching for Home in the Cultural Supermarket*, New York: Routledge.

Miller, D. and D. Slater. (2001) *The Internet: An Ethnographic Approach*, Oxford and New York: Berg.

Murata, Y. (2002) "Nihon no kōkyō-kūkan ni okeru 'dansei' toiu seibetsu no imi" (The meanings of "maleness" in the public space in Japan), *Chirigaku Hyōron*, 75(13): 813–830.

—— (2000) "Chūnen singuru dansei wo sogai suru basho" (Places where middle-aged single men are alienated), *Jinbunchiri*, 52(6): 533–551.

Plummer, K. (1995) *Telling Sexual Stories: Power, Change and Social Worlds*, London: Routledge.

Nakanishi, M. and C. Ueno. (2003) *Tōjisha no shuken* (The sovereignty of the *tōjisha*), Tokyo: Iwanami shinsho.

Roberson, J. (1995) "Becoming *shakaijin*: working-class reproduction in Japan," *Ethnology*, 34(4): 293–313.

Roberson, J. and N. Suzuki. (2003) "Introduction," in J. Roberson and N. Suzuki (eds) *Men and Masculinities in Contemporary Japan: Dislocating the Salaryman Doxa*, London: RoutledgeCurzon.

Sawazaki, Y. (1997) "Gay men and HIV in Japan," *Journal of Acquired Immune Deficiency Syndromes and Human Retrovirology*, 14 (Suppl. 2): S47–S50.

Smith, R. (1987) "Gender inequality in Japan," *Journal of Japanese Studies*, 13(1): 1–25.

Stibbe, A. (2004) "Disability, gender and power in Japanese television drama," *Japan Forum*, 16(1): 21–36.

Sunagawa, H. (2003) "Nihon no gei no rekishi" (Japan's gay history), in N. Fushimi (ed.) *Dōseiai nyūmon* (Introduction to homosexuality), Tokyo: Potto shuppan.

8 Being male in a female world
Masculinity and gender in Okinawan shamanism

Matthew Allen

Introduction

This chapter employs the case of Akihiro, a transgendered boy who was initiated as a shaman as a 14-year-old, to expose a number of culturally specific factors that relate to shamanism, religion, mental health, and gender in Okinawa, Japan's southernmost prefecture. I am particularly interested in how gender informs people's choices about how to deal with their psychological or spiritual problems, and what the consequences of these choices are. In Akihiro's case, a male can present as a female, and in the process become a *more* legitimate religious practitioner than had he attempted to follow his chosen path as a man, while still being held within the purview of the mental health system. The reasons for this are related to Okinawa's history, its cultural exposure to shamanism, gender-specific religious knowledges, the open-minded and eclectic belief systems employed by Okinawans, and the interface between Okinawan religion and psychiatric practice. I raise this last issue because gender issues have an impact on psychiatric care in Okinawa. A topic that has generated considerable discussion in Japanese since the 1980s, the impact of shamanic healers' practices on mental illness in the prefecture, is of particular relevance to this case. While schizophrenia rates are high in Okinawa, the skewed gender results are statistically anomalous: women are less likely to be institutionalized as schizophrenic than men (Ogura 1996).[1] It could be argued that this is because more women than men choose to employ religious specialists to intervene in cases which could be diagnosed as schizophrenia. I examine this phenomenon in the context of the case of Akihiro.

Below, I start with a brief historical context in which to locate Okinawa, religion, and gender. I then examine the place of religious interaction, with a special focus on women's and men's roles. This enables me to provide a context in which to view Akihiro's case.

Okinawan religion in historical perspective

George Kerr's classic *Okinawa: The History of an Island People* provides us with a succinct summary of the islands' history:

> The history of Okinawa is essentially the story of a minor kingdom with few resources, and of an unwarlike people, forever seeking balance between powerful neighboring states . . . The most noteworthy feature of their social history has been subservience to, and willing acceptance of, two quite different alien standards.
>
> (1958: 15)

Known as the Ryukyu Kingdom until 1879, Okinawa had enjoyed a tributary status with China since the fourteenth century. This meant that its culture, religion, politics, and society were influenced in many ways by successive Chinese Emperors, who sent trading missions to Okinawa, spreading Chinese culture, trade goods, and philosophy. Ryukyu sent tribute to China in return, and scholars, priests and merchants went to China to study. In the kingdom, territorial lords (the *anji*) controlled a population that was hierarchically ordered, with the majority working as peasants on the "harsh, thin soil" in resource and materially poor circumstances, with intermittent typhoons devastating crops and property (Kerr 1958; Smits 1999). From 1609, however, the kingdom was under the effective, but subversive power of the Satsuma fief in southern Kyushu. Although nominally independent, Ryukyuans then had two sets of allegiances: to China and to Satsuma. But Okinawan indigenous culture continued to coexist with these alien cultural and material influences.

From the fifteenth century, the island kingdom employed religious and political practices which were divided along gender lines; men controlled the political sphere (secular), and women controlled the religious sphere (cosmological or spiritual), in a way that was quite at odds with mainland Japan's formal Shinto and Buddhist practices, which were highly patriarchal (Sonoda 1987; Anesaki 1963). Formalized state religion was led by powerful women, connected closely through blood ties with each other and with the political status quo. A nation-wide system of priestesses was in existence, which mirrored the masculinized political structure, and which overlapped in areas of juridical authority on occasion. Women in villages also dominated formalized religion, and retained strong links with the centralized state apparatus of religious practice in Shuri, the capital since the fourteenth century. These women were mostly hereditarily appointed, and often were of high status (see Ohashi 1996; Allen 2002a, 2002b).

In contrast, shamans, who occupied a liminal place in Ryukyu religious orthodoxy but were widely used by the general public, were mostly lower-class females (Ohashi 1996; Allen 2002a). Their lives were dominated by the relationships they enjoyed with gods and ancestors, and they were self-selected for their work, usually following notification by the gods (Lebra 1979). This experience of being born of high spirit potential, or of being afflicted by attacks by spirits or gods, is well documented, particularly by psychiatrists, ethnopsychiatrists, and anthropologists in Okinawa and Japan (see below), and is almost always troublesome for the person selected. Most males who aspired to a religious path in life fell into categories such as *sanjinsō* (fortune tellers who used sticks, the *I-ching*, and Chinese texts to prognosticate), *bōji* (*bōzu* in Japanese, Buddhist priests), or

Chinese medical practitioners, the best of whom were trained in China. All these religious practitioners used literary sources as the foundation of their power, a sign of their class and learning, in contrast to women religious practitioners who used cosmological empowerment – most commonly through divination, mediumship, and direct aural and verbal communication with gods and ancestors (Ohashi 1996; Allen 2002b).

The way each gender has had access to power and knowledge also has had implications for the gender-specific recognition and treatment of indigenous, culture-bound physical and mental health conditions in Okinawa, particularly in the years after Japanese control. In the post-World War II era, after sixty-six years of Japanese rule, Okinawa became a military colony of the United States. One positive outcome of this otherwise disenfranchising colonization was the relaxation of proscriptions against indigenous religious practice. In this more relaxed environment, shamanism and local religion underwent a revival. Two linked phenomena *sādaka unmari* (high spirit birth-rank), and *kami dāri* (attacked by the gods), and their relationship with both women and men are central to this discussion. For both genders today these Okinawan concepts remain powerful markers of identity. For women who are seen to possess either of these qualities, there are established courses of action to pursue. For men, these courses of action may not be quite so clear-cut due to the gender-stratified environment in which the recognition and treatment regimes occur. The potential consequences of gendered help-seeking are significant. While women may be able to pursue a life of shamanism or follow a religious path which relies on cosmological influences on their identified condition, only a few men choose, or are able to pursue such solutions to their problems these days. Of those who do choose this path, many have difficulty fitting into "normal" masculine roles. Lebra wrote, for example, of the number of physically handicapped men who were spiritual guides or religious figures, concluding that their inability to measure up to common standards of masculinity led to their career choice, and to their feminized behavior (Lebra 1979). The men who choose not to become focused on the religious causes of their problems face a statistically high probability of developing mental illness – psychogenic disorders, schizophrenic episodes and alcoholism are among the most common problems (Takaishi 1989, 1993; Nakamura 1982).[2]

Gender and religion in contemporary Okinawa

These circumstances lead to interesting interpretations of gender, power, and spiritualism in contemporary Okinawa. Some, like Sered, see the domination of religion by women as a sign of the existence of more gender equality than in other societies. She writes, "Whereas male-dominated religions are associated with patriarchal social institutions, the one known example of a mainstream religion led by women [Okinawan religion] is situated in a society that is neither patriarchal nor matriarchal" (Sered 1999: 248). Believing that religion empowers women through their ability to mediate in the secular, economic, and political worlds on behalf of the gods, Sered argues that women influence the political economy and social conditions in Okinawa, and that this influence has a moderating effect on gender roles. Other writers like Ohashi (1996), Takaishi (1993), Naka *et al.* (1985) and Nakamura (1982), however, see the domination of religion by women not as a sign of empowerment, but rather as a means by which the control of the household is extended in a symbolic sense. This is based on the perception that ancestor worship is itself dependent on a firmly rooted genealogical understanding, the knowledge of which is controlled by women as part of their orientation toward the household. Genealogical knowledges are commonly transmitted by women to women.

In the context of recent history, Okinawan shamanism has revived and has had a significant impact on the religious lives of many Okinawans from all classes, and of all ages, at the expense of formalized religion.[3] The fact that both are dominated by women reflects neither women's disempowerment nor their empowerment. Nor does it reflect a religious system that has become of little importance in contemporary life. While formalized priestess-led religion has become increasingly ritualistic and of limited importance to village and urban life in Okinawa, shamanism is important in contemporary Okinawan society, and its control by women in a society in which few women have ascended to positions of political, social, or economic superiority is noteworthy.

Sasaki Kokan, a researcher on *itako* (shamans) in mainland Japan, in an interview in the *Yomiuri Shimbun* said:

> I think shamans tend to be female in societies where women are suppressed or discriminated against as an inferior gender. By associating themselves with the gods, women are able to balance their power with men in such societies.
> (Fujii 2000)

Such views have some credibility in the context of Okinawa despite Sered's bland assurance that Okinawa is a "gender-neutral" society. Whether a "balance" is achieved is moot, I think. Most observers of Okinawan society have been struck by the gendered nature of social interactions and structures. Men's and women's roles in society, despite the increasing cosmopolitan influences from Tokyo and beyond, remain rooted in separate spheres.[4] In this sense, women's domination of spiritualism and religion remains intact.

For many Okinawans, animist religion is an integral part of their world-view. Supernatural intervention is not perceived as necessarily fraught with anti-scientific reasoning and has wide appeal within mainstream society. In particular in the countryside, views of the world which incorporate religious activities are overwhelmingly common (Lebra 1979; Nakamura 1992; Ohashi 1996; Tsuha 1997).[5] Within the household, it is common for more interest in religious activities to be shown by women, as it is in mainland Japan. In Okinawa, though, the "priests" are "priestesses" in formal religion, and in shamanism, almost all practitioners are women (Naka *et al.* 1985). Women too dominate their followers/audience/clientele. It should also be noted that visiting shamans can be very expensive: they are professionals, and charge accordingly. It is rumored that the better shamans do not charge – that they receive only appropriate gifts from their clients, if they feel they have been helped.[6]

Gender and shamanism

The preceding discussion raises many questions, but I would like to turn first to how one becomes a shaman and what implications this process has for the different genders. This will enable us to get a sense of how women are inextricably bound up with both the selection and legitimating process of becoming spiritually active in Okinawa.

Being of high spirit birth-rank (*sādaka unmari*) is one essential element in becoming a shaman. High spirit potential, or "high *sā*," refers to a latent talent to deal with spiritual and religious matters and can manifest itself in many ways. Another common element is spiritual notification (*kami dāri*), which commonly informs a person of their special place in the spiritual order. This refers to the often unwanted and intrusive onset of somatic problems that may include severe psychological, physical, and emotional distress, usually caused by gods or ancestors demanding that a person fulfil certain spiritual obligations. There is almost always a trial or test of the candidate's abilities, conducted by a quorum of spirits and ancestors, and commonly the onset of *kami dāri* leads to physical, emotional, and psychological stress. After shamanic intervention, the candidate learns to control the voices or images she hears, and in exceptional circumstances, is informally apprenticed to a shaman to learn about genealogy and spiritual intervention (Ohashi 1996; Allen 2002a).[7]

The conditions of *sādaka unmari* and *kami dāri* are often closely linked (Naka et al. 1985; Randall 1990). One factor which links these terms is the assessment process by which the conditions are identified. In both cases, almost without exception, initial diagnosis of the condition of being *sādaka unmari* (commonly following an episode of *kami dāri*) is made by either an older female relative, a female friend, or by a *yuta* (shaman) also almost always a woman. Being affected by *kami dāri* is something that is recognized as occurring more commonly among women than men, though it is clear that it does occur within males, particularly among those whose relatives have an orientation toward the spiritual (Sensui 2000). It is important to recognize that the identification of the condition is contingent upon the appropriate ritual knowledges residing within the individual making the assessment. Moreover, there are areas of expectation that in turn influence the diagnosis. Women are seen to be more likely to be both attacked by gods and be born of high spirit birth-rank than men. Hence, such expectations are often met.[8]

If initial assessment of a condition has been made by a family member, relative, or informed other, the client who is affected is then taken to a shaman, who confirms or disputes the diagnosis. Once a diagnosis has been confirmed, an appropriate course of spiritual action is planned and then undertaken. The result of this process is a raised consciousness about the impact of the spirit world on the secular, and a cosmological view which supersedes masculinized interpretations of prosaic political-economic and social relations.

Predominantly it is women over 40 years of age who make up the shamans' client base (although a number of men have call to visit shamans).[9] Given that shamanism is dependent on the accuracy of genealogical understanding of a specific client, and that genealogies, rituals surrounding birth, death, and marriage, and other spiritual knowledges concerning the family are controlled by women, it is not surprising to hear that women dominate this sphere. According to Yokota (1997), who found that more than 70 percent of people living in one country area had seen shamans, rural women appear to have higher rates of attachment to shamanism than those in the cities.[10] Following Ohashi, it is apparent that women's involvement in shamanism may be related to the extension of the domestic sphere.

This leads to the main questions that inform this chapter: how do men who wish to become shamans adapt to conditions within this women-dominated practice? And what is the significance of the gendered spiritual help-seeking behavior to mental and spiritual health?

The following case raises a number of issues that might cast some light on the questions above. There are many implications that can be drawn from the one case. It raises questions that are beyond the capacity of this short chapter to investigate, but in raising these questions, we can begin the process of assessing some dimensions of the topic at hand.

Akihiro, transgender and the dream goddess

This account is excerpted from the cases of Naka Koichi, Clinical Psychologist at the School of Clinical Psychology, University of the Ryukyus, in March 1985. At the time of interview Akihiro was a 14-year-old boy, the oldest of three brothers.[11]

Professor Naka saw him because he had demonstrated possible symptoms of schizophrenia and mild neurosis after being admitted to hospital following a series of fainting spells, diarrhea and hematosis (uncontrollable, often internal, bleeding and heavy bruising). He was called in to make a clinical assessment of the patient. At the onset it is important to acknowledge that Prof. Naka is Okinawan, and has been an observer and analyst of what Lebra and others labeled "culture-bound syndromes" for over 20 years (Lebra 1976). This case, though, came early in his career as a clinical psychologist, and before the relations between indigenous mental health and culture-bound syndromes had been clearly articulated in the academic literature.

Over the course of many interviews, it was revealed that Akihiro had had vivid dreams of the goddess Kannon-sama (Goddess of Mercy) since he was in Grade 5, and that these dreams were still recurring.[12] He had produced a series of astonishingly detailed and mature drawings of the goddess in different poses and in different locations.[13] Although he suppressed recognition of the significance of the dreams, they caused him some emotional discomfort. In his second year in junior high school he collapsed. He acted as though possessed, went into an autonomic trance state (*jinkaku henkan*), talking loudly in voices and thrashing about (*abarare sasetari*). It happened again a week later. Akihiro's mother believed that the violent behavior was attributable to a god who took perverse pleasure in possessing (*kakaru*) and manipulating her son.

He secretly absconded from school for two semesters after these episodes, not confiding his whereabouts to anyone, including his parents. His school was rather lax in accounting for children's absence, so he was able to "play hooky" with relative impunity. Although he left for school most days, he often did not arrive. Instead he was secretly performing "*uguan mae*" at the sites he had identified in his dreams and his drawings, sometimes traveling for hours to find the appropriate location.[14] He was often unable to find the locations he had seen in his dreams and became very frustrated.

Eventually confiding in his mother, she decided to help him in the way he wanted, even if it meant missing school. Mother and son developed a strategy to visit *yuta* of repute, and to follow their advice, regardless of the cost, and regardless of the time involved. This strategy was developed after it was clear that psychiatrists and medical specialists were not helping the boy (although it was also apparent that mother and son had an aversion to taking anti-psychotic medication, largely due to the quite severe side-effects). It was very expensive, praying and visiting religious specialists. According to the mother, they spent more than 8 million yen (approximately US $73,500 at current exchange rates) over two years on religious specialists alone. This does not include the medical hospitalization and ambulance costs incurred when Akihiro collapsed. Such amounts of money were not uncommon for clients to spend in their search to find religious cures for their spiritual problems. As Nakamura and others have pointed out, religious practitioners are very expensive and often ineffectual (Nakamura 1992).[15]

Interestingly, Akihiro's uncle, who was born on an island to the north of the main island of Okinawa, had himself been diagnosed as *sādaka unmari*. He was "something like a *yuta*," according to Naka, in that he understood religious matters and advised others about appropriate religious courses of action, although he did not dabble in prognostication. However, he was able to help in ritual matters and other things, providing advice and so on for the boy. Like his mother, the uncle recognized that the boy had potential to become a "god person" – *yuta/kaminchu* (*reiteki no kanōsei*), and that he should be involved in showing him how to proceed along the path.[16]

When he was 12 years old, Akihiro attempted to purge himself of the Goddess of Mercy (*Kannon-sama wo orosu*), in what amounted to a kind of initiation ceremony with the family gathered around. When the goddess was to be discharged – *kannon-sama wo orosu* – the boy was purged of the possession of the goddess, and in this case, he was also initiated as a potential shaman. The descent of the goddess from the boy was witnessed by all present and word spread of his initiation as *kaminchu*.[17]

Reading Akihiro and gender

So far, while some of the preceding discussion may appear out of the ordinary, to many Okinawan women and girls such scenarios are almost quotidian (with the exception, perhaps, of the uncle being involved). That is, such stories are quite common, particularly in the rural areas of Okinawa. What makes this case more interesting though is the gender of Akihiro, and his representation of self within the context of a women-dominated spiritual practice, as we see below, in an extract from an interview with Professor Naka:

> My impression of the interview was that Akihiro was quiet, settled, and was uninterested in the material world. But most importantly, I thought that he was like a woman (*Oyama-teki no fuinki* [an impression of femininity]).[18] ... the word *oyama* refers to men impersonating women, such as in kabuki.
>
> His way of speaking, his posture, and his deportment were all far beyond his years; it was as if I was conversing with a mature woman.
>
> He was an attractive boy, did not talk out of place, but was coquettish. He was incongruously attractive, more as a young girl than as a boy, and he moved his hands to cover his face when talking, as a girl would. Within his natural gestures was refinement. Indeed he appeared a refined young lady.

This raises questions about the issue of representation within the confines of the spiritually-informed gender boundaries. It also raises questions about gender and sex, and the issue of individual agency in determining these ideas. Akihiro's family was spiritually inclined; relatives in the family believed in ancestors and gods influencing the secular world and saw his problems within this context. His mother, in particular, was convinced of the relevance of spirituality in people's lives. From an indigenous perspective, the hereditary traits passed on within the family are a sign that the gods are within that family. From another perspective, the same phenomena could be described as inherited mental health problems.[19]

As we saw earlier, usually it is women in a family who identify those with *kami dāri*, and those who are *sādaka unmari*. In this case, too, Akihiro's mother's experience with family members was such that it influenced her own cosmological views. These views in turn influenced her son, as she encouraged him to recognize his problems as spiritual infestation, and to take responsibility for the ancestors and gods who were talking to him. It is important to acknowledge the role of his mother's brother in helping Akihiro adjust to his spiritual dilemma in this case, too.

Within the context of a patriarchal society (*not* a "gender-neutral" society, as Sered infers), Okinawan shamanism retains gender characteristics that set it apart from others (Lebra 1979; Randall 1990; Takaishi 1993, 1989; Allen 2002a, 2002b).[20] In a society which values "masculinity," the role that Akihiro has chosen is one fraught with *double entendres*, collapsed meanings and codified readings. His body expresses itself through his own agency as female.[21] What does this tell us?

A number of interpretations are possible. In the context of the notion that women in Okinawa have long held positions of religious responsibility while males have occupied politically dominant roles, in cases like Akihiro, he adopts the framework of reference of the most dominant paradigm. His goddesses are women, his peers, his teachers, and today his clientele are women. He moves, acts, indeed thinks as a woman, according to Professor Naka, and his credibility is based on a combination of his "femininity," his special status as someone who has crossed gender boundaries, and his talent. The concomitant assumption is that without this sympathetic ability to imitate women, his shamanic talent would be suspect. Such an interpretation was offered by Professor Naka.

Another interpretation of his actions revolves around the issue of personal and familial agency in the choice of gender representation. That is, to what extent was Akihiro himself the active agent in making choices about how to deal with his condition? To what extent did his mother influence his thinking, behavior, and orientation toward sexuality and religion? Within this context, how did his family's expectations of his future course of spiritualism influence his own decision to undertake the role of *kaminchu*? It is clear from other studies of shamanism in Okinawa (Randall 1990, for example) that the family of the shaman plays a crucial role in determining the possibility of a person adopting a spiritual persona, or indeed in being recognized as having the potential to become spiritually inclined. In Akihiro's case, it was apparent that although there were other males in his immediate family who were spiritually inclined, his preoccupation with Kannon, his highly empathetic behavior and his feminized self-image set him apart from others.

Moreover, when attempting to locate his behavioral patterns within a contemporary context, we can see that one set of responses of males to the impact of shamanic "notification" is to embrace a cosmology which foregrounds women; while the gender of the shaman is not necessarily a factor, modes of discourse, behavior, deportment, and pitch of voice indicate a significant shift in the presentation of gender. A number of ethnographers have written about this phenomenon in Indonesia, Korea and Northern Siberia.[22]

The impact of religious affect on gender

This leads me to ask obvious questions: does this infer that in order for men to be accepted as shamans in contemporary Okinawa, they need to embrace feminized behavior and characteristics? Does Lebra's observation that men with physical handicaps are more likely to work in the religious sector reflect in those who choose such paths a "lack" of masculine traits? An unsuitability for masculinized roles? Or does such an interpretation belong to an antiquated patriarchal interpretative frame? In other words, does a male *need* to have characteristics that disqualify him from membership of the maleness that is ascribed to Okinawan men in order to become a legitimate part of the spiritual landscape; that is, among the practitioners who do not employ literary foundations for their craft?[23] I think this is highly unlikely. As many men do pursue careers and hobbies that incorporate spiritual discourse in their daily lives without recourse to feminized behavioral tropes, it is unlikely that this is a prerequisite, I suspect. In Akihiro's case, though, there are elements of both his own social upbringing, and his spiritual upbringing that set him apart from many other male spiritualists, who from my observations, tend to employ literary tropes in attempting to order prognostications, counseling and the provision of advice for clients.

A further question spins from this discussion concerning the prioritization of gender in spiritualism. How is gender prioritized in the kinds of help-seeking that are applied to instances of *kami dāri* and *sādaka unmari*? The inferences here concern appropriate interventions that may have an impact on the skewed mental health statistics in the prefecture. That is, the significantly higher incidence of schizophrenia in males in Okinawa may be related to the alternative pathways available for women who are afflicted by what could be seen to be *either* an indigenous form of "notification" of spirituality, or potentially a sign of the emergence of a disabling mental illness. Men rarely become shamans as the avenues available to women for spiritual intervention are often closed to them. Moreover, many men have little sympathy with Okinawan religion, or with genealogy. The interventions in Akihiro's case were those employed typically for women and girls. I think it is quite likely that those interventions saved Akihiro to a large extent from the trauma of extensive mental health examinations and potentially debilitating drug therapy.[24] There was little doubt that those around him were strongly influenced by his transgendered personality, in that they accepted he had the right to be "tried by the spirits as a female *kaminchu*." This is in contradistinction to men who express themselves in more masculine ways, yet have similar spiritual experiences.

Gender, mental illness, and the impact of shamanism

In the context of the foregoing discussions, Okinawa's schizophrenia statistics are, from a gender perspective, quite uneven and very interesting. Globally schizophrenia's gender ratio is about even between women and men. In Okinawa, the statistics are tilted significantly toward men.[25] In 1988 Maxine Randall surveyed 384 mental hospital inpatients. She was interested in the relationship between *sādaka unmari* and mental illness. Her results demonstrate the prevalence of schizophrenic males among hospital patients (2.5 times as many males as females were admitted as schizophrenic, a statistic that is reflected in the overall number of mentally ill patients in the prefecture with men outnumbering women by a ratio of approximately 2:1). Some 74 percent of all males, and 81 percent of all females in her sample were diagnosed schizophrenic. Among those who had been diagnosed as *sādaka unmari before* hospitalization, the percentage of schizophrenic patients was considerably lower in both men and women (60 percent and 64 percent respectively), and so too was the total number of patients (Randall 1990). While it would not be unreasonable to expect to see in Okinawa the same types of statistics for the gender ratio of schizophrenia as in mainland Japan, and in other nations, this is not the case. Statistics for mainland Japan show approximately 63 percent of all hospitalized mental patients are schizophrenic. In the 1 percent or so of the population recognized to be schizophrenic, men and women are represented approximately evenly (Miyabayashi 1998). However, in Okinawa the number of men being treated for schizophrenia remains high. The gender imbalance seems quite striking; in fact, it is statistically anomalous.

How then can we balance the statistics with the gender-specific practices discussed earlier? It is clear that shamanic and spiritual interventions privilege women, and that women's potential for conversion to a spiritual course of action is higher than men. The long history of indigenous intervention in cases where people are visited by voices, visions, spiritual infestations, or simply schizophrenia indicates that while the overall rate of schizophrenia and other mental illness/disorders is higher than the national average in Japan, among women it is lower, and among men it is higher.

Help-seeking that involves spirituality seems to have a relationship with successful "normalization" policies for mental health; that is the spiritual interventions seem to have the twin and related impacts of reducing the number of women who need psychiatric treatment, and of reinforcing Okinawan folk religion (Randall et al. 1993, 1996). Men are less likely to be able to employ spirituality as a means of identifying and treating an ambivalent and problematic condition (that is, a mental health problem or a spiritual problem) than women. Among men, there is a powerful tendency to employ mental health services in the first instance, rather than consult shamans (though women often do so on their behalf) (Takaishi 1993).

Acknowledgement of the often effective interventions by shamans in cases where women are affected by either of the spiritual circumstances mentioned above is eclectic within Okinawa. Many health professionals reject any clinical value of shamanism, while some of those psychiatrists born and raised in Okinawa tend to have more liberal views, locating the subject within a framework that includes "culture-bound" syndromes and their pathoplastic or pathogenic applications. That is, they tend to see the patient's social and cultural functioning as the most important outcome of treatment (Nakamura 1982; Naka et al. 1985; Takaishi 1993, 1994; Nakamura and Suzuki 1994).[26]

What is clear is that spiritual knowledges, sustained over many years largely by a special group of women, have been mobilized to intervene in cases where the gods or ancestors have attacked a receptive person. For men, the kinds of intervention available to women remain accessible, but socialization, modernization, globalization, Japanization and so on, have all eroded the religious foundations of the belief system, and appear to have influenced many men to eschew such religious courses of action. Women, particularly those in rural Okinawa, remain genealogically sympathetic, are often connected in one way or another with shamans, and have historical ties with "local knowledges," which include shamanism, in contrast to men, who tend to have fewer such knowledges and relationships.

Akihiro has transformed *himself* into a performative *herself*. In doing so he has made himself receptive to a cosmological perspective rarely available to males. And in gaining access to this cultural knowledge he has reconstructed his gender. In constructing for himself a new, gendered personality, he has undertaken a life-changing course of action, and has in the years since Naka's case study, crafted for himself a niche among other spiritually inclined practitioners of healing and counseling in Okinawa.[27] While the foundations of Akihiro's condition – the onset of *kami dāri*, and the fixation with Kannon – were problematic for him, the support of his family, and of his mother in particular, were critical elements in enabling him to establish for himself a life outside that expected of males in modern Okinawa. By invoking his female-ness in asserting his identity, Akihiro opened himself to the kinds of interventions commonly employed with women, rather than with men. Equally, the outcome – that he practices as a shaman – is a much more common result for women than for men. By pursuing religious solutions for his problem, Akihiro has avoided continued exposure to the psychiatric profession, and has stayed out of hospital.

That Okinawan society is open enough to embrace him in his role as spiritual advisor is certainly interesting; but what is of more interest to this writer is Akihiro's ability (his agency) to make himself socially and culturally acceptable to both women and men alike through his commitment to his calling. Akihiro has made for himself a career in an area dominated by women, providing counseling and religious help to those who come to him. By becoming female, Akihiro opened himself to a transgendered spiritual experience, and in the process transcended the limitations of his maleness in the practicing spiritual world of contemporary Okinawa.

Notes

1 Ogura argues that schizophrenia rates among the Okinawan population in general are much higher than the Japanese national average, and that the number is potentially much higher than the statistics reveal, due to the presence of shamans and to the limited number of psychiatric hospital beds in the prefecture.
2 Nakamura Eitoku's book is an excellent early account of the impact of shamanism on mental health remission rates, and illustrates clear differentiation between male and female remission rates.
3 The revival of folk religion in Okinawa is closely linked with the years of American military rule. That is, when the US took over Okinawa in 1945, in attempting to differentiate Okinawans (Ryukyuans, as they were called by the US) from Japanese, people were encouraged to pursue their esoteric cultural practices. Among these was shamanism. See Allen (2002a) for a detailed account of the revival of shamanism in Okinawa in the postwar years. As far as I know, this revival was not mirrored in mainland Japan, though there were a number of cults and splinter religious groups set up in the 1950s and 1960s.
4 Ruth Ann Keyso's book on women in Okinawa is a wonderfully evocative account of life experience on the main island (Keyso 2000). It demonstrates repeatedly the patriarchal environment in which the women function.
5 Nakamura and Ohashi have produced comprehensive accounts of the dominance of local religion among psychiatric patients, while Tsuha and Lebra have written on the importance of shamanism in daily life within contemporary Okinawa.
6 This comment was made by Ms N., an office worker in rural Okinawa, who has quite frequent contact with *yuta* and is meticulous about recording whether they were useful or not.
7 Ohashi and Allen discuss the processes involved in becoming a spiritualist in a number of specific contexts both within Okinawa and in diasporic Okinawan communities. Others have also described in some detail the medical implications of becoming a shamanic practitioner within an ethnopsychiatric perspective.
8 Interview with Sayako, a *yuta* on Kumejima, September 1997.
9 Ohashi (1996) makes a strong case that shamanism provides not only counselling for women, but also fosters strong gendered identity, based on access to special knowledges.

10 Figures from Maxine Randall's (1990) study of mental hospital patients suggest that from her numbers, women are three times more likely to believe in spiritual efficacy than men.
11 Professor Naka has been a consulting psychologist with a particular interest in indigenous religion and its impact on mental health in the prefecture. He was called in to see Akihiro by a resident psychiatrist with the permission of the boy's mother. Client confidentiality prevents me identifying other details about the case.
12 It is probably worth pointing out at this stage that the goddess Kannon-sama is a relatively common visitation for patients with schizophrenia, and for those who become *yuta*.
13 These locations were significant to Akihiro because it was to these sites that he saw in his dreams that he was attracted. As a result of the visualization of these places, he became obsessed with searching out their real locations.
14 *Uguan* means going around the island from site to site to pray to gods for guidance in clarifying one's own condition.
15 See Nakamura (1992) for a comprehensive and critical perspective on *yuta* and their financial as well as psychiatric cost to the community.
16 The term *"yuta"* is generally avoided by practitioners and relatives when describing their work. Rather, the more generic, and more ambiguous term *"kaminchu"* – literally god person – is applied.
17 In this case the word *kaminchu* (god person) was used by Akihiro.
18 There are no negatives associated with this image, apparently – it was rather simply a direct observation.
19 See, in particular, Nakamura Eitoku (1992) for a comprehensive account of the dangers of misdiagnosing genuine mental health problems.
20 Blacker (1975) also offers interpretations for why gender in Japan and in Okinawa was such an important determinant in shamanism.
21 Some *yuta* do channel the voices of males, but the majority deal with females in the spirit world.
22 For comparisons with the Japanese mainland, see Blacker (1975). She supplies some extremely useful background for shamanism outside of Okinawa. The introduction is particularly useful in locating Okinawan shamanism within the broader embrace of Japanese shamanism.
23 As we saw in the introduction, most males who work in the fields of religion or spiritualism employ literary knowledge as the foundation of their status.
24 There was a follow-up series of interviews conducted in 1994, when it was discovered that Akihiro was working as a spiritual consultant – a *kaminchu*. Naka *et al.* (1985) suggest that if alternative, culturally-sensitive approaches are employed, even in cases where psychosis is involved, they can lead to better, more positive outcomes for patients/ritually-afflicted.
25 See note 1 for more detail on this point.
26 In two of his works, Nakamura (1982, 1994) incorporates paradigms that critique shamanistic practices in Okinawa, but recognizes their importance to a patient's cultural functioning. Takaishi Toshihiro's work is based on clinical practice in Motobu, and incorporates holistic interpretations of healing and cross-culturally informed "culture-bound syndromes" in his clinics. He believes that culture is a critically important determinant in patients' responses to treatment.
27 Like many other shamans, Akihiro had not married by the mid-1990s, and in an interview at that time stated that he was celibate, according to Professor Naka.

References

Allen, M. (2002a) *Identity and Resistance in Okinawa*, Lanham, MD: Rowman and Littlefield.
—— (2002b) "Therapies of resistance? *Yuta*, help-seeking, and identity in Okinawa," *Critical Asian Studies*, 34(2): 221–242.
Anesaki, M. (1963) *History of Japanese Religion*, Tokyo: Tuttle.
Blacker, C. (1975) *The Catalpa Bow: A Study of Shamanistic Practices in Japan*, London: George Allen and Unwin.
Fujii, M. (2000). *Yomiuri Shimbun*, 2000. Available online: http:///www.wurzelwerk. at/thema/schamanenblick_e10.shtml (accessed on 6 June 2003).
Kerr, G. (1958) *Okinawa: The History of an Island People*, Tokyo: Tuttle.
Keyso, R. A. (2000) *Women of Okinawa: Nine Voices from a Garrison Island*, Ithaca, NY: Cornell University Press.
Lebra, W. (1979) *Okinawan Religion: Belief, Ritual and Social Structure*, Honolulu: University of Hawaii Press.
—— (1976) *Culture-Bound Syndromes, Ethnopsychiatry, and Alternate Therapies*, Honolulu: University of Hawaii Press.
—— (1972) *Transcultural Research in Mental Health*, Honolulu: University Press of Hawaii.
Miyabayashi, I. (1998) "Japanese schizophrenics and the family," *Yongao Acta Medica*, 41: 99–103.
Naka, K., S. Toguchi, T. Takaishi, H. Ishizu and Y. Sasaki. (1985) "*Yuta* (shaman) and community mental health on Okinawa," *International Journal of Social Psychiatry*, 31(4): 267–274.
Nakamura, E. (1982) *Okinawa nanbu ni okeru shūkyū-ishiki no kenkyū* (Research into the consciousness of religion in the southern Okinawan islands), Fukuoka: Kyushu Seishin-shinkei gakkai.
—— (1992) *Seishinryo rinshō to Okinawa shamanizumu: kamidāri monogatari wo megutte* (Psychiatric practice and Okinawan shamanism: an investigation into the *kamidāri* myth), Naha: Okinawa Psychiatric Service.
Nakamura, E. and Y. Suzuki. (1994) "Okinawa no yuta to kamidāri" (*Yuta* and *kamidāri* on Okinawa), in E. Nakamura and Y. Suzuki (eds) *Shamanizumu no shinrigaku* (The psychology of shamanism), Tokyo: A–Z Books.
Ogura, C. (1996) "Okinawa ni okeru rekishi, bunka to seishin igaku, iryō" (History and culture of Okinawa in the context of psychiatric medicine and diagnosis), *Japanese Bulletin of Social Psychiatry*, 5(1): 110–118.
Ohashi, H. (1996) *Okinawa shāmanizumu no shakaishinrigakuteki kenkyū* (Social psychological research on Okinawan shamanism), Tokyo: Kobunsho.
Randall, M. (1990) "Sādaka Unmari as a cognitive element in illness interpretation and coping behaviour," in K. Naka (ed.) *Hyoken gyōsei. Iryō taio gyōsei ni kansuru sōgōteki kenkyū*, Naha: Ryukyu Daigaku Press.
Randall, M., K. Matsuo, H. Nakamoto, K. Yamamoto and C. Ogura. (1996) "A study of the Okinawa cultural phenomenon of *sādaka unmari* (high spirit-rank birth) as a possible indicator for persons at risk for schizophrenia: an ERPs, MMPI and case study assessment," in C. Ogura, K. Matsuo and H. Nakamoto (eds) *Recent Advances in Event-Related Brain Potential Research*, Amsterdam: Elsevier, pp. 558–563.
Randall, M., C. Ogura and K. Naka. (1993) "The Okinawa phenomenon of Sādaka Unmari: a dynamic element in onset and course of illness in schizophrenia," *1993*

World Congress, World Federation for Mental Health (abstracts) 95, WFMH (ed.), Virginia: WFMH.

Sensui, H. (2000) "Vernacular Okinawa: identity and ideology in contemporary local activism," unpublished PhD thesis, Oxford University.

Sered, S. (1999) *Women of the Sacred Groves: Divine Priestesses of Okinawa*, New York: Oxford University Press.

Smits, G. (1999) *Visions of Ryukyu: Identity and Ideology in Early-Modern Thought and Politics*, Honolulu: University of Hawaii Press.

Sonoda, M. (1987) "The religious situation in Japan in relation to Shinto," *Acta Asiatica*, 51: 221–242.

Takaishi, T. (1994) "Kokoro no byō ni tsuite" (On spiritual illness), paper delivered at Motobu City Health Conference, Nago: private publication.

—— (1993) "Minkan shinkyo to seishin iryo" (Folk beliefs and mental health), paper delivered at Itohman kazoku kai, Nago: private publication.

—— (1989) "Okinawa to bunka no kenko" (Okinawa and cultural health), paper delivered at Okinawa *denryoku dai 5 kai hokubu chiku denki jigyou anzen gosei taikai*, Nago: Nagoshiminkan.

Tsuha, H. (1997) "Tai Yamato no bunka jinruigaku" (On the shared consciousness of non-Yamato identity), *Nihon Jinruigaku Bunkasho*, 2(3): 46–68.

Yokota, T. (1997) "Okinawa no shakai, bunkateki kankyō no mentaru herusu ni oyobosu eikyō ni tsuite" (A study on the influence of Okinawa socio-cultural background on mental health, with special reference to religious beliefs), *Japanese Bulletin of Social Psychiatry*, 5(2): 135–143.

9 "Understanding through the body"
The masquerades of Mishima Yukio and Morimura Yasumasa

Vera Mackie

Morimura meets Mishima

Mishima Yukio (born Hiraoka Kimitake, 1925–1970) is primarily known as a novelist, as the leader of an idiosyncratic private army, and for his suicide in November 1970 in the headquarters of the Self Defense Forces backed up by some members of his private army, the Shield Society. Mishima also, however, was a tireless promoter of his own image and his own celebrity. In addition to his 40 novels, 18 plays, some 20 volumes of fiction and a similar number of critical essays, librettos and other writings, he was a regular contributor of essays to newspapers and intellectual journals and co-operated enthusiastically with journalists from around the world. He could barely buy a pair of cufflinks without writing about it in a newspaper or magazine (Mishima 1966a: 171). His English-language biographers (without considering the many critical studies which have appeared) are the journalist Henry Scott-Stokes (1975) and his first translator into English, John Nathan (1975). Much of his celebrity was achieved without the "professional articulation between the news and entertainment media and the sources of publicity and promotion" (Turner *et al.* 2000: 5) which are characteristic of the media industries of today. He also acted in plays, appeared in films, and was photographed by some of the leading photographers of the time. It is these visual images of Mishima which form the major texts to be analyzed in this chapter. My interest in Mishima was stimulated by an artist, Morimura Yasumasa, who would have been aged only 19 or so at the time of Mishima's death, and whose major works have mainly appeared since the 1980s.

Morimura Yasumasa (b. 1951) has for some time been engaged in a form of artistic practice which involves transcultural and transgendered transvestite masquerades.[1] Morimura works in a combination of photographic collage, digital manipulation of photographic imagery, installation and performance. He parodies the works of European art history and masquerades as the cultural icons of Hollywood and other popular cultural forms (Morimura 2000). Morimura has commented that, "I had an interest in art, and as I was wondering how to engage with it, I eventually came to the realization that I needed to understand it through my body" (Morimura and Horio 2001: 107). Morimura has also made comparisons between his own work and the performances of Mishima Yukio. In a surprising reflection he has compared Mishima's debate with student radicals at the Tokyo

University Komaba campus in the late 1960s with his own transvestite performance at the Komaba Festival some three decades later. While Mishima often presented himself with a hypermasculinized persona, Morimura appeared at Tokyo University masquerading as Marilyn Monroe in a famous scene from *The Seven Year Itch* (director Billy Wilder, 1955). Morimura has commented that he and Mishima had made subtly different choices with respect to gender identity: Mishima toward the masculine and Morimura toward the feminine.

> I can't get over the feeling that there would have been nothing surprising about Mishima having made the same choice as me. Whether to shift towards "man" or "woman:" I think it must have been very subtle. For that reason, I feel like you could say that my choice was that of "another Mishima."
>
> (Morimura 1999: 260).[2]

Although this comment does not do justice to the complexity of Morimura's work, the comparison is highly suggestive. Mishima, like Morimura, engaged in a series of masquerades throughout his life: as samurai, as *yakuza* (gangster), as boxer, as bodybuilder, as soldier, as Saint Sebastian. Mishima participated in a series of photographic shoots directed by photographer Hosoe Eikoh, collected in a publication which appeared under the title *Barakei* (Ordeal by Roses) (Hosoe 1963, 1971, 1984, 1985). The photographs place Mishima's body in a range of visual environments, some photographs drawing on the European artifacts and art works in his residence, others staged in a disused factory building.[3]

This chapter will focus on photographs of Mishima, and on selected photographic collages by Morimura. The body is important to both artists: Mishima engaged in bodybuilding and military training, while Morimura's masquerades can be described as "embodied critical practice." Both are engaged in dialogues with Japanese and European traditions. Mishima's house is full of European art works and his writings (particularly the critical writings) refer to the European literary and philosophical tradition. Morimura's work quotes extensively from European art history. Nevertheless, they both insert themselves into their local traditions in various ways. I am most interested, however, in their engagements with masculinity and femininity, and the place of the body in their enactment of gendered identities. Mishima and Morimura each display different ways of dealing with the disjunctions between the sexed body, gendered identity and the "imaginary body." In this discussion I also assume that visual culture is important in the dissemination, validation and censuring of desirable and undesirable models of gender identity.

Morimura's masquerades

In Morimura's artistic practice, he wears clothes, wigs, prosthetics and cosmetics and places himself in front of painted backdrops or three-dimensional dioramas in order to transform himself into figures from some of the major works of European art history such as da Vinci's Mona Lisa (Morimura 2000: 32–37) or Manet's Olympia (Morimura 2000: 53). He also places himself in American popular culture:

in a homage to Andy Warhol's portrait of Elvis Presley (ibid.: 75), as Madonna (ibid.: 23) or as Michael Jackson (ibid.: 24). Other works engage with Japanese popular culture. In his transvestism, he not only crosses gendered boundaries, but also racialized boundaries. Indeed, the boundaries of animal, vegetable and mineral are also transgressed as his face is inserted into still life compositions (ibid.: 38–43; 58–61; 64–65), and the boundaries between human and machine are questioned in the "psychoborg" performances (ibid.: 23–24). "Self-Portrait as Movie Actress (Red Marilyn)," 1994 (reproduced in ibid.: 23), is a recreation of the famous calendar shot of a naked Marilyn Monroe on a red velvet background. In Morimura's recreation, however, the prosthetic breasts which transform his body into something resembling a woman's body are clearly revealed. His gendered masquerades are always imperfect, always drawing attention to artifice.

In several works, Morimura is transformed into the Monroe character in the famous scene from *The Seven Year Itch*, where she stands over the ventilation outlet of the New York subway, the wind from the subway providing welcome relief from the oppressive New York summer heat. The wind causes the white pleated skirt of her dress to billow around her, threatening to reveal her legs and more (Figure 9.1). Morimura re-stages this scene in front of a group of students at Tokyo University, in the very lecture theatre where Mishima had his famous confrontation with the radical left-wing students of the Zenkyōtō group. In this and several other art works, Morimura places the icons of Western popular culture in a Japanese environment, thus rendering them strange. Other works insert Morimura's Japanese-looking features in the major works of European art history (Gonzalo 2000: 89–102). In this case, his performance as the icon of blonde, white femininity in a site made famous by student radicals draws attention to the strategies of enacting gendered performances. Morimura is clearly a man masquerading as a woman, but this juxtaposition suggests that other men might simply be masquerading as men (Morimura 2001).

In "Self-Portrait as Actress (Black Marilyn)" 1996 (reproduced in Morimura 2000: 24), the fantasy structure of the representations of the hyperfeminine figure of Marilyn Monroe is revealed. Polarities are reversed as the white dress of the *Seven Year Itch* scene becomes a black dress, and the fetishistic anxiety of the male who gazes on Marilyn's skirt is resolved in a surprising way as a phallus is revealed under the skirt.

To explain further, the word "fetish" originally referred to an object which held particular religious power. In psychoanalytic terms, as adapted by Freud, the fetish is a perversion whereby an object, such as an item of clothing, provides sexual satisfaction in place of genital sexual activity. The object comes to serve this function because it displaces the male's anxiety about castration, an anxiety which would be reinforced by the sight of the female body which lacks the phallus. Several critics have also identified the mechanism of fetishism as operating in filmic and photographic representation.[4]

> Psychoanalytically speaking, the photograph has prompted comparison with the structure of the fetish . . . in so far as the camera image marks the con-

The masquerades of Mishima and Morimura 129

Figure 9.1 Photograph of Morimura Yasumasa as Marilyn Monroe, Tokyo University, 2001, reproduced by kind permission of the artist.

junction of a look, an arrest, and an illusion of presence that belies the object's real absence ... [T]he interest of the photography/fetish homology for feminism resides in the social and cultural instrumentalities of photography; most specifically in the medium's tendency to emblematize repetitively the status of women as objects of the photographic gaze, bearers of meaning rather than makers of it ... In other words, the urgency of feminist interrogations of photography rests on the acknowledgement of the complicity of the camera in sustaining and perpetuating certain kinds of viewing relations that are themselves reflective of the unequal order of sexual and social relations.

(Solomon-Godeau 1992: 330)

Morimura's masquerades reveal the fetishistic anxiety behind representations of the veiled female body, and also reveal the fetishism of the photographic enterprise itself. Morimura's masquerades as Monroe reveal the parody that is at the heart of this ultimate icon of white, blonde femininity.[5] Monroe's feminine persona was achieved through cosmetics, peroxide, dress, extravagant gestures and modulation of her voice. Even during her career this was the object of parody, such as a scene in *Gentlemen Prefer Blondes*, where Jane Russell dons a blonde wig and adopts Monroe's breathless manner in a masquerade which draws attention to the constructedness of Monroe's persona (director Howard Hawks, 1953).

Marjorie Garber has also noted the connection between transvestism and fetishism, a connection which Morimura demonstrates here through artistic practice rather than academic treatise.[6] This is what I refer to as Morimura's "embodied critical practice." Indeed, this critical practice has much in common with the practice of queer theorists who attempt to deconstruct essentialist notions of gender and sexuality and, with street fashions and practices which celebrate androgyny and hybridity, challenge conventional gender norms (Fuss 1991; Burston and Richardson 1995; Creed 2004: 123–139).

Morimura's work may thus be seen to operate through citation, a recognized artistic practice which has also been seen as a form of critique (*Bijutsu techō* 1993: 27–92). Each of Morimura's masquerades cites a well-known art work or popular cultural representation, but the art work or cultural representation can never be viewed in quite the same way after it has been subjected to Morimura's embodied critical practice. Morimura's gendered masquerades also, however, highlight the citational and reiterative practice of gender which has been identified by Judith Butler. Gender difference – the cultural construction of masculinity and femininity – is not given or preordained but is produced through the constant repetition and citation of gendered performances. These performances are also *performative* in the sense that they do something – they produce the meaning of gender in society and culture (Butler 1990: 148).

Morimura's work reveals the ways in which differences are constructed through culture, a process he has reflected on, and a process which he destabilizes in his work.

> The history of humanity is the history of boundaries. Humans first became human through surrounding themselves with many boundaries. Human and nature. Country and country. Race and race. Class and class. Normality and madness. Adult and child. Bloodline, family and other groups. Man and woman. Humans have created boundaries, have given them authority and solidity and have measured the differences between themselves and other forms of existence.
>
> (Morimura 1999: 247–248)

Morimura's body may be seen as a canvas or screen on which various images can be projected. In many ways, Morimura's masquerades reaffirm the distinction between "sex" as a biological property of male and female bodies and "gender" as a set of culturally and socially constructed practices. As in drag performances, Morimura's masquerades gain meaning from the disjunction between the body which is sexed male and the feminine masquerade which he performs. Morimura adds a further dimension in drawing attention to racialization and ethnicization. Morimura dresses his body in make-up, wigs, clothes, and prosthetics, but does not modify the body itself. Morimura has contrasted his own fascination with femininity with Mishima's fascination with masculinity. Mishima and Morimura also demonstrate different attitudes to the body itself. Furthermore, Mishima's gendered masquerades start to look different if seen through the prism provided by a consciousness of Morimura's embodied critical practice.

Mishima's masquerades

Mishima, however, did more than simply choose to masquerade as "masculine" in opposition to "the feminine." Mishima ranged across a certain field of masculinities. This contributes to the theoretical understanding (for which I am hugely indebted to my colleague Romit Dasgupta) that there is no one form of masculinity, but rather a field of possible masculinities (Connell 1995: 77–81; Dasgupta 2000: 189–200; 2003: 118–134). It is certainly true that masculinity only has meaning in opposition to femininity, and that patriarchal power places men in a privileged position with respect to women. There are also, however, competing masculinities in any one cultural and social system, and the most powerful representatives of masculine and patriarchal power also have power over other men and other, less dominant forms of masculinity.

One of my major texts is a collection of photographs by Hosoe Eikoh (b. 1933), completed during the 1960s, but reissued after Mishima's death in a lavish art book designed by graphic artist Yokoo Tadanori (b. 1936), who was also responsible for many of the posters used to promote the avant-garde theater troupes of the time (Goodman 1999). The photographs were taken in and around Mishima's rococo house, or sometimes staged in other settings, often using his European furniture and artworks as props, demonstrating the complexity of Mishima's cultural references.[7] Despite his eventual association with an idiosyncratic form of militaristic ultranationalism, he was deeply steeped in European cultural and literary traditions, and his speech and writings are full of an extraordinary range of references to European, as well as Japanese philosophical and literary works. In this complexity of cultural reference points he had much in common with the intelligentsia of Japan throughout the twentieth century. In commissioning his house, completed in 1959, he is said to have commented, "I want to sit on rococo furniture wearing Levi's and an Aloha shirt; that's my ideal of a lifestyle" (Nathan 1975: 150).[8] The house was the realization of contradictory yearnings – for the high culture of Europe and the more vulgar and exuberant popular culture of the United States.

Although I will focus largely on cultural representations in the form of photographic images, it is difficult to get away from the body itself. The photographs to be examined are largely concerned with the body, and Mishima crafted his own body in a much more literal way than Morimura. Mishima transformed his own body from that of a rather sickly individual to one that was physically fit and suntanned, displaying well-developed muscles.

In his photographic representations, Mishima presents a range of possible masculinities: the ascetic, the festival shrine-carrier, the boxer, the bodybuilder, the gangster, the samurai warrior, the soldier, and the aesthete. Let us consider each of these forms of masculinity in turn, with reference to a whole corpus of photographic representations, including a collection of photographs, including press and publicity photographs, co-edited by his widow, Yōko (Mishima and Fujita 2000).

In his novel, *Kamen no kokuhaku* (*Confessions of a Mask*) (Mishima 1949) which has been assumed to have a strong autobiographical element, Mishima provides a portrait of a young man's sexual awakening. One of the first objects of the character's erotic attention is the figure of Saint Sebastian. Indeed, this is said to have prompted the fictional narrator's first sexual feelings (Nathan 1975: 95–97). Eventually, in 1970, Mishima had himself photographed as Saint Sebastian, complete with arrows piercing his torso in a recreation of Guido Reni's (1575–1642) painting of 1615 (see Figure 9.2). The photograph by Shinoyama Kishin, 1970, reproduced in Mishima and Fujita 2000: unpaginated.[9] It is even more interesting, however, that the narrator of *Confessions of a Mask* has an initial fascination with a heroic figure on a white horse, until he is told that this is not a beautiful young knight, but a woman – Joan of Arc (Nathan 1975: 12–13). In the logic of the narrative, this prefigures an unease with gender ambiguity, while the fascination with Saint Sebastian is an early indication of the fusion of masochism, eroticism and death in Mishima's work (Starrs 1994), a fusion which is also revealed in many of the photographic representations we have of Mishima.

The men who carry portable shrines through the streets at Shinto festivals are another early focus of attention for the narrator of *Confessions of a Mask*. The practice of carrying these shrines has been vividly described by Mishima's biographer and translator, John Nathan:

> The shrine, known as a *mikoshi*, is a wooden structure in tiers, ornately carved and brightly painted and weighing close to two thousand pounds. It takes from forty to sixty young men to carry it by the two long wooden bars which run its length on both sides. When the neighborhood festival parade begins, the youths shoulder the heavy shrine and begin moving through the streets, shouting rhythmically to help keep themselves in step. The shrine moves up and down and sways precariously from side to side; the bearers gradually accelerate until they are weaving down the street almost at a run, a tangle of feet and sweating bodies, shouting at the top of their lungs and somehow just managing to keep the swaying wooden edifice upright above them.
>
> (Nathan 1975: 128–129)

Figure 9.2 Photograph of Mishima Yukio as St Sebastian, by Shinoyama Kishin, 1970, reproduced by kind permission of Shinoyama Kishin.

Mishima himself explained the attraction of the shrine carriers:

> Through it all there was only one vividly clear thing, a thing that both horrified and lacerated me, filling my heart with unaccountable agony. That was the expression on the faces of the young men carrying the shrine – an expression of the most obscene and undisguised intoxication in the world.
> (Mishima 1949, translated in Nathan 1975: 129)

Mishima also participated in such festivals and there are several extant photographs of Mishima at festivals in loincloth and *happi* coat, a joyous expression on his face (see photographs in Mishima and Fujita 2000: unpaginated; Nathan 1975: unpaginated section). These can be dated to the period after he commenced his program of bodybuilding in the mid-1950s, when he can be assumed to feel more comfortable with his own body. The carriers of the portable shrines can be seen as a form of "peasant" masculinity, in distinction to the mainstream white-collar, middle-class masculinity of the world he inhabited.[10] Mishima also appears to have had a fascination with the Japanese gangsters, the *yakuza*, another non-hegemonic form of masculinity. He appears in the film *Karakkaze Yarō* (Tough guy) (director Y. Masumura, 1960), taking the part of a *yakuza*. Publicity photographs for the film show him wielding a pistol, one of the many phallic symbols to be seen in the photographs of Mishima (see photograph of Mishima in *Karakkaze Yarō*, by Nogami Tōru, reproduced in Mishima and Fujita 2000).

In the early 1950s, Mishima took up boxing training and then commenced bodybuilding in July 1955, a practice he continued for the rest of his life (Nathan 1975: 123; photograph of Mishima at Kōrakuen gym, 1958, in Mishima and Fujita 2000: unpaginated; Mishima 1959: 259–260). He has commented in several places on the reasons for his desire to transform his body in this way. One of his comments has been paraphrased by biographer Henry Scott-Stokes.

> Early in his life, he says, he felt a loathing for his body. He put all his emphasis on "words," on the pursuit of literature: "words" tended to corrode his being – as if white ants were eating into his person – and he sought a second "language," the "language of the flesh."
> (Scott-Stokes 1975: 185)

Just before his death, there was an exhibition devoted to Mishima at the Tōbu Department store in Tokyo. Mishima suggested dividing the exhibition into four sections, with the titles "The River of Writing," "The River of Theatre," "The River of Body" and "The River of Action" (Mishima 1970a: 506), and these were adopted as subtitles for sections of Scott-Stokes' biography of Mishima. Some of Hosoe's photographs were included in the exhibition, along with commentary by Mishima himself:

> I had been dissatisfied for quite some time by the fact that my invisible spirit alone could create tangible visions of beauty. Why could not I myself be

something visibly beautiful and worthy of being looked at? For this purpose I had to make my body beautiful. When at last I came to own such a body, I wanted to display it to everyone, to show it off and to let it move in front of every eye, just like a child with a new toy. My body became for me like a fashionable sports car for its proud owner. In it I drove on many highways to new places. Views I had never seen before opened up for me and enriched my experience . . . But the body is doomed to decay, just like the complicated motor of a car. I for one do not, will not, accept such a doom. This means that I do not accept the course of Nature. I know I am going against Nature; I know I have forced my body onto the most destructive path of all.

(Mishima 1970a: 507–508, translated in Scott-Stokes 1975: 184)

Unlike Morimura, whose masquerades may be characterized as a complex and multilayered form of quotation, citation and transvestism, Mishima must transform the physical body itself. Mishima's body becomes a form of sculpture rather than a mere canvas. It seems that he is unable to reconcile any disjuncture between his physical body and his imagined identity, or what Moira Gatens has called "the imaginary body" (1996: 3–20). In this, he seems to have much in common with those who undertake sex change operations or other forms of bodily modification.[11] In Mishima's case, however, it is not a case of transforming a female body into a male one or a male body into a female one. Rather, he needed to make his male body more closely approximate his ideal form of masculinity and maleness.

Mainstream masculinities

There were other possible masculinities not espoused by Mishima, and it is necessary to bring these into the discussion in order to appreciate the figures he was defining himself against. The greatest absence is the middle-class salary-man, which was rapidly becoming the archetypal model of postwar masculinity in Japan (Dasgupta 2000, 2003). Mishima had rejected the figure of the salaryman both literally and figuratively. As Hiraoka Kimitake, he had completed secondary education at the elite Peers' School (Gakushūin) and entered the Law Faculty of the Imperial University (now Tokyo University). On graduation from the Law Faculty he entered the Finance Ministry, the most elite echelon of the bureaucracy. He survived nine months in the Finance Ministry before convincing his father to allow him to resign and write full-time (Nathan 1975: 88–90). Except for the extraordinary discipline with which he pursued his writing, his subsequent lifestyle was a rejection of the mundane lifestyle of the white-collar worker. He had an active social life in the evenings, wrote from midnight to dawn, rose at noon, and spent the afternoons in body-building or *kendō* (Japanese fencing) practice.

The other absence is any contemporary figure of the soldier. The soldiers Mishima identifies with are the samurai of the pre-Meiji period, or the right-wing army officers who failed in their attempts to restore the authority of the Emperor in the 1930s. Mishima appeared in the samurai film, *Hitogiri* (director Gosha,

1969), playing a character he described as a "single-minded terrorist" (Mishima 1969a: 108; 1969b: 189–190; Scott-Stokes 1975: 20) and there are countless photographs of Mishima, often in loincloth (*fundoshi*) and sometimes with a headband (*hachimaki*) wielding a samurai sword (see photographs in Mishima and Saitō 2000: unpaginated; photographs by Yatō Tamotsu in Nathan 1975: unpaginated section; photograph by Shinoyama Kishin in Scott-Stokes 1975: unpaginated section). He also displayed several of these photographs in his own house (Shinoyama 1995: unpaginated).

What are missing are the members of the postwar Self Defense Forces (who were the object of his perorations in his speech at the Self Defense Force Headquarters in November 1970), and the police: the major representatives of the state monopoly on violence. Mishima regretted the fact that Japan had given up the right to belligerence in the postwar constitution, and criticized the hypocrisy of the Self Defense Forces that were created under this regime. Mishima's ideal soldiers are the young officers of the 1930s who attempted several times to conduct *coups d'état* to restore the political power of the Emperor. His story, "Patriotism" (*Yūkoku*) (1960), depicts the final day of one of these officers, who commits double suicide with his wife due to the impending failure of the plot. The story was completed late in 1960, soon after the Ampo crisis of June 1960, when record numbers of demonstrators turned out in the streets of Tokyo to protest against the renewal of the Japan–US Security Treaty, which allowed the continued stationing of US bases on Japanese soil, and maintained Japan's subordination to US security policies in East Asia. Mishima also appeared in a film version of the story in 1966, playing the part of the young officer who commits ritual disembowelment (producers Dōmoto and Mishima, 1966; see poster for the film of "Patriotism," showing Mishima in military uniform with samurai sword, reproduced in Mishima and Saitō 2000: unpaginated).

It is in the 1960s that Mishima established his private army, the Shield Society (*Tate no Kai*). In 1967, in preparation for establishing the Society, he obtained permission to undertake two months' training alongside new recruits to the Self Defense Forces. He was a 42-year-old man training alongside young men in their twenties (Mishima 1967: 303–304; 1968: 311–312; 1969d: 287). Scott-Stokes was one of the few individuals allowed to observe a practice session of the Shield Society, which commenced in 1968. Scott-Stokes commented archly on their uniforms: "Fantastic uniforms – yellow-brown with rows of shining, brass-buttons which gave wasp-waists to Mishima's young men. Mishima's taste for kitsch exemplified" (Scott-Stokes 1975: 19; see photograph in Mishima and Fujita 2000: unpaginated; for Mishima's own views on the beauty of military uniforms, see Mishima 1969c: 65; on the design of the *Tatenokai* uniforms, see Mishima 1969d: 282).

Militant masculinities

There is another marginal form of masculinity that was intimately entwined with Mishima's fantasies of violence in his latter years. These are the students of the left-wing movements who were an important part of the political spectrum in the 1960s and 1970s. In the largest demonstration against the renewal of the US–Japan Security Treaty on 15 June 1960, the Diet building was encircled by over 100,000 demonstrators, some affiliated with political groups, some simply seeing themselves as concerned citizens. A group of students from the Zengakuren student organization attempted to storm the Diet building. In the ensuing mêlée a 23-year-old female Tokyo University student, Kamba Michiko, was killed. By the late 1960s (in parallel with what was happening in France and the Anglophone countries) students had occupied several university campuses and engaged in confrontations with riot police. The students started to go to demonstrations armed and wearing crash helmets (Packard 1966; Mutō and Inoue 1985). Their demonstrations in the streets of Tokyo and their occupations of university campuses are well documented in the photographic record (see, for example, Abe and Hosono 1960; Akane and Shibata 2003). As the decade of the 1960s progressed, the students came to resemble the riot police more and more, in their wearing of crash helmets which identified their particular political faction and in their wielding of rocks and sticks in opposition to the batons, shields and helmets of the riot police. The riot police, however, also had the backing of the state and the option of using water cannons and tear gas.

Mishima defined himself against these students, and also engaged in a debate with them on the Tokyo University Komaba campus about aesthetics, politics, revolution, and violence. In these discussions there was an implicit triangle of possible masculinities – on one point of the triangle that of Mishima and his right-wing private army, on another point that of the left-wing students who were not afraid to engage in violent confrontation, and on the third point that of the riot police who represented the state's monopoly of legitimate violence. The debate was recorded and appeared in a best-selling publication which is still available as a paperback (Mishima and Tōdai Zenkyōtō [1969] 2000). Mishima and the students split the proceeds, and he commented that, "[t]hey probably used the money to buy helmets and Molotov cocktails. I bought summer uniforms for the Shield Society. All concerned are satisfied" (Mishima 1969d: 284; translated in Nathan 1975: 250).

Mishima's own fantasies reveal this triangulated structure of possible masculinities. Scott-Stokes has commented on his apprehensiveness before the debate with the students, but also his recognition of the similarities between them:

> Mishima had a moment of paranoia when he approached the hall at Komaba, fearing that the students would seize and murder him on the spot. Afterwards he remarked: "I was as nervous as if I was going into a lions' den but I enjoyed it very much after all. I found we have much in common – a rigorous ideology and a taste for physical violence, for example. Both they and I represent new species in Japan today. I felt friendship for them. We are friends between whom there is a barbed wire fence. We smile at one another but we can't kiss."

(Scott-Stokes 1975: 184)

Mishima fantasized about the Shield Society intervening when the riot police, the representatives of state-sanctioned violence, were unable to exert control over the students. In each version of the fantasy, the members of the Shield Society die in violent confrontation:

> In the fantasy Mishima entertained until late in 1969 . . . the Left would initiate violence in the form of mass demonstration too large for the police to handle. The Prime Minister would be obliged to mobilize the Self-Defense force to keep the peace. During the interval of chaos while the police were being overpowered and before the Self Defense mobilized, the [Shield Society] would defend the Emperor with its collective life . . .
> There was also a second, more exciting version, in which the [Shield Society] would spearhead an attack on the Diet together with the [Self Defense Forces]. When the Diet had been occupied, the [Self Defense Forces] would demand revision of the war renunciation clause in the Constitution and restoration of supreme command to the Emperor. Since the [Shield Society] was to lead (and thus inspire) the attack on the Diet casualties would be high.
> (Nathan 1975: 244–245)

Mishima's masquerades range across a field of culturally intelligible forms of masculinity. All the forms of masculinity he adopts are legible to the viewers of the time. However, the final performance of all takes Mishima into the realm of the pathological, with annihilation the logical conclusion. It must be said, however, that this pathological conclusion – committing suicide by ritual disembowelment, with the assistance of a second who beheaded him at the crucial moment – was another culturally intelligible, although no longer culturally valorized, form of masculinity. Mishima's masculinity may thus be seen as a "necrophiliac masculinity."[12]

Ordeal by Roses

Having considered the range of possible masculinities espoused by Mishima in his photographic representations, produced in collaboration with some of the major photographers of the time, let us return briefly to a consideration of some of the photographs included in *Ordeal by Roses*. These photographs do not partake of the fascination with violence evidenced by some of the other photographic representations considered in this chapter. Rather, Mishima surrendered to the surrealistic impulses of the photographer Hosoe (Mishima 1963: 29–32). Mishima is posed in either a white or a black loincloth, naked, in Levi's jeans, or in white leggings with a military cap (Figure 9.3). At times he is wrapped in a garden hose in a pose suggestive of sadomasochist practices. At other times he poses with other people – sometimes the body of a woman, man or child is clearly identifiable; at other times the bodies are indeterminate. In several photographs, roses feature: clasped between his teeth or draped around his neck. In the Japanese edition of 1971, the frontispiece includes Yokoo's colourful drawing of a hirsute Mishima, his naked body strewn with red, red roses.

Figure 9.3 Photograph of Mishima Yukio, in Hosoe Eikoh, *Barakei (Ordeal by Roses)*, Denville, New Jersey: Aperture, 1985, unpaginated, reproduced by kind permission of Hosoe Eikoh

For mainstream readers, these photographs simply seem surrealistic. For those familiar with the underground perverse press of the time, however, there are other associations, perhaps not so obvious to a mainstream audience. The loincloth (*fundoshi*) and the samurai sword were staple elements of representations of sado-masochism. In subsequent years several journals of the underground homosexual press adopted titles including the word "rose" (*bara*) (McLelland 2005);[13] Mishima performed a song "The Sailor who was Killed by Paper Roses" with transvestite chanteuse Maruyama [Miwa] Akihiro (Mishima 1966b: 173–174; Scott-Stokes 1975: 191); and one of his plays had the title "Roses and the Pirate" (Mishima 1958: 134–135; 1970b: 504–505). In reading these visual texts, then, we need to be alert to the possibility of alternative readings. A reader of the weekly magazines of the 1960s and 1970s, a reader of the perverse press of the 1960s and 1970s, a reader schooled in the visual conventions of European art history, or a reader schooled in twenty-first-century theories of visual semiotics, gender studies and queer theory will each provide alternative readings of the photographs.

Let me now provide a reading of some of the photographs in *Barakei* through the prism provided by the work of Morimura. Despite my comments about the different attitudes to the body displayed by Morimura and Mishima, there are some fascinating similarities in the images produced by Morimura and those produced through the collaboration of Mishima and Hosoe. We have noted how Morimura provided a sense of strangeness by placing the figures of European popular culture in a Japanese context or by placing a "Japanese" face in the works of European art history. Let us look again at Mishima's masquerade as Saint Sebastian in this context. We could also consider the photographs in *Barakei* where Mishima appears before a painted backdrop. When Mishima appears in a black loincloth before a painted backdrop of trees and sky, this seems to be a precursor of the Saint Sebastian photograph staged by Shinoyama Kishin. When Mishima appears standing on a stool, wearing white leggings, holding a large clock stopped at 12 o'clock in one hand and a tennis ball in the other hand, this suggests a quote from the Dadaists and Surrealists of the early twentieth century. When Hosoe produces complex collages where Mishima's body is superimposed on a Renaissance painting of Venus, this seems to prefigure the strategies of the photographic collages of Morimura Yasumasa.

Mishima and Morimura display different ways of dealing with the disjunctions between the sexed body, gendered identity and the "imaginary body." Morimura's work revels in these disjunctures and plays with them. His body is a screen on which various fantasy representations can be projected. Morimura's masquerades provide an embodied critique of the history of artistic representation, and reveal the fetishistic anxiety at the heart of the photographic enterprise. Mishima, on the other hand, worked to banish any ambiguity as he transformed his physical body into something which more closely approximated his ideal "imaginary body." His body was a sculpture rather than a screen. Reading photographs of Mishima through the prism of the work of Morimura also, however, reveals their complex engagement with both European and Japanese artistic traditions, reflecting the range of cultural reference points deployed with great confidence in the intellectual worlds of twentieth-century Japan.

Acknowledgements

Research for this chapter was completed as part of a project on "The Politics of Visual Culture in Modern Japan," funded by the Australian Research Council from 2001 to 2003. Papers related to this chapter have been presented at the Workshop on Genders and Sexualities in Japan, Institute of Advanced Studies, University of Western Australia, April 2004, the Workshop on Genders, Transgenders and Sexualities in Japan, Centre for Critical and Cultural Studies, University of Queensland, April 2004 and in a public lecture hosted by the Centre for Critical and Cultural Studies and held at the Mayne Centre, University of Queensland, April 2004. I am indebted to the audiences on those occasions for feedback and comments, and to Leigh Dale, Romit Dasgupta and Mark McLelland who commented on an earlier draft of this chapter. Thanks also to Leigh Dale for letting me read her forthcoming article, from which I have learned a great deal (Dale, forthcoming).

Notes

1 Morimura's art works may be seen online at: <http://www.telefonica.es/fat/catayasu/yasumasa01.html> (accessed 18 July 2004).
2 Translations from Japanese are my own unless stated otherwise.
3 There are at least three Japanese editions of the collection of photographs. The first Japanese edition of *Barakei*, published in 1963, was known under the English title "Killed by Roses." Mishima, Hosoe, and graphic artist Yokoo Tadanori were working on the second edition in the months before Mishima's death. This was eventually issued in 1971. By this time it had been agreed that "Ordeal by Roses" was a better English translation of the title. A new Japanese edition, which employed a similar sequence of photographs to the original 1963 edition, was issued in 1984. This was the basis of the English edition which was issued by the US-based publisher of photography, Aperture, in 1985.
4 For definitions of the fetish, fetishism, and fetishization, see Freud (1927: 147–158); Erwin (2002: 414–416); Wright (1992: 41–45, 113–120, 327–331). See also Mulvey ([1975] 1984: 361–373).
5 As Marjorie Garber explains with reference to magazines which include photographs of transvestites:

> The social critique performed by these transvestite magazines for readers who are not themselves cross-dressers is to point out the degree to which *all* women cross-dress as women when they produce themselves as artefacts. This is yet another way in which transvestism creates culture, produces and is produced by the Symbolic.
> (1992: 49)

6 According to Garber:

> That the fetishistic patient is sometimes *in fact* a transvestite renders more complex but also more plausible the argument that the transvestite on stage or in culture is himself/herself a fetishization. The fetish is a metonymic structure, but it is also a metaphor, a figure *for* the undecidability of castration, which is to say, a figure of nostalgia for originary "wholeness" – in the mother, in the child. Thus the fetish, like the transvestite – or the transvestite, like the fetish – is a sign at once of lack and its covering over.
> (1992: 121)

7 On Mishima's house, see Shinoyama Kishin's (1995) collection of photographs.
8 I have made every effort to trace the original sources of quotes in the biographies by Scott-Stokes and Nathan, but this has not always been possible.
9 Compare with Guido Reni's painting at: <http://www.comune.roma.it/museicapitolini/pinacoteca/visita/sala6_reni_sebastiano.htm> (accessed 18 July 2004).
10 Although such festivals are carried out in urban areas as well as rural areas, and the festivals Mishima participated in would have been in the Tokyo metropolitan area, I suggest that this is a "peasant" form of masculinity because of the links with rural Japan and the Shinto rituals involved with the cycle of planting and harvesting.
11 For scholarly literature on transgenderism, see, *inter alia*, Califia (1997), Stryker (1998: 145–158), Mackie (2001).
12 I have adapted this phrase from Macciocchi's (1979) description of the "necrophiliac femininity" which was cultivated under Italian fascism.
13 I am indebted to Mark McLelland for discussion of this issue, and for kindly letting me read relevant sections of the manuscript of his book (McLelland 2005).

References

Abe, K. and T. Hosono (eds). (1960) *Zengakuren: Okoru Wakamono* (Zengakuren: angry youth), Kyoto: Ryokufūsha.
Akane, S. and H. Shibata. (2003) *Zenkyōtō* (University joint struggle committee), Tokyo: Kawade Shobō.
Bijutsu Techō. (1993) Special Issue: "In'yō no kairaku" (The pleasure of quotation), March 1993, *passim*.
Burston, P. and C. Richardson (eds). (1995) *A Queer Romance: Lesbians, Gay Men and Popular Culture*, London: Routledge.
Butler, J. (1990) *Gender Trouble: Feminism and the Subversion of Identity*, New York: Routledge.
Califia, P. (1997) *Sex Changes: The Politics of Transgenderism*, San Francisco: Cleis Press.
Connell, R. W. (1995) *Masculinities*, Sydney: Allen and Unwin.
Creed, B. (2004) *Pandora's Box: Essays in Film Theory*, Melbourne: Australian Centre for the Moving Image.
Dale, L. (forthcoming) "'The sensuality and the suffering:' Reading Mishima and Tsiolkas".
Dasgupta, R. (2003) "Creating corporate warriors: the 'salaryman' and masculinity in Japan," in K. Louie and M. Low (eds) *Asian Masculinities: The Meaning and Practice of Manhood in China and Japan*, London: Routledge.
—— (2000) "Performing masculinities: The 'salaryman' at work and play," *Japanese Studies*, 20(2) 189–200.
Erwin, E. (ed.). (2002) *The Freud Encyclopedia: Theory, Therapy and Culture*, New York: Routledge.
Freud, S. (1927) "Fetishism," in J. Strachey (ed./trans.) *The Standard Edition of the Complete Works of Sigmund Freud*, vol. 23, (1953–1966), London: The Hogarth Press.
Fuss, D. (ed.). (1991) *Inside/Out: Lesbian Theories, Gay Theories*, London: Routledge.
Garber, M. (1992) *Vested Interests: Cross-Dressing and Cultural Anxiety*, New York: Routledge.
Gatens, M. (1996) *Imaginary Bodies: Ethics, Power and Corporeality*, London: Routledge.
Gonzalo, P. (2000) "The Body as sign: Yasumasa Morimura and the identity of the expanded body," in Y. Morimura, *Historia del Arte*, Madrid: Fundación Telefónica.

Goodman, D. (1999) *Angura: Posters of the Japanese Avant-Garde*, New York: Princeton Architectural Press.
Hosoe, E. (1985) *Barakei: Ordeal by Roses: Photographs of Yukio Mishima* by Eikoh Hosoe, Denville, NJ: Aperture.
—— (1984) *Barakei: Hosoe Eikō Shashinshū*, new edition, Tokyo: Shūeisha.
—— (1971) *Barakei: Hosoe Eikō Shashinshū*, Tokyo: Shūeisha.
—— (1963) *Barakei: Hosoe Eikō Shashinshū*, Tokyo: Shūeisha.
Macciocchi, M. (1979) "Female sexuality in Fascist ideology," *Feminist Review*, 1: 67–82.
Mackie, V. (2001) "The transsexual citizen: queering sameness and difference," *Australian Feminist Studies*, 16(2): 185–192.
McLelland, M. (2005) *Queer Japan from the Pacific War to the Internet Age*, Lanham, MD: Rowman and Littlefield.
Mishima, Y. (1976) *Mishima Yukio Zenshū* (Mishima Yukio complete works), 35 vols, Tokyo: Shinchōsha.
—— (1970a) "Untitled," *Mishima Yukio Ten Katarogu*, November 1970, reproduced in *Mishima Yukio Zenshū*, vol. 34.
—— (1970b) "'Bara to Kaizoku' ni tsuite" (On "Roses and the Pirate"), program for "Bara to Kaizoku," Gekidan Roman Gekijō, October 1970, reproduced in *Mishima Yukio Zenshū*, vol. 34.
—— (1969a) "'Hitogiri' Tanaka Shinpei ni funshite" (To Tanaka Shinpei of "The Assassin") *Yomiuri Shinbun*, 1 July 1969, reproduced in *Mishima Yukio Zenshū*, vol. 34.
—— (1969b) "'Hitogiri' shutsuen no ki" (On appearing in "The Assassin"), *Daiei Kurabu*, August 1969, reproduced in *Mishima Yukio Zenshū*, vol. 34.
—— (1969c) "Otokorashisa no bigaku" (The aesthetics of masculinity), *Danshi Senka*, May 1969, reproduced in *Mishima Yukio Zenshū*, vol. 34.
—— (1969d) "'Tate no kai' no koto" (On the "Shield Society"), *Tatenokai Isshūnen Kiken Panfuretto*, November 1969, reproduced in *Mishima Yukio Zenshū*, vol. 34.
—— (1968) "Jieitai to Watashi" (The Self-Defense Forces and me), *Shūkan Yomiuri*, 13 September 1968, reproduced in *Mishima Yukio Zenshū*, vol. 35.
—— (1967) "Untitled," *Shūkan Shinchō*, 17 June 1967, reproduced in *Mishima Yukio Zenshū*, vol. 35.
—— (1966a) "Oshare Ippin" (An accessory), *Sankei Shinbun*, 3 July 1966, reproduced in *Mishima Yukio Zenshū*, vol. 35.
—— (1966b) "Untitled," Maruyama Akihiro Charity Recital Program, July 1966, reproduced in *Mishima Yukio Zenshū*, vol. 35.
—— (1963) "'Barakei' taikenki" ("Ordeal by Roses:" my experience), *Geijutsu Seikatsu*, July 1963.
—— (1960) "Yūkoku," *Mishima Yukio Zenshū*, vol. 13, translated as "Patriotism," in Y. Mishima, *Death in Midsummer and Other Stories*, New York: New Dimensions, 1966.
—— (1959) "Jimu kara dōjō e: pen wa tsurugi ni tsūzu" (The office and the gym; the pen and the sword), *Chūō Kōron* (Zōkan), 20 January 1959, reproduced in *Mishima Yukio Zenshū*, vol. 35.
—— (1958) "Bara to kaizoku ni tsuite" (On "Roses and the Pirate"), *Mainichi Mansurii*, April 1958, reproduced in *Mishima Yukio Zenshū*, vol. 35.
—— (1949) *Kamen no Kokuhaku*, *Mishima Yukio Zenshū*, vol. 3, translated by M. Weatherby (1958) as *Confessions of a Mask*, New York: New Directions.
Mishima, Y. and M. Fujita. (2000) *Shashinshū: Mishima Yukio '25~'70* (Mishima Yukio:

Photographs 1925–1970), Tokyo: Shinchōsha, originally published in 1990 as *Gurafikku: Mishima Yukio*, Tokyo: Shinchōsha.

Mishima, Y. and Tōdai Zenkyōtō. ([1969] 2000) *Bi to kyōdōtai to Tōdai tōsō* (Beauty, community and the Tokyo University struggle), Tokyo: Kadokawa Bunko.

Morimura, Y. (2001) Postcard, in collection of author.

—— (2000) *Historia del Arte*, Madrid: Fundación Telefónica.

—— (1999) "Onna? Nihon? Bi? Nōto" (Notes on Women? Japan? Beauty?), in T. Kumakura and K. Chino (eds) *Onna? Nihon? Bi? Aratana Jendâ Hihyō ni Mukete*, Tokyo: Keiō Gijuku Daigaku Shuppankai.

Morimura, Y. and M. Horio. (2001) "Tanabata Taiwa: Morimura Yasumasa x Horio Makiko, Furiida Kāro ni deau tabi" (Conversation at Tanabata Festival: Morimura Yasumasa and Horio Makiko on their encounter with Frida Kahlo), *Bijutsu Techō*, 53: 810, September.

Mulvey, L. (1984) "Visual pleasure and narrative cinema," in B. Wallis (ed.) *Art After Modernism: Rethinking Representation*, New York: Museum of Contemporary Art.

Mutō, I. and R. Inoue. (1985) "The New Left, Part 2," *Ampo: Japan-Asia Quarterly Review*, Part I, 17(2): 20–35; Part II, 17(3): 54–73.

Nathan, J. (1975) *Mishima: A Biography*, Tokyo: Tuttle.

Packard, G. (1966) *Protest in Tokyo: The Security Treaty Crisis of 1960*, Princeton, NJ: Princeton University Press.

Scott-Stokes, H. (1975) *The Life and Death of Yukio Mishima*, Tokyo: Tuttle.

Shinoyama, K. (1995) *Mishima Yukio no ie* (The house of Mishima Yukio), Tokyo: Bijutsu Shuppansha.

Solomon-Godeau, A. (1992) "Photography," in E. Wright (ed.) *Feminism and Psychoanalysis: A Critical Dictionary*, Oxford: Basil Blackwell.

Starrs, R. (1994) *Deadly Dialectics: Sex, Violence and Nihilism in the World of Yukio Mishima*, Honolulu: University of Hawaii Press.

Stryker, S. (1998) "The transgender issue: An introduction," *GLQ*, 4(2): 145–158.

Turner, G., F. Bonner and P. D. Marshall. (2000) *Fame Games: The Production of Celebrity in Australia*, Cambridge: Cambridge University Press.

Veijola, S. and E. Jokinen. (1994) "The body in tourism," *Theory, Culture and Society*, 11(3): 125–151.

Wright, E. (ed.). (1992) *Feminism and Psychoanalysis: A Critical Dictionary*, Oxford: Basil Blackwell.

10 An introduction to men's studies

Kimio Itō

Editors' introduction

As the chapter by Futoshi Taga in this volume outlines, while there had been earlier developments, the sudden "boom" in men's studies and the widespread interrogation and questioning of masculinity as a construct only became visible throughout Japanese society in the 1990s. The rapid transition from the confidence of the 1980s' "bubble economy" years to the growing sense of cultural malaise occasioned by the economic slowdown of the 1990s formed the backdrop to this inquiry into masculine values. In many respects, Japan's industrial success, particularly in the postwar decades, had been premised on a hegemonic gender ideology which equated femininity with the private household sphere, and masculinity with the public, work domain. Consequently, men's lives – at least as far as the hegemonic ideal was concerned – came to be defined primarily through work. However, as many of the assumptions – guaranteed lifetime employment, for instance – that had underpinned hegemonic masculinity in postwar Japan started to unravel in the 1990s, men's lives, and indeed, masculinity itself, came under increasing public scrutiny. These critiques of hegemonic masculinity ranged from mainstream media coverage of such social problems as *karōshi* (sudden death due to excessively long work hours and stressful conditions) among middle-aged male employees, and the rise in suicide rates among men, through to personal accounts and reflective essays by men, to more academic and/or activist writing seeking to "deconstruct" Japanese masculinities. Many of these voices and strands started coalescing in the early to mid-1990s into a loose (yet distinct) social movement centered on men's studies/men's issues. The first of these "men's groups," the *Menzu Ribu Kenkyū Kai* (Men's Liberation Research Association) was set up in western Japan in the early 1990s, and similar groups formed in other regions throughout the 1990s. Underlying the thinking of most of the groups and individuals involved was the recognition that while men *did* benefit as a group from the patriarchal dividends of hegemonic masculinity, individual males could also be "victims" of the ideological expectations of patriarchy and hegemonic masculinity. What was needed was the provision of forums where men could talk about issues pertinent to their lives, such as relationships, work, and sexuality, and where the expectations of hegemonic masculinity could be publicly questioned and interrogated.

The fact that discussion of masculinity and "men's issues" entered the domain of public discourse in these years was in no small measure the result of the efforts of individual activists and researchers committed to drawing attention to the issues at stake. One individual, in particular, was instrumental in bringing the issue of masculinity onto the public stage, and extending its profile beyond the reaches of the academy. The person in question is Professor Kimio Itō, an academic at Osaka University, who in many respects came to represent the public/community face of men's studies in Japan in much the same way that figures like Tokyo University academic Ueno Chizuko came to represent the public face of Japanese feminism. Drawing upon a legacy of involvement with the student movement and women's activism in the 1970s, Itō has worked tirelessly through numerous academic and community channels to draw attention to masculinity-related issues. These included offering the very first courses in men's studies at a Japanese university (at Kyoto University in 1991), being one of the founders of the first men's group (the *Menzu Ribu Kenkyū Kai*) and men's center (the Men's Center Japan), speaking at a range of academic and public forums across Japan in an effort to raise community awareness, and being discussed extensively in the mainstream media. Professor Itō has also published widely on the topic of masculinities (as well as on other areas of research interest), both for an academic readership and for a broader public. It was through publications like *"Otokorashisa" no yukue* (How masculinity is changing; 1993), *Jendā de manabu shakaigaku* (Studying sociology through gender, co-edited with Muta Kazue; 1996), and *Danseigaku nyūmon* (An introduction to men's studies; 1996) that awareness about issues of masculinity extended out into the wider community. The issues he touched upon in these and other works resonated with concerns about men's lifestyles experienced by growing numbers of men and women in 1990s Japan. While some of these concerns were also being articulated elsewhere (for instance, discussion in the popular press about married men's lack of communication with their partners and children, or about the alienation felt by men after retirement), what was significant about Professor Itō's work was the linking of these social phenomena with masculinity as a construct.

Yet despite his impressive profile, and despite the influence his works have had on public awareness about masculinity in Japan, Kimio Itō remains largely unknown outside of Japan.[1] As we have argued in the Introduction, there needs to be far greater awareness among English-language readers of the richness and vibrancy of new research in Japanese in the areas of gender and sexuality and it is for this reason that we have translated selected excerpts from one of Itō's best-known works from the 1990s, *Danseigaku nyūmon* (An introduction to men's studies).[2] An indication of the significance of this work may be gauged from the fact that a new, revised version of the original 1996 edition is to be published in 2005.

We have deliberately chosen to draw upon this earlier work from the 1990s, however, since, as outlined above, the 1990s was the decade when many of the debates and issues related to masculinity first became visible in Japan. The excerpts we have translated here, from the Foreword and the first chapter of the book, provide a snapshot of some of the concerns which went on to shape men's studies in Japan. These translated excerpts cannot provide a comprehensive introduction to the range of Itō's scholarship, but by providing a brief background to his ideas, we hope to demonstrate the need for more comprehensive translation projects to be undertaken in the future.

Mark McLelland and Romit Dasgupta

Foreword

Towards the end of 1989 I made a certain prediction. It was as follows: "The decades of the 1970s and the 1980s were the period of 'women's issues,' issues which are likely to gain increasing significance in the future. Following on from this trend, the 1990s will see the beginning of the age of 'men's issues'." This prediction has certainly come true. Over the past few years, at places like Osaka University and Kyoto University, I have been delivering lectures under the title of "men's studies." The number of students wishing to attend these lectures has greatly exceeded expectations (in 1995, numbers at Kyoto University increased to 2,900), and I have been quite surprised by the level of interest in "men's issues" shown by both male and female students. Furthermore, at women's centers all over Japan, "men's seminars" aimed at members of the community are being organized more and more often and, as one of only a handful of individuals associated with men's studies, I am frequently invited to attend. The popularity of these seminars, especially with middle-aged men at an impasse in their lives, is remarkable, and often the audience number greatly exceeds the capacity of the venue.

Mass media such as magazines, newspapers, and television have also started addressing many men's issues and related concerns. Most noticeably, these have included the "Fuyuhiko phenomenon,"[3] and the "shy man syndrome"[4] as well as the increasing numbers of "single men who want to get married but can't," the "sharp increase in suicide" and "*karōshi*"[5] among workaholic salarymen. Other issues include the various lifestyle-related problems of elderly men, including the rising number of "post-retirement divorces," the "*nureochiba* tribe" who are completely dependent on their wives,[6] or the "*washi* men,"[7] and so on. The present day really is the age of "men's issues!"

Men's studies, of course, has emerged in relation to the prior development of women's studies which was a discipline created by women who were seeking to construct a society where they would be able to more fully realize their potential through their own abilities, and, through this, lead richer, more fulfilled lives. Similarly, men's studies is best seen as research investigating men's lives which seeks to understand and alleviate the many problems faced by men in contemporary society. Nothing would make me happier than if this book were able to help men, and women concerned about their relationships with men, to become more aware of the troubled state of masculinity in contemporary Japanese society and, through helping them reflect on masculinity, change the way they think, feel and live so as to create more fulfilling lives.

Weak-kneed young men

Once, when we held a meeting for lecturers who were teaching women's studies and gender studies courses, a female lecturer remarked: "The number of male students and female students who attend my tutorials in gender studies are almost the same. It is easy for me to deal with female students because they have relatively strong critical minds. However, it is very difficult to deal with the male students who make up almost half of all tutorial groups because they do not have any special interest in women's studies. I think they chose this tutorial because the lecturer is a woman. That is, they probably expect me to play the role of mother. Therefore, when I make provocative remarks about the power and authority of men, they do not listen to me, although they do not contradict my opinions. Since they seem so feeble, I don't know how to deal with them." Many lecturers, especially female lecturers, agreed with her. Comments such as these were common: "Compared with men in the past, male students today seem quiet and their use of language is gentle, but there are many male students who cannot clearly state their own opinions;" "The number of male students who, instead of walking with a swagger, look weak-kneed, is increasing;" "Today's male students may seem more tenderhearted but their way of thinking is still male-oriented," etc.

I would like to state my opinion clearly so that readers will not misunderstand my purpose in describing the above scene. Women's studies – and men's studies which is emerging as a corresponding area of research – are often misunderstood as implying that the desirable types of men are those who are simply tenderhearted (at least I think so). Yet, this type of man who seems tenderhearted but is lacking in independence is criticized just as much as those men whose thoughts are typically male-oriented. What is really important – for both men and women – is that they are able to create equal relationships with others as independent individuals outside the traditional stereotypical models of masculinity or femininity. This is surely one of the primary goals of men's and women's studies.

In fact, I often hear that male students these days are somewhat effeminate and I tend to think so, too, when I am mixing with male students of this generation. Compared with students of the past, male students these days are taller and wear nicer clothes and there are relatively few who act like traditional masculine types or who walk with a swagger. Male students today are not stereotypically masculine in terms of their behavior or manners. After all, this is the era of so-called "young men who are tenderhearted." The emergence of popular phrases such as *"asshii-kun"* (young men who are used as a chauffeurs by young women), *"messhii-kun"* (young men who treat young women to meals at restaurants) and *"mitsugu-kun"* (young men who buy expensive gifts for women even if they are not their boyfriends), reflects the increase of tenderhearted young men. Yet, to what extent have young men's attitudes towards masculinity really changed?

Adherence to masculinity

As many lecturers have pointed out, despite the fact that young men these days may seem enervated and delicate, in terms of their mindset, they do not actually resonate with the "women's era" and have, in fact, changed their way of thinking very little. To illustrate this point, some years ago I conducted a questionnaire to determine whether respondents thought of themselves as a "masculine type" or a "feminine type" and the reasons why. The results were interesting. The majority of responses from female students went something like "I find the idea of femininity strange. I want to live as I am, and not according to some stereotypical notion of femininity." Of course, there were responses saying "I am feminine," but even in these cases, the majority of respondents stated that they understood the position of women in the current male-centered society and chose such a lifestyle of their own accord.

On the other hand, most male responses could be divided into two types with few exceptions. One set of responses went something like "I am a masculine type. I am tall. I have a male sexual organ. I am excited when I look at women." The other set of responses mentioned things like "I am not a masculine type because I am small. I have never been good at sports since I was a child. I am not physically strong." I was also impressed that many responses from female students were relatively long whereas most male responses were simply two or three lines.

I was impressed by the fact that, compared with the responses of male students, female students were able to see their gender conditioning more objectively. In contrast, both groups of male students, those who answered that they were masculine types and those who answered that they were not, showed that they had very conventional understandings of masculinity. They seemed unable to think of their masculinity in objective terms.

Although many male students may seem gentle, deep down they still hold to traditional stereotypes of masculinity, just as their fathers' generation did. That is, even though they look delicate, their ways of thinking are characteristic of a "masculine type." Evidence of this can be seen in the fact that the number of Japanese who accept the division of labor at home is much greater than other countries. For example, the recently released results of the fifth survey of "young people's thoughts in the world" conducted by the *Sōmuchō* (Prime Minister's Office), shows that the number of Japanese young people who agreed with the opinion that "men should work and women should stay at home" was the third largest, alongside Russia and the Philippines (although unlike the past dishonorable situation, Japan was no longer the top nation).[8] This result indicates that although Japanese society is one which emphasizes "equality between men and women" in public, the stereotypically sexist view that "boys should be masculine, girls should be feminine" is still largely accepted in practice.

The dilemma of being masculine

However, despite this situation, the general trend is definitely towards less acceptance of the division of labor. This decline is naturally linked to the increasing number of women who are participating in social movements worldwide and the changing ways of thinking among women which have taken place in the past 20 years. The view that "it is natural for women to participate in social movements" is shared by women of all generations. Indeed, the majority of my female students often express opinions in their essays such as, "I do not like radical feminism because it forces us to accept particular values, but I basically agree with what feminists have said." However, as I mentioned, male students are different. The majority of them agree with "equality between men and women" in theory while at the same time sticking to the notion that "men should work and women should stay at home" in everyday life.

The reason why this has happened is that despite the fact that social structures and values have changed rapidly in the last 20 years, and irrespective of the changes in women's thinking, men still tend to hold on to strongly stereotypical and sexist views of masculinity. While their fathers' generation could see "masculinity" reflected in their own image, the lifestyle of the sons' generation is no longer so stereotypically "masculine." Yet, despite this, young men are still attached to the traditional myth of masculinity. Another reason why the number of young men who seem weak-kneed and who cannot become independent has been increasing might be the formation of the so-called "*maza-kon*." This "mother complex" refers to young boys and men who have developed an Oedipus complex due to the strong ties between mothers and their sons. This complex was parodied in the very popular TV drama *Fuyuhiko-san* which depicted Fuyuhiko as a son who followed his mother's advice in everything even after he got married. Indeed, as scholars in the US who research men's studies often point out, such strong ties between mothers and sons are characteristic of situations where fathers are rarely at home. This tendency can be seen in many families in which husbands are salarymen who are workaholics and largely absent from the home. The problem is that, on the one hand, boys are ideologically conditioned to be masculine, whereas on the other hand, they have not had enough communication with masculine role models – particularly their fathers. The result is a mental condition in which boys do not develop sufficient self-confidence and they always feel vulnerable and anxious.

The 1990s – the era of men's studies

The social value of men seems to be slipping quite rapidly. For instance, in the past the majority of parents wanted to have sons but today the majority state they would prefer to have daughters.[9] Against this background it is not surprising that, as I predicted would happen, since the 1990s various media have started to debate men's issues. In particular, the number of magazines which feature articles on men's issues has been increasing. It was early in the summer of 1992 when the women's magazine *CREA* and the men's magazine *Monthly Playboy* started to feature articles on "men who have become weakened." Since then, *SPA*, *Jiyūjikan* (Free time) and *POPEYE* have frequently featured articles on issues such as "what is masculinity?" "men's liberation" and "gays." From 1994 to 1995, articles such as "respect women, scorn men" as opposed to the traditional adage "respect men, scorn women"[10] and "wives who are older than husbands" have been featured in young men's magazines such as *SPA*, *BART*, and so on. This trend can also be seen in magazines read by middle-aged men. Of particular interest is a series of articles which appeared in *Jitsugyō no Nihon* (Business Japan) in summer 1995, discussing "men who are excellent workers are also good at doing housework." These articles were described as "detailed housework manuals for men," offering advice on everything from doing the ironing to cooking *à la carte* dishes. Other men's magazines, too, have followed this lead. For example, since January 1996 *Men's EX*, which contains many photo spreads, has run a series entitled "supplementary lessons for men;" I myself was interviewed in an article entitled "an introduction to men's studies" for the first issue. Furthermore, manuals such as "cooking for men" and "housework for men" have been increasing in number. The trend in cooking advice has recently changed from the preparation of special luxurious meals to cooking everyday dishes.

Men in an aging society

An indication of the widespread attention being paid to men's problems is the fact that you now often hear of such events as workshops on men's lifestyles or men's studies being organized by various bodies. As one of a handful of men's studies' specialists in Japan, I get invitations to speak from every part of the country. Speaking from my experience, if you look at the men attending the seminars by generation, men in their fifties are the largest group. Speaking to them you realize that these men, who until recently had dedicated themselves to becoming "corporate beings" (*kaisha ningen*), as they approach retirement age, they start to reflect on the meaning of their lives as well as worrying and thinking about what their lives will be like after retirement. The reality is that the problems associated with the overall aging of society have much in common with problems associated with Japanese masculinity.

For instance, Hyogo Prefecture recently carried out an attitude survey of senior citizens living alone. According to the survey, the top-ranked concern for female seniors living alone was financial difficulty. However, for male seniors loneliness was the major concern. In addition to highlighting the loneliness faced by older men, the survey also revealed the problematic nature of relationship patterns between men and women in Japan. In other words, the financial difficulties faced by female senior citizens living on their own reflects the difficulties women face in achieving economic independence within a patriarchal society. At the same time, I believe that the loneliness faced by male seniors living on their own points to the fact that men, having thought of themselves as "work beings" (*shigoto ningen*) are unable to function effectively as "lifestyle beings" (*seikatsujin*). Sadly, after their wives pass away, few older men have anyone they are close to with whom they are able to communicate at a deeper, more personal level.

There is even more depressing data in relation to elderly men – this is data relating to the average life expectancy for men and women over 60 after the death of their spouse. The average life expectancy for men after their wives die is less than three years but for women whose husbands die, it is around 15 years. While a gap between men and women may be expected, given that the average longevity for women exceeds that of men by around six years, and given that in most cases the marriage age for men is higher, a difference of 12 years is still excessive. I believe that these statistics point to older men's dependence on their wives within the household as well as their lack of ability to function effectively as social beings.

It is in this context, then, of over-dependent, weak-kneed younger men and alienated, socially dysfunctional older men, that we can understand the need for increased study of and discussion about men's issues in contemporary Japan.

Notes

1 However, it should be noted that major researchers in masculinities studies writing in English, like R.W. Connell do mention his work.
2 The original translation was made by Noriko Hagiwara and it has been edited and revised by Mark McLelland and Romit Dasgupta.
3 The reference here is to the main character of a popular early 1990s' television serial, *Zutto anata ga suki datta* (I've always liked you). The central theme of the serial was the main character Fuyuhiko's pathological relationship of dependence on his mother. Following on from the serial, the term "Fuyuhiko syndrome/phenomenon" (*Fuyuhiko genshō*) came to be applied to describe excessively co-dependent mother/son relationships (known in Japanese as *maza-kon*).
4 This refers to a term originally deployed by Brian Gilmartin in a 1989 work, *The Shy-Man Syndrome*, to refer to men who lack the self-confidence and social skills to communicate and interact effectively with women, despite wanting to do so.
5 Sudden death caused through work-related stress, including excessively long working hours.
6 The expression "wet leaves" (*nure ochiba*), which cannot be swept away easily, was applied to men who after retirement found themselves completely dependent – emotionally and physically – on their wives. Unlike their wives who had led far more rounded, socially engaged, emotionally rich lives, these men had had few interests and networks outside their jobs and hence after retirement became a burden on their wives.
7 *Washi* is a term of self-address (corresponding to "me" or "I") associated with older men who often get a bad press for being stubborn, narrow-minded and dull.
8 "Japanese young people compared with those in the rest of the world," part of the fifth survey of the thoughts of young people conducted by the Youth Policy Centre, Management and Coordination Agency.
9 According to statistics published by the Prime Minister's Office in 1995 the percentage of parents hoping to have a boy fell from 52.1 percent in 1972 to 24.3 percent in 1992. Conversely, the share of those hoping for a baby girl rose from 19.2 percent to 75.7 percent over the same period.
10 This traditional slogan of male dominance was "*danson johi.*"

11 Rethinking Japanese masculinities
Recent research trends

Futoshi Taga

Introduction

This chapter presents an overview of some of the challenges facing Japanese men by outlining the history of the study of men and masculinities in Japan. As elsewhere, recent research into men and masculinities in Japan has had a twofold significance. First, in contrast to earlier gender research which tended to view men as a homogenous group and take manhood for granted, recent research has revealed both the diversity which exists among men as well as the constructed and unstable nature of men's gender identities. In addition, the results of this research into men and masculinities have prompted many men to rethink their taken-for-granted notions of manhood and take a more proactive stance in the construction of new forms of masculine identity and behavior.

Obviously the amount of material written about men in Japanese is considerable. Indeed, most studies which have been conducted on human society in the humanities and social sciences have in effect been studies about men since they have tended to take male experience as the human norm and have excluded women from consideration. However, these studies clearly fall outside of this chapter's focus. Also excluded from this chapter is a discussion of the growing body of material published on gay men's experience in Japan (see, for example, Vincent *et al.* 1997). Although important, gay studies in Japan have largely developed independently of heterosexual men's studies and since this material is explored by McLelland and Lunsing in this volume, I will not consider it here. I will also limit my discussion to the trends apparent in Japanese-language material since one of the main purposes of this volume is to introduce Japanese-language scholarship to English-speaking readers and, despite the translation into Japanese of a few key English texts, studies published in foreign languages do not seem to have had much *direct* influence on the growing field of men's studies in Japan so far. The main focus of this chapter will therefore be on those studies published in Japanese after the impact of *josei gaku* (women's studies) and which deliberately focus on men as gendered beings.

In this chapter I argue that the emergence of the study of masculinities in Japan is basically an indigenous development and not the result of direct Western influence. In the following sections I will first introduce some of the pioneering works on men and masculinities which were published during the groundbreaking decade of the 1980s, a period when men's issues were barely recognized as a field of study even among academics. I will then go on to look at the widespread social changes and the development of various men's groups which provide the background for this new research field. I will then look at the wider dissemination of *dansei gaku* (men's studies) and introduce some of the important findings of recent Japanese research on men and masculinities before finally making a few suggestions for the further development of the field.

The groundbreaking years

Before the 1990s in Japan "men's issues" were hardly ever taken up as a topic for inquiry by the academic community, let alone by the general public. Most research into gender issues (albeit the term "gender," in Japanese *jendā*, was not yet widespread) was undertaken by feminist researchers who identified gender studies with women's studies. At this time, the notion that "gender" might also be problematic for men was not widely discussed, although there were a few pioneering works published in the 1980s which were to serve as a basis for more critical reflections on men and masculinity in the next decade. Indeed, some pro-feminist men's groups had already emerged by the late 1970s. These included *Otoko no Kosodate wo Kangaeru Kai* (Group for considering men's child rearing)[1] and *Otoko mo Onna mo Ikuji Jikan wo Renraku Kai* (Network concerning child care hours for men and women),[2] established in 1978 and 1980 respectively. These organizations both advocated greater participation in housework and childcare for men. A few years later, in 1984, Murase Haruki published a book describing his experience as a househusband, but these developments hardly impacted on the majority of men at the time.

Despite the small number of men in the groups described above, it was generally female journalists and researchers who introduced debate about men and masculinities into the public realm. In the early 1980s, for instance, discussion of men's issues in the US was introduced to the Japanese press through the efforts of journalists such as Shimomura Mitsuko who translated *The Hazards of Being Male* (Goldberg 1976), a book which argued that masculinity was also a repressive force in the socialization of men. In her own book *Amerika no otokotachi wa ima* (American men at the moment; 1982), she also described the emergence of the men's movement and outlined the important issues facing American men at the time. Two years later, two other key texts were translated into Japanese – the *Dilemmas of Masculinity* (Komarovsky 1976) and the *Peter Pan Syndrome* (Kiley 1983), both of which portrayed the conflicts male youth were experiencing due to the rapidly changing nature of the US sex and gender system.

In the late 1980s, female researchers in Japan conducted some excellent empirical studies on the gender oppression and conflict experienced by men. Sekii (1989), for instance, employed quantitative psychological methods to reveal that the personality traits of individual men often did not match up with the social norms they were required to embody, and pointed out that the gap between individual inclination and social norms could result in a sense of oppression for many men. Kasuga (1989), too, portrayed the complex experience of different men within patriarchal society through her case study of a single-fathers' circle. She observed that the single fathers in her study were at a disadvantage both in the workplace and in the wider community because their parental role as primary caregivers and their single status failed to live up to normative gender expectations. This research led to the important discovery that patriarchal social institutions, which in general allow men to dominate women, are supported not only by the marginalization of women but also by the marginalization of other men who fail to embody hegemonic codes of masculine behavior.

While in the 1980s research into men's issues in Japan was mostly pioneered by women, male psychologist Watanabe Tsuneo described for the first time the creation of *dansei gaku* (men's studies) in his influential book *Datsu-dansei no jidai* (The age of deconstruction of men), published in 1986. Employing psychoanalytic theory in a case study of male transvestite associations, Watanabe problematized the manner in which modern society requires the repression of femininity in men and argued for the necessity of men's liberation and men's studies as a complement to women's liberation and women's studies. Although his argument was criticized by some feminists because of its blindness to power relations between the sexes (Ueno 1995), his book is thought to have had a strong impact on a large number of young activists and academics who are now working in the field of men and masculinities (Ōyama and Ōtsuka 1999). Watanabe went on to edit the first interdisciplinary collection of research into men and masculinities which included chapters by male and female researchers writing from a variety of perspectives, including sociology, psychoanalysis, sexology and anthropology (Watanabe 1989). Although his subsequent work has not exerted as much influence, he is widely recognized as the founder of the discipline of men's studies in Japan.

Also published in the 1980s were some other excellent works which indirectly focussed on issues concerning men and masculinities, such as Satō's (1984) ethnographic research into *bōsōzoku*.[3] However, despite their innovation, these studies were not understood to be *gender studies* texts at the time since the notion of "men's studies" had not yet taken hold in the Japanese academic community.

Social change and the burgeoning men's movement

If the 1980s in Japan can be described as a decade dedicated to women's issues, then the 1990s can be seen as the decade in which men's issues came to the fore (Itō 1996). Reasons for this are complex but social changes which began in Japan in the late 1980s began to challenge the previously secure and dominant lifestyles enjoyed by many men.

At least three conspicuous trends brought increased public attention to men's issues. First, new government policies began to undermine the legitimacy of chauvinistic male behavior and to impact on men's work-centered lifestyles. In 1985, the last year of the United Nation's Decade for Women, the Japanese government ratified The Convention for Elimination of All Forms of Discrimination against Women and started to develop laws aimed at realizing gender equity. The government enacted *Danjo koyō kikai kintō hō* (the law for equal employment for men and women) in 1985, further revising it in 1997 in order to prohibit sex discrimination more rigidly and to include sanctions against violations. In 1991 the *Ikuji kyōgyō hō* (child-care leave law) was enacted which allowed both male and female employees to take parental leave for up to one year after the birth of a child. However, the government's policy encouraging more men to participate in childcare was not simply aimed at promoting gender equity. Since 1975, Japan's total fertility rate (the average number of babies born to women during their reproductive years) has never exceeded 2.08 (the minimum necessary to avoid a decrease in population) and it fell to a low of 1.29 in 2003. The government, which takes the view that men's greater participation in childcare would reduce the burden on women and encourage them to bear more children, launched a poster and TV advertisement campaign in 1999 which attracted a lot of interest. The campaign featured Sam, the former husband of Japan's most popular female singer of the time, Amuro Namie, cradling his child and saying "A man isn't called father unless he takes part in childcare." This message had a great impact on many Japanese people who had previously assumed that the responsibility for the nurture of children was basically a woman's task.

During the 1990s, prefectural and municipal governments also began to run courses for men to help them rethink their lifestyles and social attitudes. According to research conducted by Amikas (formerly the Fukuoka Women's Center), from April 1993 to July 1995, the total number of such programs held all over Japan was 1,033 (Amikas 1995). One of the most famous of these early courses was *Dansei kaizō kōza* (Course to re-create men) held in Adachi-ku, Tokyo (Adachi-ku Josei Sōgō Sentā 1993). Another course held in Osaka from 1995 to 1996 included lectures and seminars on such topics as "rethinking work-oriented life," "men and violence," "the meaning of family for men," "developing self-expression" and "practical cooking" (Itō 1997). Now most of the public centers for gender equality promotion all over Japan organize such men's courses at least once a year either for free or at a moderate charge.

The second trend which brought men's issues to greater public consciousness was the economic recession and deteriorating employment conditions that followed the bursting of the "bubble economy." The recession began to threaten the material base of men's power and undermine their identity. According to the *Rōdōryoku chōsa* (labor force survey) which is conducted monthly by the government, though the unemployment rate was only around 2 percent in 1991, it rose to over 5 percent in 2001.[4] In addition, according to statistical data collected by the *Keisatsuchō* (national police agency), the number of suicides by men worried about work had increased. In 1998, when personnel downsizing went into full swing, the number of men's suicides per 100,000 in the population rose rapidly from 26 to 37 in one year, while that of women rose from 12 to 15. In 2002, suicides motivated by economic or occupational problems made up 49 percent of suicides among men whose motives were specified while the corresponding figure among women was only 14 percent.[5] These changes, alongside men having to take increased responsibilities for housework and childcare as more married women entered the workplace, resulted in the identity of the salaryman husband as sole breadwinner becoming more fragile.

A third trend which had a strong impact on men's lives was changes in the demographic make-up of Japanese society. According to estimates by the former *Kōseishō* (Ministry of Health and Welfare), the average life expectancy of Japanese men and women, which was 64 and 68 years respectively in 1955, had increased to 76 and 83 years by 1995.[6] This extension of the average lifespan brought a new problem of *daini no jinsei* (second life) to late-middle-aged men. Many men found that they experienced an excessive dependency on their wives during their long period of retirement because their previous over-identification with their careers had resulted in isolation from community networks and a complete lack of housework skills (Itō 1996: 55–74). One phrase which became popular in the 1990s was *teinen rikon* or "retirement-age divorce" – where a wife divorced her husband upon his retirement since she did not want to look after such a dependent partner. Indeed, the divorce rate among couples where the wives' age was over 50 increased from 2 percent in 1950 to 10 per cent in 1997 (Inoue and Ehara 1999: 17). Furthermore, a rapidly expanding elderly population together with a sharp decline in the birth rate has resulted in an increase in the number of middle-aged men who need to take care of aged parents or an infirm wife (Harris *et al.* 1998)

Against the background of these social changes, various discussions about men and their problems have surfaced since the early 1990s. One trend has been an appeal to men to change through the use of parody. This approach included a popular collection entitled *Dansei junan jidai* (The age of men's calamity; Ichikawa 1992) which features caricatures of a wide range of men including young men who cannot find a bride because of their social immaturity, middle-aged men who are afraid to come home because there is no "place" for them, and older men who have nothing to do after their retirement and consequently cling to their wives like *nure-ochiba* (wet leaves). Other books have criticized Japan's work-oriented society which produced these easily identifiable stereotypes and argued for a reappraisal of men's work culture (Ōsawa 1993; Kashima 1993). Some other male writers have looked at men's issues through a variety of men's narratives. Nakamura (1993), for instance, explored men's new lifestyles based on personal-advice columns in the newspapers and his own experience of nursing his wife. Toyoda (1997) questioned the pressure many men experienced to present themselves as manly through his own experience and the life histories of other young men. As a result of the growing debate about men's issues, a collection reviewing recent books about men was also published (Nakamura and Nakamura 1997).

These discussions created a trend toward the formation of more men's groups (Ōyama and Ōtsuka 1999). In 1991, one of the most influential groups, *Menzuribu Kenkyūkai* (Study group for men's liberation) was founded in the Kansai district around Osaka. This group has conducted regular consciousness-raising meetings every two months. Some of the members of this group established the Men's Center Japan in Osaka in 1995 (Menzusentā 1996). Dozens of similar groups have now sprung up in various regions in Japan (Menzusentā 2002). One of the characteristic features of Japanese men's groups has been that many were founded by former participants in the education courses run by municipal governments. One such example is *Passport* in Tokyo, founded in 1995 by former participants in *Dansei kaizō kōza* mentioned earlier. It seems that new groups are constantly being created while established ones split up or fall apart. Though the size of the groups is generally small (less than ten people in most cases), their activities and policies are often well known to individuals who are interested in gender issues through their bulletins and reports on their activities published on the Internet or in the mass media. Following a suggestion from the Men's Center, a regular *Otoko no fesutibaru* (men's festival) has been held since 1996, which is a national annual conference aiming to solve a variety of men's problems, and providing a venue for exchange between men's groups (Menzusentā 1997).[7]

Although some men's groups are indifferent to women's issues, the majority have not adopted the same anti-feminist stance as is conspicuous among some US men's groups. Despite the fact that backlash voices criticizing government policies supporting gender equality and advocating a return to "traditional" roles for men and women have become stronger since the turn of the century (Itō 2003a), these conservative opinions do not seem to have impacted upon men's groups so far. On the contrary, some men's groups have recently been involved in pro-feminist activities such as *Otoko no Arikata wo Tou Kai* (Group for rethinking the way of being a man) which organized a signature-collecting campaign demanding the resignation of Diet members who defended suspects in a gang-rape case in 2003.[8] Another example is White Ribbon Campaign Japan whose members asked the male candidates for the Upper House election in 2004 to sign an oath repudiating domestic violence and published the response of every candidate on the Internet.[9]

The establishment of men's studies

As a result of these various developments, the notion of men's studies had already gained prominence by the mid-1990s and *dansei-gaku* began to be referred to not only by academics but by people more generally. One effect of this heightened visibility was that men's issues increasingly began to be included in government-sponsored higher education courses and in the extracurricular adult education courses sponsored by local authorities.

Feminist thinkers also played an important role at this time in furthering the establishment of *dansei gaku*. For instance, when several of Japan's leading feminist theorists edited the seven-volume collection *Nihon no feminizumu* (Feminism in Japan), they included a volume dedicated to *dansei gaku* as an addendum (Inoue *et al.* 1995). Apart from Ueno Chizuko, one of the series editors who provided the Introduction, all the other contributors to the volume were Japanese men who had been influenced by feminist ideas. Though most of the essays reprinted in this volume were non-academic, they did raise issues that were also of interest in academic circles, including discussions of men's liberation, men's studies, sexuality, family and labor.

Rethinking Japanese masculinities 159

The most influential academic to emerge in the field of men's studies in the 1990s was Itō Kimio, a professor of sociology of Osaka University and one of the founding members of *Menzuribu Kenkyūkai* and the Men's Center Japan. Like some other pioneers of *dansei gaku*, Itō had had some connection with feminist activism in the 1970s and 1980s and was well informed about feminist scholarship. His writings therefore not only had an impact on men who were encouraged to rethink their lifestyles but were also widely accepted by feminist scholars. Itō is important because he contributed to the establishment and dissemination of *dansei gaku* both within and outside the academy. It is reported that Itō taught the first *dansei gaku* class in Japan in Kyoto University in 1992 (Itō 1996). The number of such courses has rapidly increased; according to the *Kokuritsu Josei Kyōiku Kaikan*'s (National Women's Eduation Center, Japan) database, 2,068 classes related to the topic of gender were taught in 531 colleges and universities all over Japan in 2002, and of this number, 61 classes were related to *dansei gaku*.[10]

By the late 1990s, *dansei gaku* had come to be seen as a legitimate research field by the academic community. In 1998, for instance, a substantial men's studies panel was held at a conference of the Japan Sociological Society for the first time; chaired by Itō Kimio, the panel included five male researchers, myself among them. The presentations included the methodology of men's studies, the gender formation of men, men who were poor performers in sport, the sexuality of disabled men and the history of the Japanese men's movement. In response to such developments, by 2000 the Japan Sociological Society and other relevant bodies were including *dansei gaku* as one of the key terms for gender studies papers in their indexes. Today, the term *dansei gaku* is mentioned as a key term in the list of research fields for scientific research grants offered by the Japanese government.[11]

As mentioned above, *dansei gaku* has developed not only as an academic field but also as a range of practical approaches for those interested in understanding men's problems (and gender issues in general) and in working out ways to solve them. Consequently, *dansei gaku* is now recognized as important by the wider community. After Itō published his *Dansei gaku nyūmon* (Introduction to men's studies) which outlined in simple terms the basics of men's studies and men's issues for non-academic readers (Itō 1996), the term *dansei gaku* and the topics associated with it were adopted by the adult education courses run by prefectural and municipal councils. In 2003, a serial course on men's studies aimed at a mainstream audience was aired on TV for the first time by NHK's educational channel. Entitled *Otokorashisa to iu shinwa* (The myth of "manliness"), the series featured eight lectures by Itō about the social construction of masculinities and men's issues in contemporary Japan (Itō 2003b).

Recent expansion of research on men and masculinities

Given the now widespread dissemination of the term *dansei gaku* and the increased public scrutiny of men's issues, there has been an exponential increase in the number of studies dedicated to Japanese masculinity since the end of the 1990s. A characteristic of these more recent works has been a change in focus from "men" to "masculinity," the adoption of a social constructionist position and the deployment of more qualitative methodologies such as representative analysis and ethnography. More researchers have brought not only "hegemonic masculinity" but also "subordinated" and "marginalized" masculinities (Connell 1995) into view, along with an increased focus on men's private lives, sexuality and violence. The range of disciplines where this kind of research is carried out has expanded from sociology to such fields as geography, history, anthropology and literary criticism.

Some of this recent research has paid attention to dominant forms of masculinity. Osa (1999), for instance, looked at the modernization of Japanese masculinity through an analysis of portraits of the Meiji Emperor, Mutsuhito, and his family. Following the Meiji Restoration of 1868, the Emperor was suddenly cast as a politician and military leader despite the fact that under the previous regime he had been regarded as an effete noble and exercised little political power. In photographs taken during the Restoration year, Mutsuhito still appears an androgynous figure, dressed in traditional court costume because at that point in time it was more important that his nobility, as opposed to his masculinity, be stressed. However, in a portrait painted in 1888, he was depicted in a style which was used to confer dignity on European monarchs in the nineteenth century – he appears sitting on a chair bearing a sword, and wearing Western ceremonial military dress, with moustache, beard and thick eyebrows. As head of state, the Emperor's masculinity was increasingly emphasized from this point on. While female Empresses had succeeded to the throne in their own right in the past, the Imperial Constitution of 1889 specifically restricted the succession to male descendants and the Empress was reconfigured as an auxiliary support for the Emperor rather than as a political figure in her own right. By 1905, images of the Imperial family in the press clearly represent the Emperor as husband and father.

After Japan's defeat in World War II, the hegemonic depiction of Japanese masculinity underwent various transformations. The Emperor was stripped of political power and the Constitution redefined him as a symbol of the unity of the Japanese people. During Japan's period of high economic growth starting in the 1950s, the figure of the "salaryman" emerged as the hegemonic depiction of Japanese masculinity (Dasgupta 2000; see also Chapter 12 this volume). Through an analysis of articles in postwar Japanese newspapers, Okamoto and Sasano (2001) have outlined the changes which took place in depictions of the salaryman. At the beginning of the postwar economic boom of the 1950s, the term salaryman signified any person (including women) who received a salary from employment. In the latter half of the 1960s, however, salaryman began to be used to refer to a majority of all adult male workers and the salaryman was represented as a good breadwinner and taxpayer. In the recession following the oil crisis in the early 1970s, while the gendered division of labor in the home was highlighted, the salaryman was also expected to go straight home after work and perform *kazoku sābisu* (family service), that is, spend time with his family on weekends and holidays. In the bubble economy years during the first half of the 1980s when many male employees worked long and hard, more articles began to depict the negative side of a salaryman's life, such as his heavy tax burden and the repression of individuality demanded by corporate life. Since the 1990s, these so-called "traditional" images of the salaryman, which actually became normative only during the period of high economic growth, have been problematized.

Research on family life in Japan has long included analysis of men as husbands and fathers but as the gendered division of labor has recently been reexamined, men's roles in the family and the community more generally have come under the spotlight. Indeed, more recent studies on the family have begun to focus on the husband/father rather than the wife/mother. Research on fatherhood began to look not only at men's socializing role but also at the self-development of fathers through parenting (Kashiwagi 1993; Makino et al. 1996). In addition, in response to the increasing numbers of men who are required by circumstance to care for their elderly parents, other research has been conducted into the problems faced by such male caregivers (Kasuga 1999). Regarding men's lives after retirement, Yamato (1996) conducted research into possible remedies for men's poor social networking, and discovered that the more men took part in housework and community activities in middle age, the wider were the social networks they could tap into in old age. In an empirical sociological investigation into how men could strike a better balance between work and family life commissioned by the Tokyo Metropolitan Women's Foundation (1998), it was found that although the majority of men strived to keep a balance between work and family life in theory, they were forced to live work-centered lives in practice. The report's conclusion called for government initiatives to ensure better working conditions in which the performance of domestic labor by men would not be prejudicial to their chances of promotion.

Given the widespread changes in notions of masculinity taking place in contemporary Japan, recent research has shown that adolescent males in particular are experiencing difficulty in forming adult masculine identities. Based on life history interviews of 23 middle-class young men, I explored the types of conflicts that arose regarding masculinity and how my informants reacted to these conflicts (Taga 2001, 2003). Various types of conflict were reported by informants. Some wondered how both paid work and housework should be divided between husband and wife, and/or questioned the validity of male dominance over women while others were required to rethink "traditional" gender relations because they fell in love with career-oriented women. The manner in which informants dealt with their conflicts was also varied. Some responded by changing their sexist views to anti-sexist ones, thus managing to maintain relationships with career-oriented girlfriends, while some tried to ignore the conflicts by postponing thinking about such issues until they were approaching marriage or in steady relationships. Others avoided such conflicts altogether by choosing a wife who shared the man's own sexist beliefs. In this way, a considerable number of informants were engaged in reappraising "traditional" notions of masculinity. Despite being required to engage with changing ideas about masculine identity, however, most informants took it for granted that they would seek a permanent job, get married to a woman and have children at some point in the future. For these young men, the meaning of "becoming a man" seemed to be fundamentally unchanged (see also Dasgupta, Chapter 12 this volume).

While much research has looked at dominant forms of masculinity, some researchers have developed unique approaches toward the construction of subordinated forms of masculinity. Based on interviews with men who consider themselves to be *hage* or bald, Sunaga (1999) argues that the interaction between a "bald man" and the people who deride him contributes to the reproduction of dominant images of masculinity. In Japan, while young men have become more invested in their appearance (Miller 2003), the notion that men should not be overly concerned with looks is still prevalent. Hence, most bald men think that there is no solution other than to put up with the taunting, because, if they tried to conceal their baldness or reacted with anger, they would be perceived as unmasculine.

Another unique investigation of subordinated Japanese masculinity is Ukai's (1999) case study of "train-spotters," a predominately male subculture of train fanatics who spend their leisure time seeking out and taking pictures of (especially rare) trains, and collecting train-related goods such as tickets and registration plates. Conventionally, train-spotters are regarded as being alienated from the workplace, the family, normal dress codes and relationships with women and consequently often face ridicule. However, despite failing in mainstream society, within their own circles these men are highly competitive about their knowledge of trains and the collection of train goods. Ukai suggests that such men have retreated from the competition for hegemonic masculinity in the wider social context and are instead pursuing masculine status within a more localized context.

Though most studies of men's sexuality have so far focused on homosexuality (see discussions by Lunsing and McLelland (Chapters 6 and 7 in this volume), studies which investigate the sexual attitudes and behavior of heterosexual men are increasing. One unique project is Shibuya's (2003) historical research tracing the changing attitudes toward male virginity through the twentieth century in Japan. In the 1920s, elite students and some intellectuals thought that being a virgin before marriage was of great worth not only for women but also for men. In the 1960s, however, some tabloid magazines lamented that the number of male virgins was increasing while the number of female virgins was on the decline and by the 1970s the discourse regarding male virginity as a failure of masculinity became dominant.

There are also numerous studies which look at masculinities in relation to violence. At a time when the Japanese public is paying more attention to the problems of domestic violence, Nakamura (2001) has investigated the background and the behavior of batterers and introduced a program of violence prevention for men based on Western psychological research and his own experience in a citizen's group.

Apart from the development of psychological research on sex differences and sex roles (Sugihara and Katsurada 1999), most studies on men and masculinities have so far been concentrated in the field of sociology. However, recently we can see signs of interest in other disciplines. Within the discipline of geography, Murata (2000) explores the alienation felt by subaltern categories of men based on interviews with middle-aged single men. His research also explores the meaning of masculinity in the context of differing public spaces and in terms of sexuality (Murata 2002). Other studies have taken a historical approach to masculinities. One excellent example of this type of work is Kaizuma's (2004) research into disputes about fatherhood in the early twentieth century. She reveals that Japan's modern understanding of fatherhood was by no means homogenous but included a variety of positions, some of which were based on a clear division of labor while other views argued for fathers' contribution to housework and/or criticized the gendered division of labor.

Conclusion

As outlined above, research on men and masculinities in Japan has been expanding rapidly. The number of studies and the range of the literature in this field in Japan are far ahead of studies in other Asian languages and compare favorably with many European countries. Despite the parallel rise in prominence in men's studies in Western societies, it seems that Japanese men's studies has been developing not only through the direct translation and import of Western men's studies but also largely in response to widespread social changes taking place in Japan itself. The results of the research speak volumes about the challenges facing many Japanese men and the plurality and instability of Japanese men's identities. In conclusion, I would like to make a few suggestions about how research on Japanese men and masculinities might develop.

First, through rereading the vast number of already extant studies on Japan in terms of masculinity, we will be able to reassess this information in the light of new gender theories. Given that most studies of Japanese society prior to the advent of women's studies were, by default, "studies on men," this material will surely lend itself to the study of masculinity. For example, Ueno (1995) points out that although public discourses such as politics and the economy have been seen as gender-neutral, they have in effect been a male realm and women have often been systematically eliminated from these spaces.

Second, we should look at more diverse types of masculinity in Japan. Despite the increased attention being paid to the plurality of men and masculinities, the subjects of most studies (especially those written in Japanese) have tended to be drawn from a narrow demographic base – urban adults from middle-class background. For a more detailed understanding of Japanese masculinities, further research into rural areas, male childhood and working-class conditions needs to be undertaken.

Finally, the establishment of a more productive dialogue with feminism is desirable. There have been some feminist critiques of *dansei gaku* such as Shibuya (2001) who points out that *dansei gaku* has a tendency to focus on personal issues or on the relations between plural masculinities and has failed to locate men in wider patriarchal-institutional contexts, and therefore contributes to the maintenance of existing power relations between the sexes. If *dansei gaku* is really interested in contributing to greater gender equity, then the discipline should be open to such criticism. On the other hand, excessive emphasis on the "institutionalized privilege" of men as a group over women as a group easily leads to essentialism, and can make "the costs of masculinity" and "differences and inequalities among men" (Messner 1997) less visible. Hence, for a more detailed understanding of gender relations in Japan, it is necessary to pay greater attention to the theoretical links between feminism and the findings from *dansei gaku*.

Notes

1 Details about the *Otoko no Kosodate wo Kangaeru Kai* are available online: http://homepage2.nifty.com/otokono-kosodate/hyoshi.html (accessed 12 July 2004).
2 Details about the *Otoko mo Onna mo Ikuji-jikan wo Renraku Kai* are available online: http://www.eqg.org/ (accessed 12 July 2004).
3 *Bōsōzoku* are groups of young men (and sometimes women) who show off their *bōsō* driving (driving automobiles and motorcycles at breakneck speed with loud noise). See Satō (1991) for more details.
4 The statistics are available online: http://www.stat.go.jp/data/roudou/ (accessed 12 July 2004).
5 The statistics are available online: http://www.npa.go.jp/toukei/index.htm (accessed 12 July 2004).
6 Trends of life expectancy at birth are available online: http://www.mhlw.go.jp/english/index.html (accessed 12 July 2004).
7 Details about *Menzuribu Kenkyūkai*, the Men's Center Japan and the *Otoko no festibaru* are available online: http://homepage2.nifty.com/akira-na/ (accessed 12 July 2004).
8 Details about the *Otoko no Arikata wo Tou Kai* are available online: http://www.thinking-men.jp/ (accessed 12 July 2004).
9 Details about the White Ribbon Campaign Japan are available online: http://www.bouryokudame.org/ (accessed 12 July 2004).
10 The database is available online: http://www.nwec.jp/ (accessed 12 July 2004).
11 Researchers are not always in agreement about what this emerging field should be called. While the field has generally been called in Japanese *dansei-gaku*, it is also sometimes called *dansei-kenkyū* (research on men) or *danseisei-kenkyū* (research on masculinity).

References

Adachi-ku Josei Sōgō Sentā. (1993) *Dansei kaizō kōza* (Seminar for changing men), Tokyo: Domesu Shuppan.
Amikas. (1995) *Heisei 7 nendo danseimondai-kōza jisshi-jōkyō hōkokusho* (Report on the condition of courses about men's issues in 1995), Fukuoka: privately published.
Connell, R. W. (1995) *Masculinities*, Cambridge: Polity Press.
Dasgupta, R. (2000) "Performing masculinities? The 'salaryman' at work and play," *Japanese Studies*, 20(2): 189–200.
Goldberg, H. (1976) *The Hazards of Being Male: Surviving the Myth of Masculine Privilege*, New York: Signet.
Harris, P. B., S. O. Long and M. Fujii (1998) "Men and elder care in Japan: a ripple of change," *Journal of Cross-Cultural Gerontology*, 13: 177–198.
Ichikawa, K. (ed.) (1992) *Dansei junan jidai: menzuribu kara hyūmanribu e* (The age of men's calamity: from men's liberation to human liberation), Tokyo: Shibundō.
Inoue, T. and Y. Ehara (eds). (1999) *Josei no dēta bukku: dai san pan* (Women's data book: third edition), Tokyo: Yuhikaku.

Inoue, T., C. Ueno and Y. Ehara (eds). (1995) *Dansei-gaku* (Men's studies), Tokyo: Iwanami Shoten.

Itō, K. (2003a) *Danjo-kyōdō-sankaku ga toikakeru mono* (What gender-equal policy problematizes), Tokyo: Inpakuto Shuppankai.

—— (2003b) *Otokorashisa toiu shinwa* (The myth of manliness), Tokyo: Nippon Hōsō Kyōkai Shuppankai.

—— (1997) "Dansei taishō no jendā kōza no genjō to kadai" (The present situation and the tasks of courses teaching gender issues for men), *Kokuritsu Fujin Kyōiku Kaikan Kenkyū Kiyō*, 1: 77–88.

—— (1996) *Dansei-gaku nyūmon* (Introduction to men's studies), Tokyo: Sakuhinsha.

—— (1993) *Otokorashisa no yukue* (How masculinity is changing), Tokyo: Shin'yōsha.

Kaizuma, K. (2004) *Kindai Nihon no fuseiron to jendā poritikusu* (The dispute on paternity in modern Japan and gender politics), Tokyo: Sakhuhinsha.

Kashima, T. (1993) *Otoko no zahyōjiku: kigyō kara katei shakai e* (The configuration of men: from business to home and community), Tokyo: Iwanami Shoten.

Kashiwagi, K. (ed.) (1993) *Chichioya no hattatsu-shinrigaku* (Development psychology of the father), Tokyo: Kawashima Shoten.

Kasuga, K. (1999) "Dansei kea-wākā no kanōsei" (The possibility of male carers), in Y. Nisikawa and M. Ogino (eds) *Kyōdō-kenkyū dansei-ron* (Discussions about men: a collaboration), Kyoto: Jinbun Shoin.

—— (1989) *Fushikatei wo ikiru: otoko to oya no aida* (The single-father's family: living as a man and a parent), Tokyo: Keisō Shobō.

Kiley, D. (1983) *The Peter Pan Syndrome: Men Who Have Never Grown Up*, New York: Dodd Mead.

Komarovsky, M. (1976) *Dilemmas of Masculinity: A Study of College Youth*, New York: W. W. Norton & Company, Inc.

Makino, K., Y. Nakano and K. Kashiwagi (eds) (1996) *Kodomo no hattatsu to chichioya no yakuwari* (Child development and father's role), Kyoto: Mineruva Shobō.

Menzusentā. (2002) *Dansei gurūpu ichiran* (List of men's groups), Osaka: privately published.

—— (1997) *Otokotachi no watashisagashi* (How are men seeking their new selves?), Kyoto: Kamogawa Shuppan.

—— (1996) *Otokorashisa kara jibunrashisa e* (From manliness to selfness), Kyoto: Kamogawa Shuppan.

Messner, A. M. (1997) *Politics of Masculinities: Men in Movements*, Thousand Oaks, CA: Sage Publications.

Miller, L. (2003) "Male beauty work in Japan," in J. E. Roberson and N. Suzuki (eds) *Men and Masculinities in Contemporary Japan: Dislocating the Salaryman Doxa*, London: RoutledgeCurzon.

Murase, H. (1984) *Kaiketsu hausu hazubando* (House-husband the hero), Tokyo: Shōbunsha.

Murata, Y. (2002) "Nihon no kōkyō-kūkan ni okeru 'dansei' toiu seibetsu no imi" (The meanings of "maleness" in the public space in Japan), *Chirigaku Hyōron*, 75(13): 813–830.

—— (2000) "Chūnen singuru dansei wo sogai suru basho" (Places where middle-aged single men are alienated), *Jinbunchiri*, 52(6): 533–551.

Nakamura, A. (1993) *Watashi no dansei-gaku: jinsei-sōdan ni miru ie-ishiki* (My men's studies: the Japanese traditional family system seen in personal-advice columns), Tokyo: Kindai Bungeisha.

Nakamura, A. and T. Nakamura (eds). (1997) *Otoko ga mietekuru jibunsagashi no hyakusatsu* (One hundred books for self-exploration of men), Kyoto: Kamogawa Shuppan.
Nakamura, T. (2001) *Domesutikku baiorensu to kazoku no byōri* (Domestic violence and familial pathology), Tokyo: Sakuhinsha.
Nishikawa, Y. and M. Ogino (eds). (1999) *Kyōdō-kenkyū dansei-ron* (Discussions about men: a collaboration), Kyoto: Jinbun Shoin.
Numazaki, I. (2002) *Naze otoko wa bōryoku wo erabu no ka: domesutikku baiorensu rikai no shoho* (Why men choose violence: introduction to the understanding of domestic violence), Kyoto: Kamogawa Shuppan.
Okamoto, T. and E. Sasano. (2001) "Sengo Nihon no 'sarariiman' hyōshō no henka" (Changes in representations of "salaried men" in postwar Japanese newspapers), *Shakaigaku Hyōron*, 52(1): 16–32.
Osa, S. (1999) "Tenshi no jendā: kindai tennō-zō ni miru otokorashisa" (The Emperor's gender: masculinity in the image of the modern Emperor), in Y. Nisikawa and M. Ogino (eds) *Kyōdō-kenkyū dansei-ron* (Discussions about men: a collaboration), Kyoto: Jinbun Shoin.
Ōsawa, M. (1993) *Kigyō-chushin-shakai wo koete: gendai Nihon wo jendā de yomu* (Beyond the company-centered society: looking at contemporary Japan in terms of gender), Tokyo: Jijitsūshinsha.
Ōyama, H. and T. Ōtsuka. (1999) "Nihon no dansei undō no ayumi 1: menzuribu no tanjō" (On the history of men's movements in Japan 1: the birth of the *menzuribu* movement), *Nihon Jendā Kenkyū* (Japanese Journal of Gender Studies), 2: 43–55.
Satō, I. (1991) *Kamikaze Biker: Parody and Anomie in Affluent Japan*, Chicago: The University of Chicago Press.
—— (1984) *Bōsōzoku no esunogurafii* (The ethnography on *bōsōzoku*), Tokyo: Shinyōsha.
Sekii, T. (1989) "'Danseisei' ni kansuru jisshōteki kenkyū," *Kazoku Kenkyū Nenpō*, 15: 65–83.
Shibuya, T. (2003) *Nihon no dōtei* (The male virgin in Japan), Tokyo: Bungeishunjū.
—— (2001) "Feminisuto dansei-kenkyū no shiten to kōzō" (A view and vision of feminist studies on men), *Shakaigaku Hyōron*, 51(4): 447–463.
Shimomura, M. (1982) *Amerika no otokotachi wa ima* (American men at the moment), Tokyo: Asahi Shinbunsha.
Sugihara, Y. and E. Katsurada. (1999) "Masculinity and femininity in Japanese culture: a pilot study", *Sex Roles*, 40(7/8): 635–646.
Sunaga, F. (1999) *Hage wo ikiru* (Getting through hairlessness), Tokyo: Keisō Shobō.
Taga, F. (2003) "Rethinking male socialization: life histories of Japanese male youth," in K. Louie and M. Low (eds) *Asian Masculinities: The Meaning and Practice of Manhood in China and Japan*, London: RoutledgeCurzon.
—— (2001) *Dansei no jendā keisei: otokorashisa no yuragi no naka de* (The gender formation of men: uncertain masculinity), Tokyo: Tōyōkan Shuppansha.
Tokyo Metropolitan Women's Foundation. (1998) *Dansei no jiritsu to sono jōken wo meguru kenkyū: dankai sedai wo chūshin ni* (A study on men's independence and its condition: around the baby-boomers), Tokyo: privately published.
Toyoda, M. (1997) *Otoko ga "otokorashisa" wo suteru toki* (When men discard "manliness"), Tokyo: Asuka Shinsha.
Ueno, C. (1995) "'Oyaji' ni naritakunai kimi no tame no menzuribu no susume" (The recommendation of men's liberation for those who do not want to be *oyaji*), in T. Inoue, C. Ueno, and Y. Ehara (eds) *Dansei-gaku* (Men's studies), Tokyo: Iwanami Shoten.

Ukai, M. (1999) "Tetsudō Mania no Kōgengaku" (Ethnography of train-spotters), in Y. Nishikawa and M. Ogino (eds) *Kyōdō-kenkyū dansei-ron* (Discussions about men: a collaboration), Kyoto: Jinbun Shoin.

Vincent, K., T. Kazama and K. Kawaguchi (1997) *Gei sutadiizu* (Gay studies), Tokyo: Seidosha.

Watanabe, T. (ed.). (1989) *Danseigaku no chōsen: Y no higeki* (The challenge of men's studies: the tragedy of Y), Tokyo: Shin'yōsha.

—— (1986) *Datsu dansei no jidai: andorojinasu wo mezasu bunmeigaku* (The age of deconstruction of men: the study of civilization toward androgyny), Tokyo: Keisō Shobō.

Yamato, R. (1996) "Chūkōnen dansei ni okeru sapōto nettowāku to 'musubitsuki shikō' yakuwari to no kankei" (The relationship between support networks and "connectedness-oriented" roles in late-middle-aged Japanese men: from the viewpoint of gender role), *Shakaigaku Hyōron*, 47(3): 350–365.

12 Salarymen doing straight

Heterosexual men and the dynamics of gender conformity

Romit Dasgupta

Introduction

As many of the chapters in this volume have shown, the visibility of non-dominant and non-hegemonic modes of gender and sexual practice in Japan has recently increased. These chapters also draw attention to the richness and diversity which have *always* been a part of the gender and sexual landscape in Japan. Yet, while it is vital that we continue to draw attention to this diversity and multiplicity, nevertheless, as Chapters 7 and 10 in this volume by McLelland and Itō show, hegemonic expectations about gender and sexuality are a real concern for many Japanese. Thus, in order to fully appreciate the shifts occurring in the contours of gender and sexual ideology and practice, we also need to examine and explore the dynamics that operate *within* hegemonic discourses and ideologies of gender and sexuality.

This chapter seeks to draw attention to some of the dynamics informing the day-to-day operation of hegemonic masculinity.[1] Specifically, it looks at the ways in which individual men negotiate with the hegemonic cultural ideal of the man as husband, father, and provider. This cultural ideal has traditionally been embodied in the image of the *daikokubashira* – literally the central supporting pillar of a house, but applied metonymically to the male breadwinner "supporting" the household (Gill 2003: 144, 245). I show in this chapter that despite the increased visibility in recent years of alternative lifestyle options for men (see Taga, Chapter 11 in this volume), this hegemonic cultural ideal premised on a specific gender ideology of *regulated* heterosexuality is still firmly entrenched, and continues to exert a powerful influence on the lives of *all* men, regardless of whether or not they fit into the category of husband, father, and provider. However, at the same time, it is through engagements between individual men and the expectations of hegemonic masculinity, that the contours of hegemonic masculinity get shaped and re-shaped. These engagements may involve dynamics of active resistance or subversion, such as the strategies adopted by the gay salarymen McLelland discusses in Chapter 7. However, even men close to the "center" in terms of hegemonic masculinity may also affect the contours of the discourse while ostensibly *conforming* to the cultural ideals. In a different way, their negotiations with hegemonic expectations may be just as complex and nuanced, as those engaged in by men on the "margins" of hegemonic masculinity. Thus, in order to fully understand the range of gendered and sexual practice, there is a need to investigate the complexities of *conformity* to hegemonic expectations as well as the complexities of dissent.

In discussing these issues, I will be drawing upon fieldwork conducted in the late 1990s. My research focused on the ways in which a particular discourse of masculinity embodied in the responsible, married, white-collar salaryman emerged as the hegemonic form of masculinity over the postwar decades. Specifically, I explored the ways in which young men who had recently entered the workforce negotiated the sometimes complex transition from a discourse of non-productive, pre-*shakaijin* (literally, "social person," but more generally, "responsible, adult member of society") student masculinity, to an adult "socially responsible" *shakaijin* masculinity, as embodied in the white-collar salaryman. Most of my informants were employees of one of two private sector organizations in a prefecture in northern Japan. One of the organizations, Northern Energy, was a large-scale corporation in the energy sector, with a workforce of several thousand employees. The second organization, Northern Print, was a medium–small firm (*chūshō kigyō*) in the printing industry, based in a medium-sized regional city.[2] In this chapter, I will draw upon the voices of informants and explore the ways in which the cultural ideals of hegemonic masculinity – the man as provider, husband, and father – have shaped their sense of being a salaryman *and* being a man. It is through these voices that we can get an appreciation of the day-to-day operation of the dynamics of gender *conformity* in contemporary Japan.

Masculinity defined through work: the *daikokubashira*

An appropriate way to introduce the voices of my informants is to explore the ways in which they conceptualize the role of work in defining their sense of masculine self-identity. This is of particular significance given the various socio-economic and cultural shifts in recent years which have contributed to the unraveling of the work/masculinity nexus. These forces include the ongoing economic slowdown which has resulted in spiraling unemployment rates among younger men (in the 15–24 age bracket) and middle-aged men (in the 45–54 age bracket). For instance, whereas the unemployment rate for men in the former age cohort had been 4.5 percent in 1990, by 2002 this had climbed to 11.1 percent. Similarly, the unemployment rate for middle-aged men rose from 1.1 percent in 1990 to 4.3 percent in 2002 (Japan Institute of Labor 2003: 22). There appear to be two interrelated fallouts from these shifts. First, large numbers of middle-aged men who had come of age during the high economic growth years of the 1960s and who had largely assumed that the compensation for their dedication and self-sacrifice would be guaranteed lifetime employment were unexpectedly faced with the possibility of retrenchment. Given the extent to which most salarymen identified with the corporate culture, this called into question their self-worth as *men*. Such instability has resulted in a growing awareness of the constructedness of masculinity and the increasing visibility of men's studies and men's support groups as discussed by Itō and Taga in Chapters 10 and 11 in this volume (see also Roberson and Suzuki 2003).

Second, among younger men, responses include circumventing or even actively resisting the ideological assumptions underpinning the man as *daikokubashira* model. A manifestation of this trend is the increase in the numbers of younger men (supposedly) not interested in finding regular, full-time work, who are opting instead to work as "freeters" (from the Japanese *furiitā*) and undertaking casual or contract work for hourly wages rather than regular salaries. The number of male freeters increased from less than 200,000 in the late 1980s to close to 400,000 in 1997 (Odani 2001: 24).

Yet, important as these shifts may be, it is necessary to recognize the persistence of the ideology which defines and determines hegemonic masculinity primarily through work. This was clearly expressed by my informants when, during the initial focus group interviews, I asked them to talk about the significance of "work" in their lives. The following range of responses provides a sample of the views expressed:

> I'd say I have an image of what you'd call a *daikokubashira* working diligently to support a family.

> Well ... in this day and age, I think "work" still ... occupies a big part in a man. There's the consideration of how this will change in the future. But for now ... I think work is probably by and large the main thing ... I think work occupies a big part of myself.

> Of course I think work's important, but I think men, in contrast to women, need to support, financially as well as mentally, their families, or else women. Of course I think there are areas where men are given support by women, but I personally think men should be the mainstay.

> At the point I joined this organization ... I expected to continue in this job for life; and thought I'd get married, and after a child was born, on the salary I receive, would support a family; that was my thinking. And, since now that I'm married and have a family, I still think that.

This sample of voices would appear to reinforce the dominant paradigm of work being almost unconsciously accepted as pivotal to a man's sense of being male. This notion of masculinity being inextricably bound to work came through even more sharply in individual interviews with my informants. Ogasawara Takurō, a 25-year-old Northern Energy employee, best summed up this connection between work and masculinity when he told me that the time he "most felt his 'masculinity'" was when he had successfully accomplished a task at work. Elsewhere, talking about a particularly challenging project which he had successfully completed, he talked about the sense of strength or empowerment he had gained: "Once I was able to finish it, naturally, how do you say it ... I was able to gain confidence in myself? I achieved the ability to say to myself that 'No way am I going to lose'."

While this statement does not specifically mention *masculinity*, given his prior statement about the significance of work in constructions of masculinity, it would be hard not to see the underlying extension of this sense of achievement to his own *masculine* self-esteem. Indeed, what best summed up the centrality of work to his sense of masculine self-esteem was his explicit condemnation of men who did not work: "the [kind of] man I dislike is someone who doesn't work and . . . pays no attention to his household – his own family."

This statement summed up the sentiments of many of my informants regarding the "fundamental" qualification for *shakaijin* masculinity – becoming a *daikokubashira*, that is, supporting and looking after a family.

This kind of sentiment – almost the antithesis of what "freeter" masculinity is seen as signifying – came through in my discussions with another Northern Energy employee, 30-year-old Murayama Satoshi who worked in the General Affairs (*sōmu*) section of the organization's Head Office. During the course of our interview, the discussion turned to the question of whether he thought he would have been a different person had he not been in his present job, or if he was not working. The thought of not working (being unemployed) did not sit comfortably with him.

> [I]f I didn't have a job, just thinking about a situation when I may not have a job is scary! . . .
>
> [*in response to my question "why?"*] It's frightening . . . it's like you become an animal which can't hunt/find its food. Because an animal which can't get its own food, at that point, probably, within the animal kingdom that signifies death.

Earlier in our discussion he had noted with disapproval what he labeled his younger brother's "lax/cheap" lifestyle. His brother had apparently "drifted" through university and had not been able to graduate even after eight years! At the time of our interview the brother had just found a job. Elsewhere, Murayama-san expressed his disapproval of unemployed men "who hang around the Labor Exchange and get an allowance, and use that to live or go off and do things like play *pachinko*." This led me to again ask him what he would do if, in his forties or fifties, he was suddenly laid off. The ensuing exchange between us conveys the importance of the concept of *work*, any kind of work, being crucial to this informant's self-worth as a man:

Murayama (M): If I'm laid off, umm, ah, you mean if I'm told not to come in to work from tomorrow?
Romit (R): Yes.
M: In that case, I'd think that my own ability is really poor, and would get quite depressed. [*laughs*] Things like I must be a completely useless person . . . why when there's also "A-san," "B-san," "C-san" . . .
R: [So you'd want to ask] Why me . . . ?

M: I'd think it was because I'm disliked, the line's being drawn at me, and at such times, I think I'd worry about why there was this disparity.

R: In other words, would that mean, that it's not just losing the job, but . . . your whole sense of being itself receives a shock?

M: You know, I, well, even if there were a drop in income, if I could find another job, the shock would be softened considerably. Any kind of job I could go into . . . For instance, in the worst case scenario, I'd even want to live by making *rāmen* [noodles] in a stall, pulling a hand-cart . . .

Here masculinity is defined not just through work *per se*, but work that is linked to the hegemonic ideology of the man as provider.

Marriage and becoming an *ichininmae no shakaijin*

Thus, within the ideological framework of hegemonic masculinity, becoming a fully responsible social adult – in other words, a *shakaijin* – involves more than merely entering into paid work upon completion of education. Rather, as Wim Lunsing (2001: 74) points out, for both men *and* women, linked to the status of becoming *shakaijin* is the notion of becoming "*ichininmae no shakaijin*" (a fully adult social being) through marriage. The implicit assumption behind this line of reasoning is that a person is not fully adult unless married with the accompanying responsibilities. Walter Edwards also draws attention to the parallels between the public validations of adult *shakaijin* status when entering into productive labor, and when getting married. Discussing speeches given at weddings he notes that:

> Wedding speakers . . . use shakai [*sic*] and shakaijin [*sic*] to assert a change in the status of the bride and groom. Because of their marriage, the speakers will say, the couple now enter society anew or have finally become full members of society. Such statements often preface injunctions to the couple to conduct themselves in a socially responsible manner.
>
> (1989: 117)

For the groom, acting in a "socially responsible manner" involves being the *daikokubashira*, and for the bride, it translates to being a wife and mother sustaining and nurturing the household from within. This is despite the reality in the post-World War II decades (and to an extent, in the prewar era too) of women *always* having played a significant role within the paid employment sector (not to mention the generally unpaid, household/family business sector). However, regardless of the reality, femininity in its construction and representations has been inextricably linked to notions of *ryōsai kenbo* (good wife, wise mother) and *sengyō shufu* (professional housewife). Until quite recently paid work for a woman was ideologically constructed as a sort of "finishing school" between the end of study and the commencement of the "real" career as housewife and mother (see Ogasawara 1998).

Thus, for both men and women, marriage signifies acquiescence to widely held socio-cultural notions of *jōshiki* (common sense, what is considered normal, natural) (see Lunsing 2001; also McLelland, Chapter 7 in this volume). It also signals conforming to the expectations of good citizenship – the hegemonic "ideal" of which is embodied in the salaryman/professional housewife pairing.

Conversely, *not* getting married carries the implication of being not *ichininmae*, but rather, "*hanninmae*, . . . half of a person . . . not independent individuals but like children waiting to grow up, no matter what their age is" (Lunsing 2001: 75). Indeed, not getting married may be seen as non-compliance to, or even active rejection of, the responsibilities of good citizenship. Examples of men who may be regarded as revoking – or at least, opting out of – these requirements of proper male citizenship would be the day laborers discussed by Tom Gill (Gill 2001, 2003), men who remain single into middle-age (Murata 2000), the freeters referred to above, or the gay men discussed by McLelland in Chapter 7 in this volume. Such men, in many respects, represent the antithesis of the model of responsible salaryman masculinity. Moreover, one of the findings that emerges from Murata's study on single, middle-aged men is the ways in which men who do not conform to this married/provider discourse, can be marginalized and excluded in the workplace (see also Lunsing 2001: 112). Murata's informants talk about such things as being passed over for promotion beyond the level of *kachō* (section manager) as a consequence of being unmarried, or anger at the expectation that not having a family means that you have more time, and hence should not complain about a heavier work-load (2000: 541).

What emerges from the above is that rather than heterosexuality *per se*, it is a *specific* model of *regulated* heterosexuality revolving around being the family provider that gets privileged in the context of the dominant gender ideology. At the same time, what also need to be borne in mind are the complexities involved in the engagements with these expectations of hegemonic masculinity. While the pressures to conform to the expectations of married, *daikokubashira* masculinity may indeed be very real, it is not a simple case of naked coercion, or of individuals being brainwashed into subscribing to the hegemonic expectations. Rather, individuals can, and do, engage in a variety of (sometimes contradictory) interactions in their negotiations with the hegemonic ideal. The remainder of this chapter will explore the ways my informants imagined and constructed notions of "marriage," "fatherhood" and being the *daikokubashira* provider.

The meaning of marriage

Miura Tōru was a Northern Energy employee who had been in the workforce for less than six months when I first interviewed him. At 20, he had barely entered adulthood. Yet he already had clear ideas about what marriage meant to him. Marriage to him represented "not being alone." When I then asked him why he saw getting married as a necessary condition for companionship, given that it was possible to be with someone without getting married, he came up with the following response: "Somehow, it just seems the natural thing. Maybe that's because, possibly, I've grown up seeing everyone else get married as a matter of course. Possibly, you want to do the same things as everyone else, don't you?"

This notion of marriage as an antidote to loneliness was echoed in the words of a number of other informants. Takahashi Yoshio, a 23-year-old Northern Print employee wanted to get married before he turned 30. To him, getting married represented a solution to the loneliness of "living alone." In his view, the loneliness of being single was associated with "such things as food not tasting good." Satō Hiroshi, 23 at the time of the interview, also wanted to be married by 30. Marriage, in his view, was "part of the course nature takes." Giving birth to children through marriage was "one of the main reasons for living," something that he had never questioned. Indeed, as he put it, the "major role for marriage was to raise children to be responsible adults (*ichininmae*)." Kobayashi Kazushi, another Northern Energy employee in his mid-twenties, also linked marriage to something that was akin to a natural part of the lifecycle; to him it was "something that one does."

Another association with marriage that cropped up in discussions was marriage as a conduit to adulthood – a means of channeling the "wildness" and unpredictable nature of youth. Thus, for Saiki Yasuo, a 23-year-old Northern Print technician, marriage signified "settling down." He described his present lifestyle as one where he found himself "wandering aimlessly." This consisted of "playing hard," specifically "drinking, picking up girls." In his view, this was a condition that only marriage could rectify. Expanding on this notion of "settling down" he noted: "I suppose, the first thing would be supporting a family properly, . . . strange as it may sound . . . living a normal life, having children, raising them properly, that's how I interpret 'settling down.'"

Significantly, with only two exceptions, not only were all of the informants discussed above unmarried, but also, at the time of the interview, none were involved in steady relationships. Yet, despite the fact that they had no particular partner in mind, they all seemed to have very specific ideas about the role and significance of marriage.

Marriage and workplace status

The relationship between marital status and a man's access to the privileges of hegemonic masculinity in the workplace came out in several of the discussions. Ogasawara Takurō of Northern Energy commented that "within the context of a Japanese organization, after a certain age, [being married] makes the biggest difference as to whether or not you're able to gain society's trust." Indeed he was quite honest about his own prejudices in this matter, stating that although "in my head I know that it shouldn't be a consideration in evaluating people, yet, to tell you the truth, if I see someone unmarried at 40 or 45, I end up thinking 'I wonder if there isn't something wrong with him?'" This sentiment was also echoed by Satō

Hiroshi who noted that regardless of what the company's official line might be in the matter, "I myself do take it [i.e. marital status] into account a little. I suppose, I'm concerned with what others think."

This connection between work and marriage, and more generally the relationship between marriage and societal validation, was made particularly visible in the conversations with recently married informants as they reflected upon the ways in which colleagues had responded to their change in marital status. Fujita Yūji was a 27-year-old Northern Print employee who had been married for four years at the time of our discussion. Prior to his marriage he and his partner had – somewhat unusually in the context of Japan – cohabited together for a number of years. He admitted that their decision to get married after many years of already living together had an element of wanting to make the relationship "official." As he put it:

> [E]ven if you're living together, when you're not married, well, people are taken by surprise . . . if you say things along the lines of "we're living together," they get taken aback. But if you're married and say "we're married," that's where it [the curiosity] ends.

As he admitted, however, this was not the only consideration at stake; there was also an element of "it was the right time . . . as we'd already been together for five or six years." Moreover, once married, he discovered that marriage "turned out to be of far greater significance than I had thought." This "great significance" hinged on the "responsibility" he now had towards immediate family, relatives and friends, as the husband in the husband–wife pairing.

Kajima Daisuke was another married Northern Print employee. He represented an interesting combination of several diverse masculinities within himself. On the one hand, he seemed to be the perfect embodiment of the ideal of hegemonic masculinity – not only was he respectably married (and on the track to fatherhood), he was also, although only 28 years old, already a *kachō* (section manager). Yet, on the other hand, he had a darker history of getting involved in fights and even into trouble with the police, and had spent years of hard drinking. At the time of our interview he had been married for over a year. One of the considerations behind his decision to get married after a (relatively) short period of time dating his partner was the sudden death of his father and the "desire to comfort" his mother, something compounded by people around him urging him to get married with comments like "hurry up and give your mother some peace of mind." Although marriage, according to Kajima-san, had not resulted in any kind of significant change within himself, he felt that it would eventually lead him "to some extent, to seek greater stability." Moreover, while he himself did not think a person being married or single was relevant to the workplace, he was aware that others might regard things differently. As he put it:

> I think management takes the view that your performance and your sense of responsibility get stronger when you get married. I was told that myself, when

I got married – something along the lines that I'd become a proper adult (*ichininmae*).

Murayama Satoshi had also been married for just over a year. His comments on what getting married had meant to him reflected many of the wider assumptions underpinning marriage. His reason for getting married was: "because it was something that was inevitable. You know, becoming a 'unit' . . . So since there was someone I really liked I got married, it was just a matter of course."

In response to my question about why he felt the need to make "official" his relationship with his wife-to-be, instead of just cohabiting together, he made the following observations:

> If you ask me why, well . . . I think I have a strong need to be validated by society . . . So, admittedly although we live in a world where things like having sex without being married don't constitute an illegal act or anything, but . . . you know at some level I think that if you are able to marry and don't, it's almost like an anti-social act.

His marriage represented an example of a classic "salaryman" marriage, where a work colleague or superior becomes an intermediary (see Rohlen 1974: 235–242; Edwards 1989: 75, 76). He and his wife had been introduced through a workplace superior. Thus, his marriage, in his view was "somewhere in between" the traditional arranged *o-miai* marriage and contemporary *ren'ai* or love marriage. He had not really anticipated getting married through such formal channels; however, in what came across as a stereotypically salaryman response, he mentioned "a lack of free time [to meet prospective partners]" as the reason for allowing his marriage to be "semi-arranged."

Like Kajima Daisuke, Murayama-san also perceived a change in the way people interacted with him as a consequence of his newly married *ichininmae* status. The comment he made in relation to the issue captured beautifully both his own feelings and the importance of married heterosexual respectability to salaryman masculinity: "Yes I got the feeling they [i.e. people's attitudes] changed. Could a mere ring on my finger make such a change? – that's what I felt!" He then went on to illustrate with an example the extent to which the *appearance* of married sobriety is of importance:

> I've heard that [men] working in banks are told to wear their wedding bands at work after they get married. It's like it's one way of creating an impression to gain trust, [by visually stating] "I'm married, I've got a family to support." I myself can really relate to that.

For Murayama-san himself, the dividends of marriage extended beyond strengthened respect and esteem from colleagues and superiors at work. He related in no uncertain terms that getting married had "taken a load off my shoulders" since he was able to hand over to his wife the responsibility of looking after his diet, his clothing and the management of the household. As he laughingly commented to me: "I've been liberated from an irregular diet." Moreover, he saw himself as having become more culturally "refined" thanks to marriage; his wife had exposed him to "a world I didn't know . . . like ballet . . . art, also theatre, the artistic side I didn't have has been able to come out."

Being a father and *daikokubashira*

As pointed out above, rather than heterosexuality *per se*, it is a specific discourse of heterosexuality that is privileged within the framework of salaryman masculinity. At its core lies the notion of the husband and father as the *provider* for a dependent family – the *daikokubashira* of the household. Various socio-economic changes in the first decades following the end of World War II have helped reinforce the ideological grip of this discourse. These include such socio-economic and cultural shifts as rapid urbanization; the growth of suburbs leading to the distancing of the home from the workplace; the emergence of a white-collar middle class; and a trend towards smaller nuclear families, which ironically focused the role of women on motherhood and household management, and the role of men on fulfilling the productive, breadwinner *daikokubashira* role (see Uno 1993). This has shifted considerably over the past decade, not least due to recent government campaigns and initiatives to encourage mothers to remain in the workforce by providing support for childcare, and through the encouragement of fathers to take on a more active role in child-rearing (see Roberts 2002; Ishii-Kuntz 2003; also Taga, Chapter 11 in this volume). The best example was the highly publicized "Sam Campaign" of the mid-1990s, which featured the partner of a well-known female rock star, Amuro Namie, on Ministry of Health and Welfare posters holding their baby. However, while there might be a greater degree of public validation of the need to move to new gender expectations, the reality (particularly in the context of a tight job market) is that the notion of masculinity being defined by being a *daikokubashira* is still firmly entrenched.

The continuing centrality of this *daikokubashira* discourse can best be gauged by a comment made by Kajima Daisuke, the 28-year-old Northern Print section manager whose views on marriage were discussed in the preceding section. At the time of our discussion Kajima-san had been married for over one year, and he and his wife were considering starting a family. Talking about what marriage and family life meant to him, he made the following observation:

> When you're single, if you lose your job or something, well, you only need to worry about your own survival. But when you have children, well, then, the whole family has to survive together, don't they? Since you can't let your family starve by the wayside . . . you can no longer think along lines like "this job isn't interesting so I'll quit."

This notion of the man needing to be there to support/feed a dependent wife and children came out in several of the accounts. When I presented Murayama Satoshi with a scenario where he was not working and was dependent on his wife's income (in other words, the antithesis of the *daikokubashira*), he was quite explicit in telling me that such a situation would be unacceptable. He used the analogy of a "male animal not going out to hunt," something which he would "not be comfortable with." Perhaps the importance he placed on living up to the expectations of being a *daikokubashira* came out best in his response to my question at the end of the interview about the most and least appealing aspects of being a man. He felt that the best thing about being born male was, "having a family, and being able to support (literally, 'being able to feed,') that family." Conversely the worst thing was "being unable to quit your job even if you want to" due to the same responsibility.

This type of sentiment was echoed by several of the other married informants – for instance, Shin'ya Naohiko of Northern Energy, who had also recently become the father of a baby girl, made the comment that fatherhood had made it "that much harder to quit the company." Kajima Daisuke, although not a father, seemed to be conscious of the dangers of getting trapped by the expectations of this discourse. He stressed that he did not want to be like a "typical" salaryman father "tied down by kids and a wife." He equated this "domesticated" salaryman model with a parallel reading of the married provider model, one in which "marriage = the end of life," something he saw reflected in the lives of his friends and in popular culture. As he elaborated:

> "Giving up on life" – you often hear it on TV and things, and also when friends get married they say things like "Well, it's all over" . . . For all of them [i.e. his friends], you get married, and after the children are born the wife doesn't work, so on just your own income, after taking into account money needed for supporting the wife and kids, there's nothing left over for enjoyment . . . I guess it's just continuous endurance, endurance, endurance, endurance, but even then, they seem to get some basic level of enjoyment out of it!

Daikokubashira realities

Shin'ya Naohiko was a 23-year-old Northern Energy systems engineer who, as mentioned above, had very recently become the father of a baby girl. In fact, both his marriage and his becoming a father had taken place almost inadvertently. Over the period of our acquaintance he had gone from a carefree young single without too many adult responsibilities and commitments, to the married father of a new-born baby. When we first met he was living by himself in the single men's dormitory run by Northern Energy. At our second meeting, when we had our first interview, he had just started going out with a new girlfriend, but mentioned that neither had any intention of getting married, particularly as his girlfriend had just returned to full-time study. However, shortly after that first interview they found out that she was pregnant and decided to get married. All of this was unknown to me, so it came as quite a surprise to see him in this new incarnation of husband and father, at our second interview.

His feelings about fatherhood and living up to the *daikokubashira* ideal were especially complex, displaying both the process of conforming to the hegemonic ideal of father and provider, and also having more ambivalent emotions about his new status. The visibility of this contradiction may have perhaps been due to the suddenness with which he had had marriage and fatherhood thrust upon him. His new status as father had not quite sunk in – the realization that he was a father was more a result of being told that by those around him, rather than any sense of "fatherly feeling" coming to the surface of its own accord. He reflected on the complex interplay of emotions and reactions he was going through.

> Well, there's some sort of realization. Or rather, a real feeling of being a father came about through it being reinforced by people around me. Just chatting in the corridors at work and being congratulated by everyone I talk to, being told that time and again, I gradually started to feel a sense that I've become a father being born within me. But the child is still largely immobile, so somehow it still feels too early to feel any sense of social responsibility.

Shin'ya-san expected this sense of responsibility as a father to strengthen as the child grew older and as the responses demanded of him as a father became concrete. At the moment though, fatherhood seemed to carry associations of disruption and chaos. He mentioned having to try and juggle his work commitments, his ice-hockey coaching duties, as well as the household cleaning, cooking and washing and bathing the baby, as his wife was still too weak to look after such things. Comparing his present situation with the time prior to marriage and the birth of the baby, he reflected that:

> I guess my thinking's changed. Well, I suppose the fact that I've ended up being married at 23, when I really thought I'd marry after 30 . . . I guess, in other words, before my child was born, my thinking about [marriage and being a father] was quite naïve and simplistic. I guess now, looking at myself married at this age I started to get a sense of the gravity of the matter. I'm not saying that it's causing me to suffer though.

He was also aware of the restrictions now placed on his ability to fulfill many of the dreams he had recounted to me in the first interview. In that first interview, he had elaborated on two possible courses he saw his life-path taking in the future. One vision of himself – the way things actually turned out – was a future where he would be married with possibly one child, and still working at Northern Energy. In the alternative scenario he presented, he was no longer in Northern Energy, but was doing things like studying to become an interior architect, or designing the lighting for famous buildings. Now, less than a year down the track, he realized that with a child to look after "it is that much harder to quit the company." Elaborating on how his new status as husband and father had shifted relationships within the workplace he noted:

I suppose, as a result of having a child to raise, I've started to place more importance on interpersonal relationships at work. On the other hand, I feel that the distance with which others used to regard me has shrunk as a result of me becoming a father. Now, because I've had a child, from the time I announced the birth of the child, it's like "You're a father too, aren't you? Just like us, a father!" ... While I was single I had a circle of unmarried friends [at work]. But, I've moved out from [that category] and have been admitted into [the circle of] more senior colleagues who are fathers, have children. Also, I've found work being passed on to me more, I guess ... I get the feeling that my trustworthiness at work has increased and things are moving in a favorable direction, that I'm trusted more.

Looking at these various voices regarding marriage and fatherhood, we get a sense of the complex interplay and shifts between various discourses surrounding these gender institutions, structures and practices. On the one hand, there is the continuing importance placed on "proving" masculinity through work – being the breadwinner, the outside provider, upon whom the whole family is dependent. At the same time, there also appear to be shifts from previous practices. For instance most of my informants (both married and single) articulated a discourse of active involvement by fathers as being a priority for themselves. This seemed to convey a sense of fatherhood somehow being "cool," as reflected in the statement by Miura Tōru that "being a young papa is good ... [because] you want to play [with your child]." Most of the other informants also stressed that they had a desire to get involved in child-rearing. My informants' positive view of fathers' roles within the family dovetails with recent government efforts to promote "active" fathering in order to counter the declining birth rate by attempting to shift some of the burden for household labor away from women. These "fatherhood is cool" views were also being articulated against a background of greater visibility of men's groups and parenting groups, such as *Ikujiren*, working for a greater recognition of men's role in parenting (Ishii-Kuntz 2003; Taga, Chapter 11 in this volume). However, while the views expressed about fatherhood may appear "progressive," the reality for most of my informants seems to still be limited to the level of statements supporting active involvement without any real shift in their expectations of masculinity being tied to being a husband and primary breadwinner.

Conclusion

As stressed in the Introduction, while there is a need to continue to draw attention to the emerging diversity and visibility of "alternative" gender and sexual identities in Japan, it is also important to investigate the hegemonic gender and sexual identities which have acted as a default against which other configurations are defined. This is necessary in order to get a sense of the overall picture of the expectations shaping genders and sexualities at the moment in Japan. This is particularly important, as there may be a tendency to be overly optimistic about the greater visibility and diversity that have emerged, and forget that pressures to conform to hegemonic gender ideologies are still very real.

Moreover, understanding the dynamics of conformity to hegemonic gender ideologies allows us to be more realistic in mapping out future directions for constructions of gender and sexuality. The voices of my informants in this chapter, as they discussed their engagements with ideas surrounding work, marriage, and fatherhood, would indicate that, as signaled in Chapter 10 by Itō, there is a gap between many men's expectations and ideas and social reality and public policy in the arena of gender. Thus, despite the very real shifts and changes in gender and sexuality practice and ideology discussed in many of the chapters in this volume, in all likelihood, hegemonic notions surrounding what constitutes masculinity (and femininity) will also continue to shape individuals' day-to-day behavior and actions well into the future.

Notes

1 "Hegemonic masculinity" is a term that has come to be associated with the works of sociologist R. W. Connell. In deploying the term Connell applied the Gramscian notion of "hegemony" to the context of gender, specifically masculinity. At any given time, in a specific socio-cultural setting there are multiple masculinities – ways of "being a male person." These various "masculinities" do not just "sit side-by-side like dishes on a smorgasbord" (2000: 10). Rather, there are definite relations of power within this matrix of multiple masculinities. The model of masculinity which exerts the greatest cultural influence – in many respects, the "cultural ideal" which occupies a position of "hegemony" – may be considered the "hegemonic" form of masculinity, one that exerts power over femininities and other subordinated, less privileged forms of masculinity (see Connell 1987, 1995, 1996, 2000).
2 The names Northern Energy and Northern Print are pseudonyms, as are the names of all the individual informants I discuss in this chapter. The research with the approximately 40 informants from these two organizations was carried out over an 18-month period in 1998/1999. The material from these interviews is discussed in my doctoral thesis, "'Crafting' masculinity: negotiating masculine identities in the Japanese workplace," Curtin University, 2004.

References

Connell, R.W. (2000) *The Men and the Boys*, St. Leonards, NSW: Allen & Unwin.
—— (1996) "New directions in gender theory, masculinity research, and gender politics," *Ethnos*, 61(3/4): 157–176.
—— (1995) *Masculinities*, St. Leonards, NSW: Allen & Unwin.
—— (1987) *Gender and Power: Society, the Person and Sexual Politics*, Cambridge: Polity Press.
Dasgupta, R. (2004) "'Crafting' masculinity: negotiating masculine identities in the Japanese workplace," PhD thesis, Curtin University of Technology.
Edwards, W. (1989) *Modern Japan through its Weddings: Gender, Person, and Society in Ritual Portrayal*, Stanford, CA: Stanford University Press.
Gill, T. (2003) "When pillars evaporate: structuring masculinity on the Japanese margins," in J. Roberson and N. Suzuki (eds) *Men and Masculinities in Contemporary Japan: Dislocating the Salaryman Doxa*, London: RoutledgeCurzon.

—— (2001) *Men of Uncertainty: The Social Organization of Day Laborers in Contemporary Japan*, Albany, NY: State University of New York Press.

Ishii-Kuntz, M. (2003) "Balancing fatherhood and work: emergence of diverse masculinties in contemporary Japan," in J. Roberson and N. Suzuki (eds) *Men and Masculinities in Contemporary Japan: Dislocating the Salaryman Doxa*, London: RoutledgeCurzon.

Japan Institute of Labor (ed.). (2003) *Japanese Working Life Profile 2003*. Tokyo: Japan Institute of Labor.

Lunsing, W. (2001) *Beyond Common Sense: Sexuality and Gender in Contemporary Japan*, London: Kegan Paul.

Murata, Y. (2000) "Chūnen shinguru dansei wo sogai-suru basho" (The places where middle-aged single men feel alienated), *Jinbun chirigaku*, 52(6): 533–551.

Odani, S. (2001) "Freeters: Japan's carefree young wage workers", *Via*, 22(4): 24–25.

Ogasawara, Y. (1998) *Office Ladies and Salaried Men: Power, Gender and Work in Japanese Companies*, Berkeley, CA: University of California Press.

Roberson, J. and N. Suzuki. (2003) "Introduction," in J. Roberson and N. Suzuki (eds) *Men and Masculinities in Contemporary Japan: Dislocating the Salaryman Doxa*, London: RoutledgeCurzon.

Roberts, G. (2002) "Pinning hopes on angels: reflections from an aging Japan's urban landscape," in R. Goodman (ed.) *Family and Social Policy in Japan: Anthropological Approaches*, Cambridge: Cambridge University Press.

Rohlen, T. (1974) *For Harmony and Strength: Japanese White-Collar Organization in Anthropological Perspective*, Berkeley, CA: University of California Press.

Uno, K. (1993) "The death of 'Good Wife, Wise Mother'?," in A. Gordon (ed.) *Postwar Japan as History*, Berkeley, CA: University of California Press.

13 Feminist futures in Japan
Exploring the work of Haruka Yōko and Kitahara Minori

Laura Dales

Introduction

This chapter explores the work of two contemporary Japanese feminists, TV personality and writer Haruka Yōko, and business woman, writer and advocate for women's erotica Kitahara Minori. While both women have adopted a number of different roles in various media, this chapter focuses primarily on Haruka's most recent non-fiction publications and Kitahara's Tokyo-based website and sales outlet, the *Love Piece Club* (LPC) which is devoted to sex goods for women.[1] Significantly, the term "feminist" is not comprehensively defined in this chapter since this would involve elisions, generalizations and categorical divisions that would occlude rather than clarify the issues under discussion. Rather, Kitahara and Haruka's works are presented as examples of the theoretical and practical criticality which Saitō suggests "adopts a female perspective rather than the traditional male value system" (cited in Buckley 1997: 263). Haruka and Kitahara are defined as feminists both through their own self-identification, and because they reflect on the positive potential of being female, supporting a feminist discourse whose "primary goal is not to be like men but to value what it means to be a woman" (Ueno, cited in Buckley 1997: 280).

The ongoing diversification of feminist theory and praxis should be seen as evidence of healthy growth and development – as Saitō Chiyo observes, "the richer the movement, the richer the range of theories" (cited in Buckley 1997: 265). Despite their wide range of publications, neither Haruka nor Kitahara can be classed as academics, and their stances on issues such as marriage place them at odds with other women who call themselves (and are known as) "feminists."

Kitahara's and Haruka's discursive and applied work point to new directions in the ongoing development of feminist discourse in Japan. The scope and style of their works may represent a shift toward a more popularized feminism, or perhaps simply a feminism which is more popular among (certain) women. The work of both authors is addressed to the everyday Japanese woman, and employs popular, non-academic themes and styles, thus engaging with feminist issues in everyday life. Both Haruka and Kitahara incorporate consumption (of fashion, beauty and sex goods) in their feminist discourse, promoting the gender subversive potential of "buying" and "appearing."

The construction of an attractive, popularly appealing feminism, as exemplified by the works of Kitahara and Haruka, is helping shape not only future feminist discourse in Japan, but also the wider depiction of women's issues in the mass media and in popular social perceptions. Their work represents a diffusion of feminist critique into mainstream youth culture, creating new spaces and terms through which feminism – and a feminist identity – might be re-interpreted. This chapter seeks to present this potential, suggesting possibilities for future feminist agendas and approaches in Japanese society. But first it is necessary to look at the manner in which "feminism" signifies in Japan.

Translating the F word

It is now well recognized that the scope of feminism in Anglophone societies is complicated by factors including sexuality, class, race, religion and ethnicity. Those who subscribe to feminist identities may qualify their choice along any/all of these lines, making for subtle and shifting understandings of feminism. Moreover, it is also evident that the word "feminism" has different import outside of English-speaking (and different import in different English-speaking) societies, and may therefore be taken up in different contexts and have different effects in countries such as Japan.[2]

The English terms "feminist" and "feminism" are laden with a variety of assumptions in Japan. Etymologically, the transliteration of the word feminism into the katakana *feminizumu* – renders it a foreign loanword (*gairaigo*) in exactly the same way as words such as curry, soccer or T-shirt (*karē, sakkā* and *tī-shatsu*) have been adapted. What is problematic about the use of *feminizumu* is that it may encourage the mistaken implication that not only the term but the concept, like the T-shirt, is of Anglo origin and therefore "not indigenous" to Japan, and that it is consequently positioned "outside the boundaries of patriarchal Japanese thought and traditional notions of female identity" (Chaplin 2001: 56).[3]

The term "*feminisuto*" was already in use in Japan before the 1970s, but rather than referring to women's rights activists, it connoted a man who was kind to women (Mackie 2003: 160). The publication of a feminist journal titled *Feminist* in 1977 reclaimed the term and its women-centered focus, and along with women's liberationists (*ūman ribu*), it took on its contemporary flavor of women's rights activism (Mackie 2003: 160–161). While not all women's rights activists deploy the term, those who do – including the tenacious Ueno Chizuko and Tajima Yōko – have brought the term *feminisuto* at least to the margins of mainstream television, newspapers and magazines.

Ueno Chizuko is Professor of Sociology at the University of Tokyo, and arguably the best-known feminist in Japan. Her academic career and numerous publications – independent and collaborative – mark her as an expert on feminist theory and critique. Tajima Yōko, a literature professor turned Diet member, is a similarly high-profile feminist whose fiery critique (as well as literary translations) have been published with titles such as "And that's why women don't count on men" (2001) and "Women become fools through love" (2004). Since Ueno and

Tajima are more strident representatives of the feminist camp, they may be perceived as distinct from "ordinary women" because of their radical politics and academic sophistication.[4]

Aside from its implications of remote academia, the often negative image associated with the word "feminist" in Japan reflects the currency of negative interpretations of feminist objectives. Stereotypes of feminists as "man-hating," "aggressive," or "biased" are frequently held up by women as grounds for distancing themselves from feminism, and by men as grounds for disparaging feminist views and theories.[5] Circumventing the actual term "feminist," official government discourse on women's issues emphasizes "gender equality" and "gender-free" (*jendā furii*) policies, and is supported by the heteronormative framework of the Basic Law for a Gender Equal Society (*Danjo Kyōdō Sankaku Shakai Tsukuri Hōhō*) (Dales 2003; Muta 2003: 124).

Anti-feminist sentiment in the mass media has tended to emphasize the role feminist ideas have played in the increase in the numbers of women deciding to remain in the workforce, and/or in delaying marriage and childbearing. Buckley (1997: 187) notes that increased media attention to feminism and feminists has had the negative effect of homogenizing a diverse field of feminist perspectives, reducing the multiplicity of women's voices to the "images and sound-bites" of a select few feminists. This false representation of uniformity narrows the goal-post area for "who can be a feminist" and the word "feminist" itself becomes synonymous with the specific work of certain women. To an extent, then, the media have constructed feminism as a distinct and unified force which exerts ideological pressure on the female population. This allows the blame for a broad spectrum of social issues and problems to be shifted from the state and onto women, rendering the political (broad social and structural inequalities) as personal (individual disenchantment, aggressiveness and dissatisfaction).

However, the role that the media, particularly television and print, have played in constructing feminist identification is multivalent. The media have also aided the direct and indirect promotion of feminist critique via the work of women such as personality Haruka Yōko and writer Kitahara Minori. Working through the mainstream media, Haruka and Kitahara have brought feminist critique into the everyday experiences of women, emphasizing the potential for change and empowerment that women possess at a personal level. Kitahara's and Haruka's work is characterized by its accessible language, familiar themes and self-awareness, and thus has the potential to become more far-reaching and distinct from, yet complementary to, academic theory and government discourse.

Haruka Yōko: from TV to *Tōdai*

Having established a career as a TV personality in the 1980s, Haruka went on to study gender theory at Tokyo University, publishing a book in 2000 about her experiences – *Tōdai de Ueno Chizuko ni kenka wo manabu* (Learning to fight from Ueno Chizuko at Tokyo University) – which became a national best-seller. Her subsequent books *Kekkon shimasen* (I won't marry), *Hataraku onna wa teki bakari*

(Working women have nothing but enemies) and *Haiburiddo ūman* (Hybrid woman) have built on this success, making Haruka one of the more popular and certainly more visible feminists in Japan. Haruka appears to be a stylish, liberal and modern woman, writing in a down-to-earth, pointedly un-academic style about her personal experiences of love, discrimination and life choices. Working with and through the mainstream media, Haruka brings feminist critique into the everyday experiences of women, emphasizing the potential for change and empowerment by women at a personal level. Incorporating radical as well as more liberal feminist approaches, Haruka's critique represents a new strand of feminist discourse which has both popular appeal and the potential to engage public and mass media interest in women's issues.

Haruka Yōko was born in Osaka, the youngest and only daughter of a working-class family with five sons. She does not give her age, but given her work history she is likely to be in her forties. Her work as a television personality or *tarento* began in 1986 and throughout the 1990s Haruka worked in television, radio and print, writing newspaper columns on subjects from working women to baseball.

While feminism and popular television may seem unlikely bedfellows, it is clear that Haruka's critique informs and is informed by her experiences in the media. She is the first to point out that as a media *tarento*, her workplace is rife with sexism and gender inequality, and that even among female work colleagues "feminism" is a foreign word. Haruka gives a particularly entertaining example of the foreignness of the word "feminism," illustrated by a vignette about a group of (male) media executives who struggled to pronounce the word *feminizumu* in discussions with her (2001: 115). Observing their difficulty with the term, and their relief at being able to use a shortened (albeit ridiculous-sounding) "*fe*" in lieu, Haruka presents the situation as ridiculous but nonetheless positive in its implications – the men were familiar with the concepts and issues of feminism, simply finding the word itself difficult to pronounce (2001: 112).

The spread of the contraction *fe* is illustrated in another context, when used by a friend to describe Haruka herself: "Yōko's studying *fe* whatchamacallit" (2001: 113). Haruka contends that if shortening the term from *feminizumu* to *fe* increases the currency of the underlying concept, then it is a positive step for feminists (2001: 115). Furthermore, Haruka reflects that while the word "feminism" has not gained sufficient currency in Japanese society to reflect its full historical import, there is nonetheless potential for the ideas behind feminism to spread (2001: 114). The transformative and subversive potential of a modified label can also be seen in the adoption of *bian* (a shortening of *rezubian*) and *daiku* (from the English "dyke") by lesbians in Japan, as an alternative to the derogatory *rezu*, which is associated with male pornography (Chalmers 2002: 38).

Haruka draws on her workplace as evidence of an existing (if obscured) feminist framework, in which feminist praxis can be seen among people "who don't particularly understand feminism but put it into practice unconsciously" (2001: 113). One example recounts the story of a full-time working female friend who apologized to her husband when asking for his help with bringing in the wash.

Then, realizing that tasks which offer benefits to both husband and wife should be shared labor, she "takes back" her apology.

What is interesting about this example is that housework features as the foil for feminist consciousness. The division of domestic labor represents a key theme in Haruka's critique, emphasizing the role of the domestic in the idealized construction of femininity. In an earlier work (I won't marry), Haruka observes that the concept of "housework" by definition requires a "housewife," or at least a wife since single people may clean, but they do not do "housework" (2000: 55).[6] Furthermore, Haruka presents herself as an antithesis to the domestic goddess (or slave) – she eats instant noodles straight from the pot, she only washes dishes once a week and she is amazed by the time and effort expended by her mother and sister-in-law in caring for their families (2001: 240). Drawing on her family as illustration, Haruka paints domestic inequality as fundamental to Japanese marriage, and is scathing of its impact on women's lives. Her observations take in both her own experiences as the youngest female, but more frequently address the demands placed on her mother and sisters-in-law, and she is upfront in her assessment, stating that "My family (*ie*) is a museum of patriarchy and capitalism" (2000: 96).[7]

Tangential to her criticism of marriage, Haruka also frequently (and critically) reflects on the implications of women's ageing, and of social mores centered on age and femininity. In an "Office Breeze" essay "Isn't there anything else you can ask?" (2001: 12–13), Haruka addresses the implications of questions about women's age and marital status, focusing on men as the particular transgressors. Such questions, argues Haruka, aim to separate women into two categories – "women" and "not-women" (2001: 12). As both youth and single status (presumably until age 30) mark women as sexually available to men, during this period they are characterized as feminine. However, to the extent that marriage and age mark women as being unavailable to men, these characteristics place older, married women outside the category of "woman." Haruka argues that the simplicity of this categorization obscures the actual diversity of women's domestic situations, inquiring "What if I was living with someone? What if I was married but had lived apart from my husband for many years? . . . What if I was single but had three kids?" (ibid.: 13).

Haruka argues that to contend with the increasing variety of women's lives, there is no solution but to increase the categories relating to femininity – to increase the number (and presumably visibility) of women who transgress (2001: 13). It is the unpredictable, "all-over-the-place woman" (*wake no wakaran onna*) who most challenges rigid ideals of femininity based on marriage and age, and by confusing these categories is therefore able to form new models of femininity.

Haruka is particularly well placed to make assessments of women's position in the media. She writes frequently of the conflicts occasioned by her work-related performance and her feminist sensibilities. As a TV personality she is aware that her value is pinned to appearance, to her decorative (and sometimes humorous) contribution on the screen. In this context it is her bodily presence, her clothes and comportment which mark her femininity, and her intellectual self is obscured.

In programs where she is invited to contribute to discussions, however, she is forced to "wear plain clothes, cover up completely, dye her hair black" in order to speak – or rather, in order to be heard (2001: 165). She is thus bound in her work to a binary of physical/intellectual selves, where the expression of one precludes the expression of the other, and where her femininity is either exploited or denied. As she says, "to sell femininity or to deny femininity, in any event there is no choice but to work while holding a self which is neither one nor the other" (ibid.: 164).

Haruka argues that while the entertainment world offers companionship and support in personal and professional issues, her feminist concerns cannot be raised or met in a workplace where "(m)ost people don't even know the word 'feminism'" (ibid.: 185). In articulating these concerns, Haruka seeks the advice of her fellow Tokyo University graduates, most of whom have gone on to further research or academic work. In painting herself as frequently confused and in need of theoretical guidance, Haruka reinforces both her own distance from the "ivory tower" of academia, and stresses the accessibility of feminism, which can after all be understood even by someone who is "just a TV personality" (ibid.: 186). She thus shows an ability to work through complex feminist theoretical issues – implicitly evidenced by her books – while still acknowledging her intellectual limitations. In doing so, Haruka presents her feminism as simultaneously flowing from everyday experiences, and stimulated by intellectual and academic engagement.

However, as her colleagues point out, it is precisely because Haruka is not an academic but a TV personality that her feminist critique is effective – "We research (feminism). We want you to spread it" (ibid.: 190), they say. The realization of her role as a promoter and public ambassador for feminism has brought about a partial reconciliation of the physical/intellectual conflict, blurring the line between work and ideology but without changing Haruka's material job requirements or performance.

The negotiation of professional development and feminist integrity features significantly in Haruka's writing, and highlights the "everyday" (as opposed to theoretical) roots of her feminist critique. While balancing social critique with an interest in fashion and beauty implies a liberal feminist grounding, Haruka seems less interested in qualifying her feminism than in promoting general feminist critique. In this sense she represents an attainable model of feminism, advocating a feminism that aims purely to make life easier or more comfortable for women. The incorporation of personal experiences and, particularly, ideological challenges and conflicts, distinguishes Haruka's feminism from distant academic feminism, and in combination with her public TV persona facilitates an accessible and reassuringly human critique.

Hybrid women

Haruka's latest work, *Hybrid Woman* (2003), is both polished and succinct. It continues her prolific publication output in the years since *Learning to Fight*. Still peppered with self-deprecation and humor, the book's style has refined the more general critique of previous works, proposing strategies for feminist living in a way that sometimes evokes the fashion editorials of women's magazines.

Agency and strategy represent key themes in this work. The aim of feminism, according to Haruka's discourse, is to make life easier for women. If women are to live easily (implying freely, without discrimination, independently), they need to develop strategies by which to plan and achieve their life goals. The decisions to marry or remain single, to court or reject men's attention can be read as examples of such strategies for living (2003: 212). However, Haruka argues that each of these strategies have limitations in their applicability and value. While women who marry are assured of social respectability (as wives and mothers) and financial security, they are constrained in their independence and career prospects. Women who remain single are free to work and play as they like, but garner pity as "unhappy women who never met the right man" (ibid.: 209). Women who play on "feminine weakness" and flirt with men alienate other women, and are bound by their dependence on men. Women who view men as enemies are stigmatized as aggressive, and constantly face criticism and alienation from men and mainstream (malestream) society.

The flaws inherent in each of these options lead Haruka to propose a new model – a hybrid which takes the best of all positions while remaining bound to none. In Haruka's theory, men are quite literally resources (*shigen*), whose value should be assessed pragmatically and without regard for the fantasy of romantic love. The key is therefore to employ the method which most suits an individual's immediate purpose, while keeping in mind the ultimate goal of "overtaking" men. By "overtaking," however, Haruka does not suggest that women should seek power over men specifically – rather, in a society where gender norms privilege the male, "overtake" means simply to live beyond these norms, or to live freely.

To this end, women must be pragmatic in their lifestyle choices. Focusing on fashion, career and romance, Haruka marks flexibility and adaptability as the keys to hybrid womanhood. The hybrid woman should take up the best of stereotypes and expectations, without compromising her integrity or sense of self-worth. In fashion, this translates as being "both mannish and feminine . . . Having no fixed notion of your sex," and incorporating the possibility of both hard and soft ("leather and organza") fashions (ibid.: 230–231).[8] This attention to fashion echoes Haruka's earlier reflections on the conflict of physical and intellectual selves, and reinforces the importance attached to the expression of self through clothing and appearance. The strategy of this approach is clear – if fashion is central to existing femininity, it also makes a good starting-point for reviewing or reforming femininity.

Regarding careers, Haruka advocates that the hybrid woman must first know her own place (ibid.: 231). Evidently if the hybrid woman is to develop her career options, she needs a map of the terrain, and an understanding of the obstacles she may encounter. For women who work in male-dominated workplaces (including, for example, office ladies or OLs), it is important to make a few firm allies among the men, to secure a stronghold from which strategic decisions can be made (ibid.: 231). The efficiency of this approach is reflected in Ogasawara's discussions of the power wielded by OLs over their male colleagues and superiors, who "curry favor" with women, through the giving of gifts and treats, to ensure a harmonious working relationship (Ogasawara 1998: 156).

Arguably the most significant aspect of hybrid womanhood outlined by Haruka is romance, or romantic relationships. Haruka is pragmatic about the need to form relationships with men. However, she argues that such relationships are only beneficial to women temporarily and furthermore that their success depends on women's flattery (*kobi*) of men (2003: 226). While women who do not flatter lose access to "male resources," women who flatter too much (that is, act "ditzy" around men) lose access to "female resources," alienating women and discrediting their own femininity (ibid.: 226). Furthermore, flatterers who marry are forced to maintain the flattery indefinitely, as part of the marital contract (ibid.: 227).

Ultimately, Haruka advises women to view romantic relationships not as a fate, but as a hobby, and one which women can live without (ibid.: 232). There are no "true" or "pure" or "genuine" romances, only those which appear so, and it is the fantasy of such romance that constrains women, preventing them from self-fulfillment (ibid.: 232). In this reading, while marriage and related long-term romantic commitments may be seen as offering security or stability, the viability and reward of such security (and thus such relationships) must continually be re-assessed in critical feminist terms. The benefits, argues Haruka, do not outweigh the risks:

> Men are not enemies – they are still viable resources. What you should know are the kinds of circumstances in which men can become enemies, and in which they can be allies. Polish your skills at using the resource wisely. And at the same time, remember that as allies they have limitations in their usefulness.
>
> (2003: 233)

For hybrid women, heterosexual relationships are exercises in strategy and power play. When the "usefulness" of the man dissipates, so does the relationship. While Haruka offers this as a slightly tongue-in-cheek analysis, her approach can be interpreted as a serious challenge to marriage not unlike the commodified romance enjoyed by some women in the host club subculture described in Chapter 14 by Takeyama.

Limitations of the hybrid model

Haruka's writing seeks to problematize gender ideals, roles and expectations in Japanese women's everyday lives. In her most recent work, Haruka proposes a new model for feminist living which seeks to solve some of the conflicts and issues raised in earlier works. The model encourages women to view romance, marriage and ultimately men, as means through which to achieve freedom and self-fulfillment (2003). Through taking "the best of all worlds," Haruka's hybrid woman seeks to redress the gender imbalances which currently constrain women, repudiating ideals which support this inequality and focusing on enjoying fashion, work and independence. Haruka, who "eats what she likes, says what she likes, sleeps when she likes" and who will not marry, represents the embodiment of the hybrid woman.[9]

However, it must be recognized that her fame, financial status and most significantly her singleness mark Haruka as different from the majority of her female audience. While numbers of single women are increasing in Japan, those of Haruka's age who are single and wealthy are a small minority. While in reality they may be delaying or rejecting marriage, young women are still expected and encouraged to marry. Older single women are still stigmatized by their lack of domestic ties, labeled "loser dogs" (*make inu*) by society and their married sisters and parents (Sakai 2003).

Haruka's promotion of the hybrid woman as an alternative feminine ideal reflects a deep dissatisfaction with the dominant models of Japanese femininity. Bold and sharp, the hybrid woman takes charge of her life and her femininity, utilizing all tools available to achieve her ends. Yet, the model does not promise happiness – Haruka is clear about its limitations. The free-living, free-moving hybrid woman cannot expect to be understood (2003: 233). If she wants self-fulfillment she must also accept solitude as its price (ibid.: 234).

This is not empty rhetoric for Haruka, who is clear about her own life path, stating that "I know that I have to live my life alone" (ibid.: 221). While the hybrid woman may represent a brave new future for Japanese feminism, the likelihood of women taking up the mantle is compromised by the social, physical and emotional ties which bind femininity to the performance of certain roles. It is her recognition that such ties exist that marks Haruka's work as a real, accessible and potentially radical feminist text for Japanese women. However, the implications behind cutting these ties may prove a barrier to the popularization of hybrid womanhood.

For Haruka and her hybrid women, heterosexual relationships are to be constructed and dismantled strategically, and romance is a luxury in which to indulge occasionally. As fellow feminist Kitahara Minori puts it so succinctly in the title of one of her books, "Men are good to have around sometimes."

Kitahara Minori: feminism, erotica and the *Love Piece Club*

While Haruka touches briefly on (hetero)sexuality in her writing, Kitahara Minori places sexuality at the center of her feminist activities, textual or otherwise. Kitahara is a writer, businesswoman and self-described advocate for feminist erotica. The founder of online and Tokyo-based shop *Love Piece Club*, and editor of *Vibe Girls* magazine, Kitahara has also published a number of books, including *Hachimitsu no baiburēshon* (Honey vibrations) (1998) and *Femi no kirawarekata* (The ways feminists are hated) (2000), in addition to Internet publications.[10] While she admits that the women who work in and on the *Love Piece Club* and *Vibe Girls* publications gather "basically because it's fun and interesting," nonetheless Kitahara depicts feminism as a core stimulus for critique and practical engagement (2000: 214).

Kitahara's publications differ from academic feminist texts in their clear and familiar style, and draw on personal experiences to illustrate issues of feminist concern or interest. Her books, for example, feature discussions of the sex industry, masturbation, contraception, love and childrearing. *Femi no kirawarekata* includes a re-crafted fairytale and concludes with a dialogue with Haruka entitled *Femi de kirei ni naru* (Becoming beautiful through feminism). This dialogue presents two women's ideas and experiences of feminist consciousness, thoughts about the term "feminist" and related stereotypes. While Haruka's feminism is informed by her studies with Ueno, Kitahara admits, "I've never really thought of feminism as 'something to study'" (ibid.: 215). Rather, for her, feminism is something she realized during childhood experiences which provoked envious reflections such as "if I were a boy I wouldn't have to feel this kind of disappointment" (ibid.: 3). She writes of these schoolyard, family and relational experiences as the source of her critical stance, and draws herself into the text through candid and emotional writing, noting that "I wrote this book while thinking about women and I wrote while I felt angry, delighted, sad and happy" (ibid.: 6).

Kitahara's writing draws on and develops sociolinguistic critique, and the themes of interpretation and reappropriation characterize her *LPC* column. The nature of the language used by Kitahara, the structure of her prose and her focus on language as used by others sharpen the critical impact of the writing. The combined effect of these features paints a picture of a woman for whom language is both a marker of gendered inequalities and a tool to be consciously wielded against such inequalities.

Kitahara acknowledges the significance of language for herself:

> Compared to when I was a teenager, life has gotten easier, and I think the reason for that is that I've become able to use my own words, my own voice. And now I can discuss things and say, "Well, you might say this but . . . . "[11]

One of Kitahara's most informative and wide-reaching projects of feminist critique is the *Love Piece Club* website. As well as online shopping, the site offers regular columns, articles and photo-essays on subjects related to sexuality, feminism and/or erotica. The feminist potential of the *LPC* as a space for resistance and agency is achieved not only through innovation and subversion of gendered sexual norms, but also through manipulation of consumption. While consumption as a feature of liberal feminism can be seen as conflicting with the radical sexual agenda of the LPC, in fact the connection between the two is both functional and essential. As Driscoll (1999: 188) observes, just as the existence of subcultures requires a mainstream, so feminist identities are tied inextricably to patriarchy. Kitahara comments:

> Selling vibrators. Selling penis-shaped dildos. Putting a vibrator into a vagina. Inserting a penis-shaped dildo deep, deep, or having one inserted. Saying no to cock while selling cock-shaped vibrators no longer makes me feel pained or contradictory. And the reason is that sexual desire is free. "Sex that isn't

based on penetration" and "sex that is based on penetration" – they're both the same. Both are completely unrelated to sexual desire. "The freedom to maybe penetrate" – maybe that's what sexual desire is.[12]

Kitahara is frank in discussing the ambiguous nexus between her theory as a feminist, her work as a businesswoman and her desires as a sexual female. Conceding the contradiction and uncertainty of the discourses she is involved in allows Kitahara to put aside details of feminist/un-feminist definition and to focus instead on the broader conditions (specifically social taboos) which have previously obscured such discussion.

On another site, the Lifestyle section of cafeglobe.com, Kitahara contributes a weekly column entitled *Futsū no sekkusu* (Ordinary sex), with the subtitle: "For sluts, nymphos, masturbators and people with no sexual appetite."[13] Emphasizing the diversity of people's (particularly women's) sexuality, Kitahara critically examines the socially constructed taboos of both high and low libido among women. In one column this examination highlights the links between the social problematization of sexless marriages and the low birth-rate – "It's no coincidence that the terms 'sexless' and 'low-birth-rate society' became common in the same year (1991)."[14] While Kitahara frankly discusses her own sexual practices (as a self-confessed "slut" and "masturbator"), she is also critical of the ways in which women's sexuality is essentialized and/or conflated with reproduction and wider social issues. "Before speaking about sexlessness as simply a danger and tragedy to women, we mustn't forget to be cautious about who decides it to be a 'danger' or 'tragedy'."[15]

In a *Gekkan kazoku* (Monthly family) column critiquing *de facto* marriage (2003), Kitahara acknowledges that she herself has lived with men twice in her life. By implicating herself in the discourse both as critic and subject, she presents feminism as fluid and grounded, set within the context of women's lives and therefore contingent upon experience and growth. The connection between experiences of sex and sexuality and feminism is underscored throughout Kitahara's publications, and represents the kind of feminist praxis that Misciagno (1997) describes as essential to positive social change.

The *Love Piece Club*

The *LPC* promotion of sexual fulfillment, not least through the consumption of sex and sex goods, squarely addresses the considerable consumer power of Japanese women, and particularly young women (see Skov and Moeran 1995: 37). Supporting this approach are postwar associations of consumption (particularly personal consumption) with femininity (Kinsella 1995: 249). To extend Kinsella's (ibid.: 251) observations, I argue that just as young women's consumption of cuteness in the 1980s and 1990s reflected resistance to social expectations of (mature, reproductive, adult) femininity, so too can the consumption of sex and sexiness be seen as a challenge to contemporary gendered norms (see also Takeyama, Chapter 14, this volume).

With an exclusively female clientele (to the shop at least) and female target market, the *LPC* relies heavily on the provision of women-centered services – namely consumer goods, creative work and information – which may otherwise be unavailable or inaccessible for Japanese women. This is evidenced by the fact that the women who create, promote and use the *LPC* choose this over (or at least in addition to) "mainstream" options. Yano Kikuko, the "Netpatrol" reviewer of women's magazine *Oggi* describes the value of the *LPC* website in terms of its relative accessibility:

> Among *Oggi* readers, there must be many who baulk at the idea of buying condoms themselves ... If even buying condoms requires courage, people who can go into so-called "adult toy-shops" must be even fewer. Most adult shops are the world of male-centered sex fantasies, and for me at least are not comfortable places.
>
> (2003: 345)

The *Love Piece Club* allows access to goods and concepts generally unavailable or considered taboo for the "average woman." In this sense the LPC represents a safe space for the exploration and deconstruction of taboo, encouraging women to critically engage with social constructions of (passive, subjective) feminine sexuality. On this level, the *LPC* promotes curiosity and critical engagement with social expectations in relation to familiar experiences of femininity. Women are encouraged to offer their opinions through *LPC* site polls, which raise issues such as methods of masturbation, names for their vagina and whether they would want to be men. The diverse themes covered in the written columns promote critical understanding of social constructions of femininity, and encourage engagement with an agenda for feminist change at specific levels.

In the context of the *LPC*, where heterosexuality is often challenged if not rejected, I argue that consumption and commoditization can be interpreted as potentially subversive. This potential is wrought first by the *LPC*'s openly and exclusively female focus, and second, by its depiction of feminine sexuality as consuming as well as consumable. As a sex-goods shop, its business depends on the consumer power of female sexuality, and in order to harness this, the site must attract the feminine gaze. The Tokyo *LPC* shop rejects masculine consumption by prohibiting men from visiting alone (that is, without women), while the website encourages women's consumption of products for personal pleasure (such as nipple-stickers for "those feminists among you who wonder how come only women have to hide their nipples").[16] Through the promotion of sex toys, the LPC challenges the socially defined borders of feminine consumption, encouraging the incorporation of sex as an ordinary feminine (consumer) need and overturning the "traditional" sex-industry construction of men as consumers and women as consumables. In so doing the *LPC* shop has much in common with the host clubs described by Takeyama (in Chapter 14).

While women's interest in and patronage of the *LPC* may be grounded in consumerism, the shop and website function to draw attention to women's bodies and sexuality in a positive and empowering way. Kitahara states:

I've had women come to the shop and break down, telling me about sexual abuse within their relationships. It's as if they have nowhere else to talk about these things. They're too embarrassed to tell their doctors, or even counselors.[17]

Such a leap from sexuality and sexual goods into sexual health and counseling is not surprising, but is nonetheless expressive of both the nature of the *LPC* and its staff, and of the wider Japanese social context. Government-run women's centers often do provide counseling services for women, and issues of domestic and sexual violence are frequently targeted in public health and education campaigns. That the *Love Piece Club* substitutes as a space for nurturing and healing women who have suffered assault reflects the inadequacy of such government services, and more significantly, the way that women's experiences of sex are buried or excluded from mainstream (patriarchal) concern.

Comparisons and connections

The accessible language and familiar themes mark the potential of Haruka's and Kitahara's work to become far-reaching feminist texts, distinct from, yet complementary to, academic theory and government discourse. While both women engage with these "official" feminist spheres in their work, I argue that it is precisely because they position themselves figuratively and literally outside these official spaces that they are popular as feminist critics and as writers. Haruka and Kitahara promote particular versions of feminist identities, sometimes linked to explicit feminist identification and at other times tied to action rather than identity.

The challenges addressed by Kitahara and Haruka to mainstream ideals of femininity reflect their own experience as single, past their twenties (and therefore ostensibly "loser dog") feminist women. Kitahara's anger at the patronizing attitudes of male doctors and sexist child-rearing practices is more than purely personal indignation, as it sketches a broader picture of the impact of gender norms on everyday aspects of women's lives (2001: 54).[18] It is in the promotion of feminist consciousness and criticality at this everyday level, in the households of subscribers and readers, that Kitahara's feminism has most impact. From everyday criticality, readers are encouraged to challenge broader assumptions of femininity, critically deconstructing gendered roles (such as wife and mother) and their related ideals.

In Haruka's critique, the implications of marriage and motherhood not only limit women's career possibilities, they limit women's potential to develop fully as individuals. Further, the expectation of marriage constrains even women who are not married, binding "woman" to "wife" – even, as in Haruka's case, where that gloss is consciously and actively rejected. Even the fantasy of romantic love is demolished, Haruka commenting that "I think marriage is a hobby chosen by people who like to play families" (2003: 15).

Critique of marriage is not new in Japanese feminist circles – psychologist Ogura Chikako made the comment "I hate married feminists" fifteen years ago, provoking dramatic and critical reaction. Ueno reflects that the resulting backlash was a "litmus test," proving the extent to which marriage was ignored by Japanese feminists (Ueno and Ogura 2002: 213). Drawing on Ogura's comment as reference, Kitahara Minori replaces "married" with "de facto" (*jijitsukon*) feminists (2003). She is critical of "(f)eminists who say 'I have no intention of marrying,' as they go home every night to a house owned by a man." For Kitahara, it is not simply whether women enter the marriage system, but rather the physical act of living with and being dependent on a man that challenges feminist integrity.

Similarly, it is not simply the act of heterosexual sex, but rather the assumptions underlying heterosexuality which stimulate Kitahara's critique. While Kitahara "sleeps with boys and also sleeps with girls," she places her heterosexual self as a premise in her discussions of sexuality, because it is this self which is most conflicted and therefore least developed.[19] Accused of "pretending to be hetero," she argues that she "must not run away from her heterosexuality," but rather should challenge the aspect of her sexual self most easily obscured in contemporary Japanese society, founded on heterosexist norms and ideals. Further, argues Kitahara, lesbians and bisexual women are not free from heterosexist ideals simply by virtue of their female partners – "(e)ven if pussy-owners (*manko-mochi*) are having sex with each other, it doesn't mean they can escape from heterosexist society."[20]

By contrast, in Haruka's work it is the inclusion of popular and familiar feminine ideals which underpins her theory – she attracts women who are not radical, whose interests include beauty and fashion, and who may otherwise avoid (or be excluded from) participating in feminist critique. Nonetheless, while Kitahara's audience (online at least) may be generally more radical with respect to sexuality and marriage, the attraction of the website is that it allows women to dip into feminist critique freely, without requiring adherence to a political agenda or requiring any knowledge of academic discourse. Contextualizing the sale and use of sex-goods within critical discussions of sexuality, Kitahara's writing encourages broader critical engagement with consumption practices, aimed at an audience of women who are more often targeted as consumers than as critics.

Conclusion

Consumption of and engagement with Haruka and Kitahara's feminist texts encourage a diversification of feminist identity beyond academia into mainstream culture and youth subculture. As feminist identification appears as much a result of as a motivation for participation in women's groups, so a re-conception of feminist identity and theory expands and develops through the media presence of Haruka and the Internet activities of Kitahara. It is the potential for feminist critique to inform change that is channeled by popular magazines, TV shows and newspapers when they address, promote or challenge the feminist agenda and identities of women such as Haruka Yōko and Kitahara Minori.

If, as Ueno suggests, feminism is about valuing what it means to be a woman, then it stands to reason that feminist analysis should evaluate practices and ideals associated with femininity for their potential to promote women's status and

Feminist futures in Japan 197

agency. For contemporary feminists such as Kitahara and Haruka, the appropriation of the "feminine" (including fashion, beauty and consumption) is more than a personal response to patriarchal pressure from society, workplace and family. It is also a proposal for a (re-)defined feminism, centered on the problems experienced by Japanese women in their everyday lives and incorporating everyday strategies in its critique. It is in this manner that Haruka and Kitahara's critique offers much to young Japanese women and to feminist discourse in Japan – through their popularization of a "(f)eminism (that) is a beauty treatment" – a way of making oneself stronger and more beautiful (Haruka, in Kitahara 2000: 210).

Notes

1 As well as online shopping, the *Love Piece Club* website offers regular columns, articles and photo-essays on subjects related to sexuality, feminism and/or erotica. Available online: www.lovepiececlub.com (accessed 12 October 2004).
2 Comparisons may be made with the situation in Singapore, Malaysia and other Asian societies, where the implications of the word "feminism" can render its use problematic by (feminist) women and women's groups (see Ariffin 1999: 422; Lyons 2000). However, while Lyons (2000: 3) notes that feminist identification in Singapore confronts "the political association of feminism with encroaching 'Western values'," in Japan the barriers seem less related to the symbolic corruption of Japanese tradition by the West, and more to the concrete social effects of what is perceived as "feminism" – for example, the "destruction of the family" (Hayashi 2000: 7).
3 Chaplin here refers to the katakana word *moga*, a Japanese-English term referring to "modern women" (modern girls) of the Taisho period (1912–1925).
4 In discussions I conducted in Kansai women's groups for my doctoral thesis on feminist identification, Ueno and Tajima tended to be seen as "aggressive and radical." Tajima's was the name which most frequently arose in discussions of negative perceptions of feminism, in the context of "Not all feminists are like Tajima Yōko!"
5 The negative connotations of *feminisuto* are arguably less widespread in mainstream Japan than, for example, Australia, because the term "*feminisuto*" has not been taken up by all women's rights activists. For examples of "anti-femi" rhetoric, see the Anti-Femi website: http://homepage2.nifty.com/antifemi/index.html (accessed 10 October 2004).
6 The Japanese word for housework *kaji* generally refers to housekeeping activities, rather than simply cleaning. While the activities performed may be exactly the same, and therefore use of the word is grammatically correct, the differing nuance means that unmarried women and men generally use the word *sōji* (cleaning) instead.
7 On her website notice-board, Haruka is asked by a male reader "Doesn't your family get mad at the way you write about them?" She reassures the fan, jokingly writing that "My parents don't read my books," and then clarifying that "Although I make fun of my family, I don't insult them." Available online: http://www.haruka-youko.net/response/index.html (accessed 19 April 2003).
8 Organza is a thin, transparent fabric, silk or synthetic in origin, often used in formal and wedding gowns.
9 Available online: http://www.haruka-youko.net/response/index.html (accessed 5 September 2004).
10 As well as online shopping, the *Love Piece Club* website offers regular columns, articles and photo-essays on subjects related to sexuality, feminism and/or erotica. In addition to Kitahara's regular column, at the time of writing there are some eleven regular columns and three "irregular" columns, written by Japanese and Korean

women (the latter comprising correspondence between a Korean author in Korea and a Japanese author in Japan). See: www.lovepiececlub.com (accessed 29 March 2004).
11 Kitahara, personal interview conducted at the Love Piece Club in Tokyo, 20 January 2003.
12 Online: http://www.lovepiececlub.com/kitaharaframeset.html (accessed 29 March 2004).
13 Online: http://www.cafeglobe.com/lifestyle/sexuality2/ (accessed 1 July 2004).
14 Online: http://www.cafeglobe.com/lifestyle/sexuality2/ (accessed 1 July 2004).
15 Online: http://www.cafeglobe.com/lifestyle/sexuality2/ (accessed 1 July 2004).
16 Online: http://www.lovepiececlub.com/shop/recommend.shtml (accessed 5 September 2004).
17 Kitahara, interview 20 January 2003.
18 Online: http://www.lovepiececlub.com/kitaharaframeset.html (accessed 31 May 2004).
19 Online: http://www.lovepiececlub.com/kitaharaframeset.html (accessed 24 February 2003).
20 Online: http://www.lovepiececlub.com/kitaharaframeset.html (accessed 5 September 2004). I have translated *manko* as "pussy", though the LPC website adopts "cunt" in its English translated front page: http://www.lovepiececlub.com/e/ (accessed 11 April 2005).

References

Ariffin, R. (1999) "Feminism in Malaysia: A historical and recent perspective of women's struggles in Malaysia," in *Women's Studies International Forum*, 22(4): 417–423.
Buckley, S. (1997) *Broken Silence: Voices of Japanese Feminism*. Berkeley, CA: University of California Press.
Chalmers, S. (2002) *Emerging Lesbian Voices from Japan*, London: RoutledgeCurzon.
Chaplin, S. (2001) "Interiority and the 'modern women' in Japan," in S. Munshi (ed.) *Images of the 'Modern Woman' in Asia: Global Media, Local Meanings*, Richmond: Curzon.
Dales, L. (2003) "Legislating for harmony: the basic law for a gender-equal society," paper presented at the Japanese Studies Association of Australia Conference, July 2003, Queensland University of Technology.
Driscoll, C. (1999) "Girl culture, revenge and global capitalism: cybergirls, riot grrls, spice girls," *Australian Feminist Studies*, 14(29): 173–193.
Haruka, Y. (2003) *Haiburiddo ūman* (Hybrid woman), Tokyo: Kodansha.
—— (2001) *Hataraku onna wa teki bakari* (Working women have nothing but enemies), Tokyo: Asahi Shinbunsha.
—— (2000) *Kekkon shimasen* (I won't marry), Tokyo: Kodansha.
Hayashi, M. (2000) "Fashizumuka suru feminizumu" (Feminism that becomes fascism), *Shokun He!*, July, 88–98.
Kinsella, S. (1995) "Cuties in Japan," in L. Skov and B. Moeran (eds) *Women, Media and Consumption in Japan*, Richmond: Curzon.
Kitahara, M. (2003) "Tsugau hito to femi" (People who couple and feminists) *Gekkan kazoku*, 1 January, 5.
—— (2000) *Femi no kirawarekata* (The ways feminists are hated), Tokyo: Shinsuisha.
—— (1999) *Otoko wa tokodoki ireba ii* (Men are good to have around sometimes), Tokyo: Bunkohan.
—— (1998) *Hachimitsu no baiburēshon* (Honey vibrations), Tokyo: Kawade Shōbo Shinsha.

Lorde, A. (1981) "The master's tools will never dismantle the master's house," in C. Moraga and G. Anzaldúa (eds) *This Bridge Called My Back: Writings by Radical Women of Color*, New York: Kitchen Table Press.

Lyons, L. (2000) "A state of ambivalence: feminism in a Singaporean women's organisation", in *Asian Studies Review*, 24(1): 1–23.

Mackie, V. (2003) *Feminism in Modern Japan*, Cambridge: Cambridge University Press.

Misciagno, P. S. (1997) *Rethinking Feminist Identification: The Case for Feminist Praxis*, Connecticut: Praeger.

Muta, K. (2003) "Danjo kyōdō sankaku jidai no [jotei]ron to feminizumu" (The empress argument in an era of gender-equal participation), *Gendai shisō – toranzunashonaru feminizumu: josei no saihaichi*, 31(1): 115–129.

Ogasawara, Y. (1998) *Office Ladies and Salaried Men: Power, Gender, and Work in Japanese Companies*, Berkeley: University of California Press.

Saitō, C. (1997) "What is Japanese feminism?," in S. Buckley (ed.) *Broken Silences: Voices of Japanese Feminism*, Berkeley, CA: University of California Press.

Sakai, J. (2003) *Make inu no tōboe* (The howl of the loser dog), Tokyo: Kodansha.

Skov, L. and B. Moeran. (eds) (1995) *Women, Media and Consumption in Japan*, Richmond: Curzon.

Tajima, Y. (2004) *Onna wa ai de baka ni naru* (Women become fools through love), Tokyo: Shueisha.

—— (2001) *Dakara onna wa otoko wo ate ni shinai* (And that's why women don't count on men), Tokyo: Kodansha.

Ueno, C. (1997) "Interview," in S. Buckley (ed.) *Broken Silences: Voices of Japanese Feminism*, Berkeley, CA: University of California Press.

—— (1988) *Onna asobi* (Women's play), Tokyo: Gakuyō Shobō.

Ueno, C. and C. Ogura. (2002) *Za feminizumu* (The feminism), Tokyo: Chikuma shobō.

Yano, K. (2003) "Web: dōdō to riyō shitai, josei ni yoru josei no tame adaruto shoppu" (Web: Adult shops we want to use without hesitation – for women by women), *Oggi*, August, 345.

14 Commodified romance in a Tokyo host club

Akiko Takeyama

Introduction

Walk anywhere at night in Tokyo's famous Kabuki-chō sex district, the largest in Japan, and you can't miss them – young males, mostly, wearing fashionable dark suits with matching leather shoes and typically smoking cigarettes. They are hosts – "*hosuto*" in Japanese – men who make a living entertaining Japan's increasingly restless and well-heeled women. Thousands of these so-called hosts prowl the streets of Kabuki-chō, making every effort to draw women's attention. With their slim bodies, tanned skin, and perfectly set medium-long hair, they show off their assets like peacocks preening for the attention of potential mates. On the crowded streets, they intercept dressed-up female passers-by, handing out their business cards. "Hey, are you going back home? Why don't you stop by our club to relax and enjoy yourself?" they implore. Many women ignore their come-ons, but a few will inevitably go on to spend tens of thousands – and in some cases millions – of yen on hosts at host clubs. To explore why women are so intrigued by the host club scene which has only recently gained notoriety in Japan, I spent two months in the summer of 2003 interviewing people who participate in this unique subculture.

While hostess clubs are well established and normalized in male-dominated Japanese society (Yoda 1981; Allison 1994; Mock 1996), establishments catering to women have received little attention until recently. The first host club that opened in Tokyo in 1966 was a highly exclusive establishment serving upper-class matrons and wealthy widows and it remained largely invisible to the public.[1] As a result of news reports and other media attention in the past five years, however, the Japanese public has become intimate with such institutions. Mainstream media coverage has included inside exposés, hidden cameras and such sensationalized reports that some hosts have become overnight celebrities. While host clubs are still mainly centered in big cities like Tokyo, Osaka, and Nagoya, they have sprung up all over Japan, with an estimated 200 clubs and over 5,000 hosts plying an increasingly lucrative trade within Tokyo's Kabuki-chō entertainment district alone – the holy ground for sex-related businesses.[2] Moreover, the host business continues to flourish despite Japan's weakened economy.

Why did this little-known subculture suddenly emerge so prominently? To some extent, the recent success of host club establishments can be viewed as another example of Japan's fad-driven consumer culture. In other ways, it reflects the undeniable economic power of Japanese women whose free-spending habits have evolved from satisfying material wants to less tangible desires. It also reflects the changing attitudes of Japanese women who increasingly choose to avoid the confines of Japan's marriage and family system.[3] According to Japanese commentators, Japanese women are now fascinated both by the notion of romantic love (in a phenomenon now called *ren'ai shijōshugi* or "romance supremacy") and by hosts themselves who sell romance as their main commodity (Ishizaki and Hamano 1998). While many housewives, office ladies, hostesses, and sex workers go to host clubs for no other reason than to have fun and escape from daily stress, others pursue a fantasy of romance, including sexual encounters. Their romantic aspirations, coupled with the rising commodification of male sexuality in the host club scene, have fostered a new form of intimacy, called *gijiren'ai* (pseudo-romance). As Chapter 13 by Dales suggests, *gijiren'ai* can be seen as yet another way in which Japanese women deploy men as "resources" to create a more woman-friendly lifestyle. As I argue, however, commodified romantic love in host clubs serves as an effective stimulus for women's greater consumption while also reinscribing gendered characteristics and hierarchical relations – paradoxically host clubs underscore the prevailing gender logic in Japan.

Such a paradox is well reflected in media representations. Western media have described the host club phenomenon as "turning the tables on the geisha club concept" and "traditional sex roles" (*Associated Press* 1996; *Marketplace Radio* 2003). In these reports, Japanese women are portrayed as being empowered. Japanese media, however, have represented female customers as the exploited victims of sleazy, manipulative male hosts. Yet neither representation adequately captures the complex relations that take place between Japanese women and their hosts. This is because the manner in which mainstream Japanese media perceive the host club phenomenon is deeply rooted in asymmetrical notions of gender and sexuality. For example, female hostesses are said to enact "natural" sex and gender roles when nurturing and comforting Japanese men. When male hosts play such "female roles," however, they are perceived as "unnatural" and therefore disingenuous. The widely held assumption is that men go to hostess clubs seeking sex, whereas women's motivations are perhaps less obvious to the public. However, it would be a mistake to assume that the sex roles in host club culture are a simple reversal of sex roles operating at hostess clubs.

Through examining the phenomenon of host clubs against the backdrop of changing, yet still pervasive gender asymmetry in contemporary Japan, this chapter demonstrates how commodified romance in host clubs transgresses while simultaneously reinforcing prevailing gender and sexual inequalities. However, in conclusion, I will suggest how consumption can become a new medium for the subversion of gender-marked heterosexual norms – men as the penetrator and women as the penetrated – operating from within Japan's late-capitalist protocol.

Late capitalism and the supremacy of romance

Japan's postwar social structure centered on the nuclear family as the basic socio-economic unit and promoted a gendered division of labor – that is, men were the breadwinners and women were homemakers and consumers (Amano 1987; Ueno 1994; Dasgupta, Chapter 12 in this volume). Since the 1980s, when Japan's so-called "bubble economy" was in full swing, however, women's lifestyles have changed dramatically. More women were being employed in the newly developing financial, service, and leisure industries and were consequently becoming financially independent. Along with shifts in the economy from production to consumption, increasing numbers of Japanese women started to postpone or avoid marriage, and married women began having fewer children in order to enjoy their increased autonomy and financial independence (Kashima 1989: 103; Iwao 1993: 63; Imamura 1996: 4; Kelsky 2001: 2).

At the same time, a small number of Japanese men began to question their social role as workers/producers through which they were discouraged from expressing their own masculine aesthetic and narcissistic pleasure through consumption (see also Watanabe 1986; Miller 2003). As Chapters 11 and 12 by Taga and Dasgupta show, the bursting of Japan's bubble economy in the late 1980s followed by the great Heisei recession intensified concerns about men's well-being. The severe *risutora* (economic restructuring) fractured the lifetime employment and seniority system, which had long protected the salaried employee in core industries. Attention was drawn to the increase in the numbers of male suicides and *karōshi* (death caused from excessive work) as manifestations of the masculinity crisis that Japanese men were experiencing. In addition, women's increasing avoidance of marriage also created men's *kekkonnan* (marriage difficulties) and further fueled the sense of crisis (Itō 1993).

Such economic and demographic transformations encouraged by Japan's late-capitalism made it difficult for the family unit to maintain its role as a basis for both production and consumption as the individual instead became the iconic model of consumption and heterosexual romance, rather than marriage *per se*, was promoted through the media (Kitano 1991; Yamazaki 1993; Miyadai 1994; Ishizaki and Hamano 1998; Yoda 2000). Young adult fashion magazines, for example, traffic not only in fashion but also dating and romance. Leisure and service industries also intensively promote heterosexual romance through advertisements that feature couples giving gifts on Valentine's Day, sharing romantic dinners on Christmas Eve and other amorous settings. Pop songs played on trendy TV dramas reinforce the precious Gestalt of romantic love and encourage the listener to share in these feelings. These messages underlie the emerging view that, whether married or not, only a couple in the throes of romantic love is living a meaningful life and that being single is inadequate.

Ishizaki and Hamano point to the intimate connection between the supremacy of romance (*ren'ai shijōshugi*) and late-capitalist economics in Japan (1998: 17; see also Kitano 1991). As they illustrate, various aspects of Japan's consumer-oriented economy are invested in promoting romantic relations. Thus, the promotion of romance does not merely encourage the development of intimate human relations in an age when marriage and family are becoming increasingly unstable and decentered but also serves as a stimulus for greater consumption. Indeed, the host club as a consumer space, where romance is easily obtainable in exchange for money, reflects and intensifies the supremacy of romance in Japan's late-capitalist period, simultaneously catering to the desires of female consumers while profiting the club, the hosts themselves and by extension the Japanese economy. Host club culture offers, I argue, a sort of microcosm of the broader socio-historical context of romance supremacy within late capitalism.

Hosting service in host clubs

Fantasy,[4] one of the largest host clubs in Kabuki-chō, employing over 90 hosts, is located in a basement and officially opens its doors at 7 p.m., but business really only gets going after 9 and typically lasts until dawn.[5] Housewives, office ladies, nurses, and college students visit the club in the relatively early hours, and hostesses and sex workers stop by late at night after work.[6] Outside the building's street-level entrance, a large glass showcase features glossy photos of the club's top-ranking hosts who entice women passing by with their celebrity-like features. Upon entering, the female customer descends into an opulently decorated open set, with gold-colored chandeliers, red carpet, mirrored walls, and green faux-leather sofas neatly arranged in rows separated by various objects such as gold-painted sphinxes and lions. The host club, which has no windows, is a totally self-contained space, suggesting to the customer that her everyday life is left outside.

As a customer arrives, hosts greet her with a familiar call of "*irasshaimase*" (welcome). Unless she is a first-time visitor, she designates her own preferred host, who usually comes with four or five "helper" hosts. Once seated, her host starts up a conversation while the helper hosts serve alcoholic beverages in order to lighten the mood and relieve stress and tension. During the conversation, the hosts make sure that drinks are always fresh and food is served on small plates to those sitting at the table. They also offer efficient, highly stylized forms of service. If a woman wears a miniskirt, for example, a host will carefully lay a lace napkin on her lap so that she can relax without worrying about men peeking at her thighs. If she stretches her hand to reach for a cigarette, a host produces the light before she has time to put it into her mouth. Her host also escorts her to the ladies' room and patiently waits outside, ready with a steaming hand towel for when she emerges.

The smooth, glossy, superficial atmosphere derived from the club's décor and the hosts' polished etiquette makes the host club and the people in it seem phantasmal. In addition, every effort is made to construct a fantasy world in which women will willingly spend money to satisfy their desires whether to escape their everyday lives or explore, if only fleetingly, the potential for romance or sex. In terms of appearance, hosts offer a seductive masculine image – slim bodies, salon-tanned skin, trendy hairstyles and expensive brand suits and accessories. Hosts are good listeners, express sympathy and concern about their clients' everyday complaints and take time to comfort them. Hosts also respond to customers' romantic aspirations and sometimes submit to requests for more intimate attention, including outside dating and sex.

In return, hosts, as well as the host club, receive money from their customers. The drinks and food are exorbitantly expensive. A bottle of champagne, for example, costs about 40,000 yen (almost 400 US dollars). The cheapest brand of *shōchū*, a potato-based liquor, available at most stores for $7 runs at about $70 at host clubs. Dishes such as spaghetti, sautéed vegetables and fruit plates cost about $50 each. Even if a female customer does not drink or eat, she is expected to pay the entire tab for the table and offer tips to the helper hosts. While an average tab at *Fantasy* is about $400 for a night's worth (an average of two to three hours) of entertainment, a customer can easily spend hundreds more and even thousands of dollars per visit. By paying eight to ten times more than regular prices for drinks and food at the host club, the women customers acquiesce in accepting the value of the service (and romance) hosts provide.

What entices female customers to pay such inflated prices and spend great sums of money at the host club? The media have reported a variety of opinions. For instance, the editor of the monthly *Seiron*, an influential opinion magazine, proposes that hosts manipulate female customers into spending. According to the editor, hosts exploit naïve and vulnerable *shōjo* (female minors), and are nothing more than "lowlifes who prey on women" (*Seiron* 2000). As evidence, the editor writes about a 17-year-old high school girl who was "deceived" by a 20-year-old host into spending two million yen (nearly $20,000) on him over half a year. Assuming that a high school girl couldn't have such a large amount of cash, the author suspects that her host forced her to work in the Kabuki-chō sex district. Interestingly, the author does not problematize the male-centered sex industry where the female minor was supposedly employed. Instead he posits the hosts as lowlifes and their female clients as victims.

The female customers in host clubs do not think that they are victims, but instead feel that going to host clubs is a personal choice. For example, a 22-year-old college student named Yōko, who is a customer and the "girlfriend"[7] of a host at *Fantasy*, says:

> Minors are not supposed to go to host clubs to start with. Apart from high school girls, there are some unwise and irresponsible customers who do not think of their financial capability and let hosts manipulate them. Like any other consumer activity, if you are not a wise consumer, you are easily manipulated into spending. If you know that and keep yourself in control, you can really enjoy host club entertainment.

Although it is expensive to go to host clubs, Yōko and other customers claim that there are few other places in Japan's male-centered entertainment world where women can safely enjoy romantic excitement.

Hosts themselves tend to explain that their stylized behavior, attitudes, and various kinds of "service" are a byproduct of Japan's male-dominated society.

Many hosts I interviewed regard their service as deriving from the Western gentleman's custom of "ladies first," providing women with courtesies not usually forthcoming from Japanese men. A 32-year-old veteran host, Ryū, for example, insists:

> Host club culture couldn't exist in the West, where men are genuinely gentle to women and ladies-first services are provided for free. Host clubs can only exist in such a male-dominated country as Japan where men are insensitive to women's psychological needs.

Hence, some hosts posit themselves as understanding, ideal "gentlemen" by aligning themselves with Western men's supposed chivalry. However, in the terms of this discourse women are once more posited as victims, this time of ordinary Japanese men's insensitive attitude toward women (see Kelsky 2001: 4).

In the above accounts, men see themselves as saviors of women. While conservative, mainstream opinions expressed by such men as the *Seiron* editor seek to rescue women from culturally deviant hosts, the hosts themselves think they are saving oppressed women from the "ungentlemanly" conduct and "insensitive" attitudes of other Japanese men. Clearly, neither perspective challenges the fundamental principles of Japan's male domination or attempts to construct relations of greater gender equality. While the editor of *Seiron* wishes to eliminate the host trade and protect the gender status quo, the hosts themselves depend upon the status quo to maintain their business. Thus, paradoxically, both perspectives support Japan's male-centered social structure.

Women's desires and social contexts

Some might ask: Are the female clients in host clubs really the victims of both social attitudes and the host clubs themselves, as conservative Japanese media and the hosts seem to argue? Or, as Western media and female customers suggest, are these women so empowered financially and sexually that their participation in the host subculture is a sign of liberation? These kinds of either–or questions, however, simplify and overlook the complex and contradictory forces at work on the host club scene.

For example, Megumi, a 31-year-old housewife and part-time worker, visits the host club *Fantasy* once a week in order to recuperate her "lost" feminine attractiveness and self-confidence. Megumi says that once they get married, women in Japan are not treated as individual women. Since her marriage ten years ago, which she insists was based on love, Megumi's husband has recently begun to show less interest in her. Her neighbors, she says, call her the wife of Mr. So and So or the mother of So and So, and she feels as if she has lost her self-identity. Megumi confides:

> In the host club, hosts call me by my first name and treat me as an individual woman. They pay attention to what I'm wearing, my hairstyle, my cosmetics,

and give me timely feedback. These comments help motivate me to make an effort to become more beautiful because there's someone who's always caring about me.

Megumi adds, "Re-recognizing my female attractiveness boosts my self-confidence in many ways."

Housewives like Megumi, who actively seek individual recognition in order to avoid being a part of the nameless "wife and mother" collective do not intend to challenge the norms of feminine appearance or overturn the existing gender hierarchy. This is because such a challenge would risk undermining the effectiveness of their feminine performance. In order to experience themselves as feminine and attractive, they need an audience of sensitive yet domineering men. Although the female clients attempt to liberate themselves from the Japanese patriarchal family system which reduces them to their roles as wives and mothers by creating a fantasy world where their unique feminine identity is recognized and cultivated, they also reinforce social norms of ideal feminine appearance. As a result, gender hierarchy is still very much manifest in host clubs, where Japanese women's self-autonomy collides with gender norms that continue to posit women's physical attractiveness as their most important attribute and the need for this attractiveness to be endorsed by an appreciative audience of men.

Hence, despite the symbolic subordination of the hosts manifest in their subservient manner and eagerness to please, gender relations at *Fantasy* are not simply a reversal of those operating at hostess clubs and more widely throughout Japanese society. In addition, gender relations are not static but are transformed as time goes on. One veteran host explains that even though women may appear to have greater power over hosts at the beginning of a relationship, they are eventually undermined. The host comments:

> At first, a host obeys his customer in order to be liked, however he will gradually, yet steadily try to shift the power relation once he is assured that she has fallen in love with him. He has to do so in a way the customer does not recognize. A capable host can do so and make his customer willingly provide whatever he wants – money, cars, expensive watches, you name it.

His assessment is supported by female customers such as Nakamura Usagi, a famous writer and host club patron, who reportedly spent 15 million yen (roughly 150,000 US dollars) in 2001 at her favorite host clubs. In an interview with the *Japan Times*, Nakamura said:

> With the host, it starts off with you being the one governing the relationship, but before you know it, he's the one in control. You just don't know when it shifts. The thing is, *if you fall for him, you lose*, because you want to listen to him so he thinks better of you . . . I think that although many customers may feel like an *odaijin* (lord) while they're in the club, they are really more like a servant of the host.
>
> (*Japan Times* 2003; emphasis added)

Nakamura suggests that the game of romance, while helping women to rediscover their female attractiveness, eventually leads them to *lose* when they let the host govern the relationship. These accounts from a veteran host and a female patron might seem to reinforce the view that hosts are manipulative and female clients are victims. However, hosts and their clients do not see it this way. Instead, hosts understand women's self-devotion and largesse as a result of women's "motherly instinct," while their female clients explain it as a matter of personal choice.

While feminist scholars have argued that many so-called gender traits are not biological attributes but socially constituted, women's "motherly instinct" is one supposed biological trait that hosts constantly refer to. Reiji, a charismatic 37-year-old host, insists that women's motherly instinct makes them feel good about their devotion to others, in particular the men they love. Technically, once they understand the logic of motherly instinct, Reiji says, hosts can take advantage of it and kill two birds with one stone – customers' satisfaction and hosts' success (Reiji 2001: 108). A typical plot involves a host asking his clients' help to achieve his sales goals, and hopefully, to become a "number one" host at the club. As all hosts know, however, the method of entreaty is the key to unlocking a bounty of riches. Instead of "Please spend more money on me," a host might instead plead, "You are the only woman I can ask. Please help make me a real man" or "Please help me achieve my goal and then I can make you happier." In this way the host thinks that he neither begs nor cajoles his customers but activates their motherly instinct to make the women submit to him voluntarily. Moreover, he avoids feeling an obligation to return the money they spend on him or guilt about what they may do on his behalf.

Akemi, a woman in her forties, exemplifies an extreme case of a female customer enabling her host. She divorced her husband of two years after falling in love with a young host and became a sex worker in order to financially support him. She spent over 100 million yen (nearly $1,000,000) on him over eight years and helped elevate him to the top rank among hosts at his club. When he opened his own host club and broke up with her, she finally realized that their romance was, after all, a pseudo-romance. Because she has spent all her income on the host and has no savings, she still lives in an apartment house and works in the sex industry. Despite these drawbacks, Akemi still believes her spending was justified by the mental support she received and the joyous times she spent with him. She says, "Although I spent so much money on him, he never asked me to do so. I voluntarily did it. I did it in order to satisfy mainly myself. The harder things got, the more love I felt for him and the more strength I felt within myself."

Akemi's understanding of her behavior as a personal choice, as well as the hosting technique employed by Reiji to take advantage of motherly instinct, shows how gendered individuals in society utilize and interpret male-centered social situations differently. Whether taking the issue as personal or biological, these views depoliticize socially constructed gender difference. Furthermore, romantic love both veils and privatizes gender hierarchy. In *Ai to shihonshugi* (Love and capitalism), a popular novel based on her own host club experience, Nakamura Usagi challenges these views by having the book's male host and protagonist ask reflexively: "Why do women believe love is something requiring self-sacrifice for others, particularly for their men? Whose value is it?" (2002: 102–103). Nakamura suggests that Japanese society, in which women are evaluated through the success of their men, underlies women's devotion to men. In her interview with the *Japan Times* Nakamura elaborates on the connection between the female clients' devotion for their hosts and the hosts' success in monthly sales competitions, saying:

> I always live with anxiety about my position in the world [because] I cannot numerically express my value as a woman, or what I do professionally. So when I entered the [sales competition] game, I was projecting myself onto my host. And when he was moving upward it made me feel as if my own value was rising as well.
>
> (*Japan Times* 2003)

Nakamura deftly captures how male-centered social structures confer a subsidiary status on the value of women and their work. Within such structures women are encouraged to devote themselves to men and live vicariously through projecting themselves onto their men. The gender imbalance at work here is made clear when it is considered how women's self-affirmation through devotion to the hosts in host clubs stands in stark contrast to the manner in which male clients present themselves as "splendid men" in hostess clubs (Yoda 1981: 27; Allison 1994: 24). Psychologist Yoda Akira describes how the male clients of hostess clubs desire to show off their own capabilities as successful and powerful men (Yoda 1981: 27). Unlike the female clientele in host clubs, men who visit hostess clubs expect the hostesses to act as a feminine audience and show great interest in their impressive stories and masculine display rather than project themselves onto their hostesses or enjoy their success vicariously through the success of their favorite hostess.

Hosting, whether in host or hostess clubs, is a profession that diagnoses the desires of the customer (who is socially situated as a gendered being) and then converts these desires into something tangible and exchangeable for money. At a host club, women may desire a variety of things – ladies-first service, stress relief, special recognition of their self-identity, cultivation of their female attractiveness, and intimate relationships. In order to satisfy their desires, the host club environment provides women with experiences that Japanese society in general fails or refuses to provide. Nonetheless, the environment is also very much embedded in the overall gender hierarchy of society and largely reproduces it. This is because desire, which derives from the frustrations of everyday life, relies on the existing social context for its recognition. In this sense, as Foucault reminds us, "Where there is desire, the power relation is already present" and therefore, total transgression is impossible (1978: 81). Nevertheless, Foucault adds, "where there is power, there is resistance" (ibid.: 95). Since power is not out there to be seized but emerges as it is exercised and negotiated from innumerable points, subversion is possible only *from within the power dynamics* (ibid.: 93–95; see also Butler 1990:

31; Kondo 1997: 152). The next section considers some transgressive elements of the gendered interactions that take place in host clubs.

Non-penetrative sex

One specific example of how normalized patterns of gender and sexuality can be subverted in the host club environment is the manner in which sexual relations are carried out between hosts and their clients. Female clients demand that hosts maintain an attractive appearance and display a sensitive, caring attitude. As Dales describes in Chapter 13, Japanese women are thinking in increasingly instrumental terms about their own sexual pleasure and it is common for women to expect their sexual partners to have the so-called "3Cs," that is, be "comfortable, communicative, and cooperative" (Miller 2003: 54). Conventional sex discourse in Japan, as in many other cultures, is centered on male erection, penetration, and ejaculation (Segal 1994: 266; Allison 1996: 62). In Japanese, for example, the phrase "*saigomade iku*" (meaning to "carry on till the end") indicates penetration and by extension ejaculation. Everything else is considered peripheral, or *zengi* (foreplay).[8] The phrase indicates a male perspective since the "end" envisaged is male and not female orgasm. In short, sex is something that is "done" by men to women, and is always already understood from the male point of view.

Women's sexual dissatisfaction relates not only to men's attitudes about sex but also to the humdrum sexual life that the marriage system unintentionally creates. Tachibana argues that the current marriage system legitimizing sex between couples and promoting it as part of a national project to increase childbirth also provides a sense of security and citizenship. This system, however, has the effect of making sex feel less than exciting and even obligatory. This is because security (*anshin*) and excitement (*kōfun*) are inversely proportional: *anshin* outweighs *kōfun* when sex receives official permission and takes place routinely in the context of marriage. On the contrary, prohibition, illegitimacy, and temporality enhance *kōfun* (Kishida and Takeda 1992: 35; Tachibana 1994: 150; see also Ishizaki and Hamano 1998: 174). Hence, the monogamous marriage and coupling system that aims to limit women's sexual contacts outside of the relationship and to maintain security ironically undermines eroticism and sensual stimuli within the relationship. Likewise, because of their illegitimacy and ephemeral nature, extramarital or unforeseen sexual relations generate increased sexual excitement.

While men (funds permitting) have unfettered access to hostess clubs and the sex trade and therefore do not have to make a choice between sex which is *anshin* or *kōfun*, Japan's double standard in sexual matters requires women to choose one and relinquish the other. Women who have chosen the safety of monogamy are socially validated as faithful wives and girlfriends, whereas those who choose sexual excitement are viewed as promiscuous. Despite these perceptions, many women today seek the excitement of commodified romance so as to revel in feelings of sensual excitement not readily experienced in monogamous relationships.

Women who are dissatisfied with male-centered sex and/or humdrum, secure sex might be able to pursue more reciprocal and stimulating sex in host clubs. While accurate statistics on women who actually have sex with their hosts is unknown, most hosts suggest that more than 80 percent of hosts have had physical relations with their clients and almost all hosts engage in some sort of sensual contact including cheek-to-cheek dancing, touching, exchange of eroticized glances, sexual conversation and kissing. The majority of hosts have also had penetrative sex with some clients. Nevertheless, I want to highlight the occurrence of *non-penetrative sex* as an alternative form of heterosexual practice that takes place in the host club environment.

Akemi, for example, admits that her ex-host often slept with her without sexual intercourse taking place. Akemi explains that hosts are often drunk or so tired after work that they have no energy for sex or have erectile difficulties. She says,

> I was rather happy to see such an unostentatious aspect of him because it meant to me that I was special enough to be shown his unperformed self. Because I really loved him, I was very happy just to be in his arms, being kissed and cuddled.

When asked if she was ever sexually satisfied, Akemi answered:

> What really matters is not sexual techniques or size of the penis but the affectionate heart and passionate feeling. If you are really passionate about the relationship, just holding hands and cuddling each other gives you an electric pulse you feel in your entire body.

Sachiko, a 46-year-old widow, also stresses such feelings in her ongoing, year-long romantic relationship with Hikaru, a 29-year-old top-ranking host. She admits that she does not have sex with him but believes that he is serious about their relationship. "After all," she says, "sex does not really matter. I guess women oftentimes just want to be held tightly. Affectionate cuddling communicates feelings much better than a fragile physical connection, and satisfies women more holistically." Miki, a 33-year-old divorced mother with two sons who has been involved in a three-year romance with a host, shares Sachiko's view. Miki explains that her marriage became sexless because of her ex-husband's inconsiderate and disinterested attitude toward her. She says that:

> [In contrast], my host is a good listener and consultant on personal matters, making me feel that he will always be there for me. This *kimochi* (heart and feeling) is more important than mere physical relations for me. Because of the *kimochi*, even just being touched on the shoulder or kissed on the forehead is very special to me.

Female clients like Akemi, Sachiko, and Miki attempt to cultivate the "3C" – comfortable, communicative, and cooperative – relations with their male hosts.

They emphasize heart and feelings in sexual matters more than sexual technique, penis size or physical intimacy. In addition, they challenge the social perceptions that place some women outside of the category of ideal "woman" based on their age and marital status (see also Dale, Chapter 13). Yet, while they actively undo the conventional understanding of ideal women as young and single and of sex as a heterosexual penetrative act, they simultaneously reinforce the assumption that unlike men, women cannot have sex without love. Some would also argue that these women are simply putting a gloss on their hosts' sexual disinterest and that inevitably this kind of affectionate or passionate feeling will fade away. Indeed, hosts say that ideally they want to make money without having "actual" sex which takes up their time and energy. In this respect, hosts who satisfy their clients with non-penetrative sex might be seen as taking advantage of women's feelings. However, in the end, the hosting business does rely upon satisfying the needs of female customers. Koji, a 25-year-old veteran host who has been a host since the age of 17, uses a common metaphor shared by hosts to explain the kind of service he aims to provide – *"kayui tokoro ni pin-pointo de tega todoku sābisu,"* – literally, service that scratches the exact point where the customer feels itchy. The metaphor suggests that even if the customer cannot verbally articulate the exact spot, the host has to locate it and know how it should be scratched.

Although Koji employed the metaphor to explain the hosting service in general, it is also applicable to sexual contexts – even if a woman does not or cannot overtly express where and how she can get pleasure, it is the host's job to intuitively find the right spot(s). When he judges that what she wants is not something he can provide, he has to find something else to substitute so as not to lose her. The customer, too, needs to negotiate with her host if she does not want to dismiss or lose the host. In this respect, romance without penetrative sex is a result of the negotiation between some female clients and their hosts. Female clients like Akemi, Sachiko, and Miki in turn prefer a more communicative and negotiable form of erotic contact rather than mere physical connection and genital pleasure.

Although these women do not overtly overturn the existing male-centered discourse about sex and female passivity in sexual matters, they do challenge the norm and create an alternative paradigm for sexual relations, one that relies on non-penetrative, non-reproductive and negotiable (albeit commodified) sex. Through prioritizing their own physical and affective needs, female customers challenge the manner in which heteronormative sex is tied up with an officially endorsed ideology of national reproduction. Non-penetrative sex is also a challenge to the gendered understanding of heterosexuality – the phallocentric assumption that sex is something "done" by men to women (Allison 1996: 92). Non-penetrative sex blurs the traditional dichotomy structuring sexual relations in which men are active and domineering and women passive and subordinate. While the multiple heterosexualities which are enacted in the host club environment may not overthrow the wider sex and gender system *per se*, nevertheless the sexual relations encouraged by the host club culture do contest common-sense notions about "good," "normal," and "natural" sexuality which is normally defined as "heterosexual, marital, monogamous, reproductive, and non-commercial" (Rubin 1984: 280).

Conclusion: cultural politics as resistance

Alternative, consumer-based forms of romance and heterosexuality, such as those promoted by the host clubs, are often viewed as mere entertainment or escapism. It is claimed that because they do not lead to organized social movements which challenge the status quo there is no real liberation (Saitō *et al.* 2001: 141; see also Miyoshi and Harootunian 1989). However, this perspective more or less assumes that consumption is a passive affair, foreclosing political possibilities for resistance. It also overlooks the fact that consumption is not simply the activity of buying ready-made commodities and meanings but rather a social enterprise leading to the creation of new markets, the cultural production of new meanings, and the transformation of social values and ethics (Miyadai 1994; see also de Certeau 1984).

Cultural production is inevitably contradictory, that is, simultaneously contestatory and complicit. It can, however, be more effective than social movements in disturbing the status quo in late-capitalist society, where power, as Foucault argues, is everywhere, not to be seized or overthrown in any one place, but "runs through the social body as a whole" (1978: 94–95; see also Kondo 1997: 184). Because of the decentered, intangible nature of power relations, subversion is possible only from within, not from outside (Kondo 1997: 152). In this sense, host club culture in Tokyo is both a part of the larger social context and a site where subversion is possible from within Japan's late-capitalist protocol. Its sporadic violation of social assumptions intensifies the transformation of gender characteristics and sexual relations, impacting on the existing heteronormative gender system. In so doing, the host club phenomenon reflects the paradoxes inherent in the rapidly changing, yet still pervasive gender logic at work in contemporary Japan.

Acknowledgements

My research in Japan has been funded by the following grants: Freeman Foundation (June–August 2002); Department of Anthropology at the University of Illinois at Urbana-Champaign (June–August 2003); NSF (July 2004); and Japan Foundation (August 2004–present).

Notes

1. McLelland (2005) describes numerous host clubs where "gay boys" served a clientele of both men and women in the early 1960s. He also points to a few establishments where *dansō no reijin* or cross-dressed female hosts entertained a similarly mixed clientele. In this chapter, however, I focus exclusively on the recent development of *josei senyō hosuto kurabu* (host clubs for women only) since the number of such clubs is rapidly increasing and receiving sensational treatment in the media.
2. Accurate official numbers are not available. Unofficial estimates suggest that the number of host clubs in Kabuki-chō is 200, employing 5,000 hosts; figures based on Nakatani (2001: 98), as well as information obtained via interviews.
3. One of the ways that women attempt to avoid the system is postponing or avoiding marriage and having fewer children. The average age of first marriage, for example,

rose from 24.4 in 1960 to 27.4 in 2003 (National Institute of Population and Social Security Research). Meanwhile, the fertility rate dropped from 2.16 in 1971 to 1.29 children per couple in 2003, a record low.
4 My analysis in this chapter is based on archival research and interviews on men's beautification practices conducted in the summer of 2002 and preliminary ethnographic research in the summer of 2003 and 2004 at a Tokyo host club called *Fantasy*. My investigation consisted primarily of participant observation as a researcher, interlocutor, and customer in and out of the club; in-depth interviews with dozens of hosts and six customers (a 31-year-old housewife, a widow in her early forties, a 33-year-old divorced woman, a 22-year-old college student, a 26-year-old hostess who used to work in the sex industry, and a sex worker in her mid-forties) and extensive media discourse analysis. All names, including that of the host club, are pseudonyms.
5 The current Entertainment and Amusement Trade Law in Japan forbids host clubs to operate between midnight and sunrise in order to eliminate "unhealthy" sexual encounters. Nonetheless, the host business prospers during those illegal hours and silent approval is given by the authorities.
6 The majority of female clients in host clubs are hostesses and sex workers who visit after work, i.e., early morning. Therefore, most host clubs open around midnight. *Fantasy* is one of a few host clubs which opens earlier to attract so-called "ordinary women" such as housewives, widows, office ladies, nurses, college students, etc.
7 Yōko believes that she is a real girlfriend of her favorite host Takuya; however, other hosts in the club assume that she is a pseudo-girlfriend because if she were a "real" girlfriend, Takuya would not let her come to the club and spend a lot of money on him. In addition, Takuya would not want her to see him flirting with other customers.
8 In the sex trade, "*honban*" (the real thing) refers to vaginal penetration.

References

Allison, A. (1996) *Permitted and Prohibited Desires: Mothers, Comics, and Censorship in Japan*, Boulder, CO: Westview Press.
—— (1994) *Nightwork: Sexuality, Pleasure, and Corporate Masculinity in a Tokyo Hostess Club*, Chicago: University of Chicago Press.
Amano, M. (1987) *Jiritsu shinwa wo koete* (Beyond the myth of independence), Tokyo: Yushindō Kōbunsha.
Associated Press. (1996) "In Japan, host clubs provide women with dream dates," 1 October.
Butler, J. (1990) *Gender Trouble: Feminism and the Subversion of Identity*, New York: Routledge.
de Certeau, M. (1984) *The Practice of Everyday Life*, Berkeley, CA: University of California Press.
Foucault, M. (1978) *The History of Sexuality*, New York: Pantheon Books.
Imamura, A. E. (1996) "Introduction," in A. E. Imamura (ed.) *Re-imagining Japanese Women*, Berkeley, CA: University of California Press.
Ishizaki, M. and S. Hamano. (1998) *Sono otoko de iino?: ai to sei ni tomadou anata e* (Are you really satisfied with that man?: For you who wander in love and sex), Tokyo: Napuru.
Itō, K. (1993) *"Otokorashisa" no yukue: danseibunka no bunkashakaigaku* (The future of "masculinity": The cultural sociology of male culture), Tokyo: Shinyōsha.
Iwao, S. (1993) *The Japanese Woman: Traditional Image and Changing Reality*, New York: Free Press.
Japan Times. (2003) "Shopping queen shelves host 'illusion'," 12 January.

Kashima, T. (1989) *Otoko to onna kawaru rikigaku* (Men and women, changing power dynamics), Tokyo: Iwanami Shoten.
Kelsky, K. (2001) *Women on the Verge: Japanese Women, Western Dreams*, Durham, NC: Duke University Press.
Kishida, S. and S. Takeda. (1992) *Gendai Nihonjin no renai to yokubō wo megutte* (About romantic love and desire among modern Japanese people), Tokyo: Besutoserazu.
Kitano, M. (1991) *Hentai-ron* (Theory of strange love), Tokyo: Metamoru Shuppan.
Kondo, D. K. (1997) *About Face: Performing Race in Fashion and Theater*, New York: Routledge.
McLelland, M. (2005) *Queer Japan from the Pacific War to the Internet Age*, Lanham, MD: Rowman and Littlefield.
Marketplace Radio. (2003) "Host club in Japan," 3 September.
Miller, L. (2003) "Male beauty work in Japan," in J. Roberson and N. Suzuki (eds) *Men and Masculinities in Contemporary Japan: Dislocating the Salaryman Doxa*, New York: RoutledgeCurzon.
Miyadai, S. (1994) *Seifuku shōjotachi no sentaku* (Choices made by girls in their sailor suits), Tokyo: Kodansha.
Miyoshi, M. and H. D. Harootunian. (1989) "Introduction," in M. Miyoshi and H. D. Harootunian (eds) *Postmodernism and Japan*, Durham, NC: Duke University Press.
Mock, J. (1996) "Mother or mama: the political economy of bar hostesses in Sapporo," in A. E. Imamura (ed.) *Re-imagining Japanese Women*, Berkeley, CA: University of California Press.
Nakamura, U. (2002) *Aito shihonshugi* (Love and capitalism), Tokyo: Shinchōsha.
Nakatani, A. (2001) *Hosutoō ni manabu 82 no seikōhō* (82 successful strategies to be learned from the king of hosts), Tokyo: Sōgōhōrei Shuppan.
National Institute of Population and Social Security Research. (2004) "Heikin kekkon'nenrei" (Average age of first marriage), "Hikonritsu" (Non-marriage rate), and "Shusshōritsu" (Birth rate). All available online: <http://www.ipss.go.jp/syoushika/syindex.htm> (accessed 10 September 2004).
Reiji. (2001) *Hosutoō no sonokinisaseru shinrisenjutsu* (Psychological tactics with which the king of hosts manipulates minds), Tokyo: Seishun Shuppan.
Rubin, G. (1984) "Thinking sex: notes for a radical theory of the politics of sexuality," in C. Vane (ed.) *Pleasure and Danger: Exploring Female Sexuality*, Boston: Routledge and Kegan Paul.
Saitō, A., T. Minami and S. Kameyama. (2001) *Otoko wo dakutoiukoto* (What it means to make love to men), Tokyo: Asuka Shinsha.
Segal, L. (1994) *Straight Sex: Rethinking the Politics of Pleasure*, Berkeley, CA: University of California Press.
Seiron. (2000) "Henshucho kara no messeji" (Message from the editor), *Seiron*, March. Available online: <http://www.sankei.co.jp/pr/seiron/koukoku/2000/0004/message.html> (accessed 15 June 2004).
Tachibana, Y. (1994) *Hontō ni konomama de iino?* (Are you really satisfied with the way it is?), Tokyo: Yamato Shobō.
Ueno, C. (1994) *Kindaikazoku no seiritsu to shuen* (Establishment and end of a modern nation-state), Tokyo: Iwanami Shoten.
Watanabe, T. (1986) *Datsudansei no jidai: andorojinasu wo mezasu bunmeigaku* (The post-men's age: enlightenment studies for the androgynous), Tokyo: Keisō Shobō.
Yamazaki, K. (1993) *Danjoron* (Discussion on men and women), Tokyo: Kinokuniya Shobo.

Yoda, A. (1981) *Otoko ni totte onna towa nani ka* (What does the woman mean to the man?), Tokyo: Nihonjitsugyō Shuppan.

Yoda, T. (2000) "The rise and fall of maternal society: Gender, labor, and capital in contemporary Japan," in *South Atlantic Quarterly*, 99(4): 865–902.

Index

abekku 38
Allison, A. 1, 98, 101

Barazoku 98
Baudelaire 73
bishōnen 50, 54–5, 73
Bluestocking: see *Seitō*
Bonjour Tristesse 58
bōsōzoku 155, 164n3
bubble economy 9, 145, 156, 160, 202
bunmeikaika 66
burakumin 85

Carmilla 73
Castle, T. 65, 71
Chamberlain, B. 1
Chie, N. 3
chigo 35
childbirth 97, 156–7, 174, 180, 202, 209; concerns about low birth-rate 193, 209
Colette 66
coming out 7, 68, 84–5, 92n8, 102, 103–4, 105
Connell, R. 96, 152n1, 181n1

daikokubashira 6, 97, 168, 170–1, 173, 177–9
Dalsimer, K. 49
dansei gaku: see men's studies
danshoku 35
dōseiaisha 65, 84, 103, 107
dōsei(no)ai 67–8, 69, 92n5, 109n7
Dower, J. 37

Ellis, H. 67, 72
ero-guro-nansensu 7, 35
eugenics 36, 38

Faderman, L. 68, 74

fatherhood 161, 163, 173, 178–80
femininity 11, 15, 20, 72, 90, 118–19, 127, 145, 149, 172, 187–91, 194–5; in men 82, 87, 90, 155; western images of 128, 130
feminism 163–4, 184–6, 191–2, 195–6; and erotica 191–2; lesbian 68; popular 5–6, 146, 183–4, 188; and queer theory 5–6, 33; radical 150
feminisuto 184, 197n5
Foucault, M. 7, 33–4, 44, 208, 212
Fujino, C. 6
Furukawa, M. 35
Fushimi, N. 6, 29n8, 45n2, 45n3, 86–8, 97, 101, 104, 107, 108n1

Garber, M. 130, 141n5, 141n6
gay 26, 104; history 33; as lexicon 27
gay boom 84, 92n4, 105
gay men 97; at work 100–5
gei 84, 88, 90
gei bōi 84
gender stereotyping 15–17, 19–20, 22, 61
Giddens, A. 2
Gide, A. 55
Greer, G. 50

Hall, R. 66, 74
Haruka, Y. 5, 183–4, 185–91, 195–6
Harvey, K. 66, 73, 75
hentai 34–5, 37–8; magazines 38–40, 42–4
homo 8, 82, 84, 88, 90–1; female 41
homophobia 6, 82–3, 85, 91, 103
Honda, M. 53, 61n5
hostesses 101–2, 200–1, 203, 206, 208
hosts 89, 200–1, 203–5

Igarashi, Y. 36–7

Internet 4–5, 81, 83, 97, 101–2, 105–6, 158, 191
Ishikawa, T. 105–6
Itō, S. 85–7, 91, 102

Japanese Story 1, 96
Japonisme 1, 66
JILGA 82, 91
josōsha 87

Kabuki-chō 200, 203–4
kakure homo 8, 99
kamingu auto see coming out
Kanai, M. 50–1, 54, 56, 59
kasutori culture 37–8
Kawabata, Y. 66
Kelsky, K. 2, 74
Kill Bill 1
Kitahara, M. 183–4, 191–5, 195–6
Korean minority 85
Krafft-Ebing, R. 67
Kristeva, J. 56

Last Samurai 1
lesbian 4–5, 7–8, 26–7, 104, 107–08, 186, 196; history 33; as lexicon 27, 45n5; in translation 65–80; *see also resubosu*
lesbian boom 84
Lost in Translation 1
LOUD (Lesbians of Undeniable Drive) 75, 109n2
Love Piece Club 183, 191–2, 193–5

Mackie, V. 2, 96
marriage 176, 202; meaning of (for men) 172–4; for women *see ryōsai kenbo*
masculinity: and aging 151–2; hegemonic 10, 96, 145, 160, 162, 167–9, 172–5, 181n1; mainstream 135–6; and marriage 172–7; see also *daikokubashira;* fatherhood; salaryman; *shakaijin*
masochism 40–1, 43
Mathews, G. 99
Matsui, S. 69
Memoirs of a Geisha 1, 11n1
men's lib 145, 157–8
men's studies 147, 163; development of 145–7, 150–1, 158–9; recent trends 159–63
Mishima, Y. 58, 66, 126–7, 131–40
Miyazaki, R. 87
mobo 36
moga 36

Monroe, M. 127–8, 130
Morimura, Y. 126–7; as artist 127–31
Murata, Y. 100

nenja 35
nihonjinron 3, 11n2; in language teaching 15, 27

Occupation period (of Japan) 34
Occur (gay-rights organization) 82–4, 85, 91
okama 81–3, 86, 91; definitions of 81, 87–9
Okinawa: and gender 113–15; and religion 111–13; shamanism in 115–16
onabe: 81, 89–90
onna kotoba 15, 20–2
onnagata 90
Orbaugh, S. 49, 52
Orientalism 1, 67
otoko kotoba 21

Pflugfelder, G. 35
Phryné 73
Plummer, K. 107
positionality: in language classroom 26

queer 34; *see also* hentai
Queer Japan 97, 102

Raichō, H. 71–2, 74, 76, 76n3
restructuring (economic) 202
resubosu 40–1, 43, 45n5, 68, 76
rezubian 45n5, 76, 90; origins of 66–8, 89, 89–90; *see also* lesbian, *resubosu*
Rich, A. 74
Roberson, J. 99
ryōsai kenbo 36, 71–2, 172

"S" Relations 69, 71
sadism 41, 43
Said, E. 1
salaryman 1, 3, 28n2, 96–9, 135, 160–1, 169, 173; 176–8; "crafting' of 98–9
Sappho 65, 68, 74
Sarashina nikki 57
Seitō 68, 71–3
Seitōsha 67–8, 70–2, 76
Self Defense Forces 126, 136, 138
seppuku 40, 43
sexist terminology 18–19
shakaijin 97–9, 169, 171, 172–3
shōjo 49–50, 54, 60, 69–70: definition 52–3,

shōjo manga 54–5, 57–8
shōjo shōsetsu 49–51, 53, 57–8
Shūkan Kinyōbi 84–6
Sōka Gakkai 83, 93n20
Sukotan Kikaku 85, 87, 102

Tajima, Y. 184–5
Takahara, E. 50, 60
Takarazuka 8, 49, 52–3, 61n1
Tale of Genji 56–7
Tanizaki, J. 66
Tezuka, O. 53
Tōgō, K. 84–5, 88
tōjisha 8, 83, 88–90, 105–7
Torikaebaya monogatari 7
transgender 2, 4–6, 81; boom 84, 87, 89–91, 101, 106, 127; in Okinawa 116–17; in *shōjo* culture 53–6

Ueno, C. 5, 34, 59, 107, 146, 184–5, 195

Venuti, L. 65–6

Wakakusa no Kai 75
wakashū 35
Watanabe, T. 155

yakuza 1, 127, 134
yaoi 8, 57, 62n12
Yoshimoto, B. 50
Yoshiya, N. 8, 52–3, 55, 60, 74
Yuasa, Y. 72, 74